JOURNEY TO GUYANA

JOURNEY
TO
GUYANA

by

MARGARET BACON

HILL HOUSE PUBLICATIONS

First published in Great Britain in 1970
by Dobson Books, London

Published in this edition in 1988 by
Hill House Publications, Highworth,
Wiltshire SN6 7BZ.

Reprinted 1993

Printed & bound by Redwood Press Ltd, Melksham, Wiltshire

ISBN 0 9513565 0 X.

Bacon, Margaret,
Journey to Guyana.
1. Guyana Description & travel
I. Title
918.8'1043

PREFACE TO THIS EDITION

This year marks the 150th anniversary of the emancipation of the African slaves in Guyana, for in 1838 the great wrong that had been done to them was finally righted. It was, however, the owners who were compensated.

1838 also saw the arrival in Guyana of the first East Indians who came as indentured labourers to work on the sugar plantations. The descendants of these two groups, African and East Indian, now make up 80% of the Guyanese people. So it seems fitting, in this anniversary year, to celebrate by bringing out a new edition of an account of a journey to that country in the early days of its independence.

I have decided not to try to update the text nor to weigh it down with footnotes for I have been surprised, on re-reading the text, at how little has changed. The armchair traveller will notice that the lovely old wooden cathedral is no longer the tallest building in Georgetown: the concrete edifice of the new Bank of Guyana overtops it. There are more cars in the city too, but bicycles and carts still hold their own and donkeys still display a fine disdain for the highway code. A new pontoon bridge spans the Demerara river six miles above the spot where the old ferry used to ply its trade—and still does. There are new roads now but they do not penetrate the bush where the rivers are still the main highways. The vast beauty of the Interior is unchanged and in its deep forests the Amerindians still maintain a way of life which spans the centuries.

I should like to thank Mr. Arnon Adams of the Guyana High Commission for his useful comments on the text and for all his willing help, given with that generosity which is typical of the Guyanese people to whom I dedicate this book.

Wiltshire, 1988.

The author, who spent two years in Guyana, gives a vivid picture of the country's many-sided life: its multi-racial population and amazingly varied terrain. She describes, too, her everyday domestic life in Guyana, setting up a home, making a garden, going to market. She tells of adventures—and some misadventures—into the Interior and of encounters with the different races which make up the Guyanese nation. She analyses the problems which confront it, which are many and grave, including poverty and mass unemployment, but behind all this she portrays a diverse people, full of resourcefulness, good humour and charm.

Margaret Bacon was educated at the Mount School, York and at Oxford, where she read History. She married a civil engineer, whose profession necessarily involved a nomadic way of life, which took them by way of the Isle of Sheppey and the Mersey Estuary to Guyana. They have two daughters and now live in Wiltshire.

Margaret Bacon's other books are:

Going Down
The Episode
Kitty
The Unentitled
The Package
Snow in Winter
The Kingdom of the Rose
The Chain
The Serpent's Tooth

For children
A Packetful of Trouble.

CONTENTS

LIST OF ILLUSTRATIONS

*Reproduced by the courtesy of the Guyana High Commission

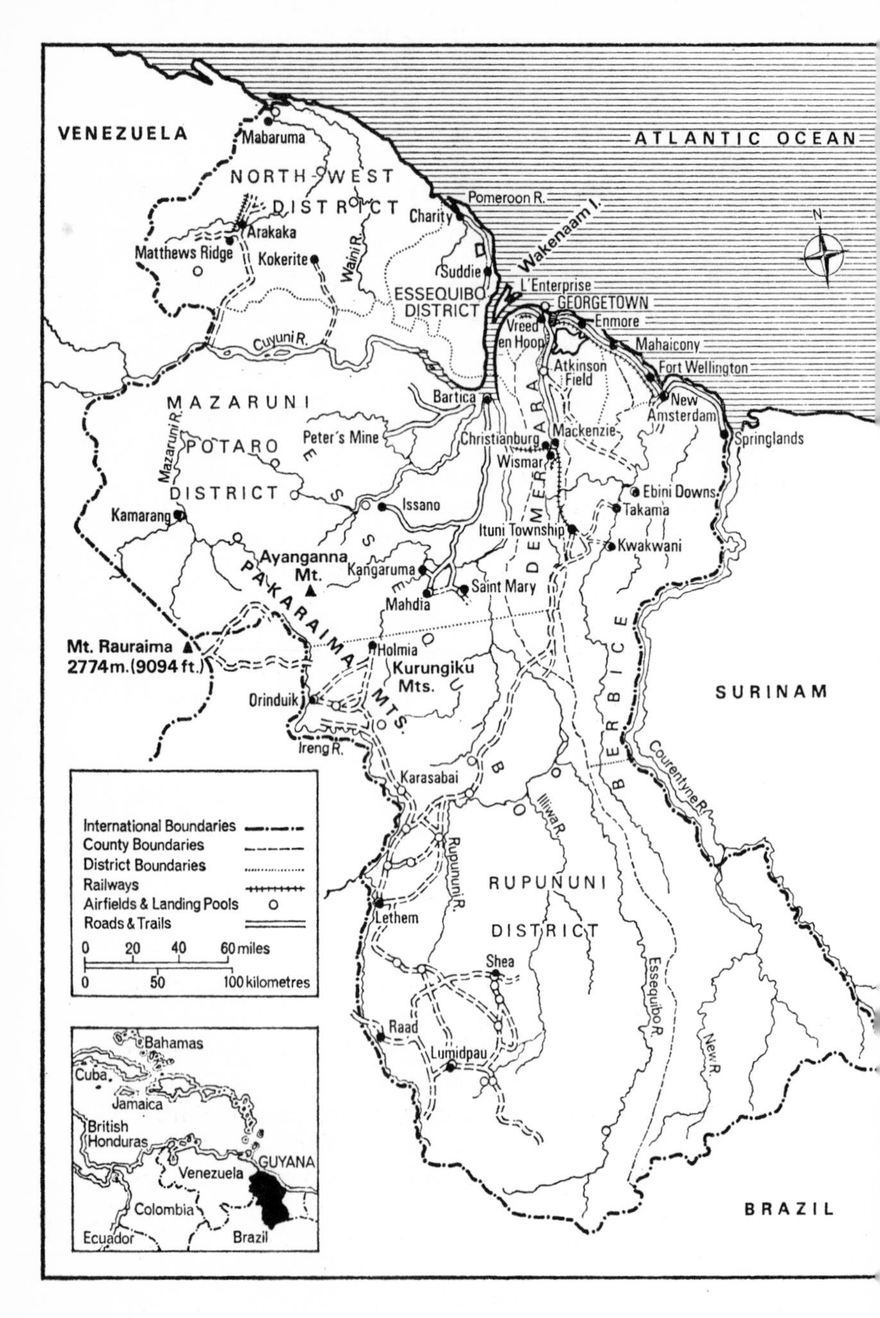
VENEZUELA
ATLANTIC OCEAN
Mabaruma
NORTH-WEST DISTRICT
Arakaka
Matthews Ridge
Kokerite
Waini R.
Charity
Pomeroon R.
Wakenaam I.
Suddie
ESSEQUIBO DISTRICT
L'Enterprise
GEORGETOWN
Enmore
Vreed en Hoop
Mahaicony
Atkinson Field
Fort Wellington
Cuyuni R.
Bartica
New Amsterdam
Springlands
MAZARUNI POTARO DISTRICT
Mazaruni R.
Peter's Mine
Christianburg
Mackenzie
Wismar
Ebini Downs
Takama
Kamarang
Issano
Ituni Township
Kwakwani
Ayanganna Mt.
Kangaruma
Saint Mary
Mahdia
PAKARAIMA MTS.
ESSEQUIBO
DEMERARA
BERBICE
Mt. Rauraima
2774m.(9094 ft.)
Holmia
Kurungiku Mts.
SURINAM
Orinduik
Ireng R.
Karasabai
Courentyne R.
Illiwa R.
Rupununi R.
International Boundaries
County Boundaries
District Boundaries
Railways
Airfields & Landing Pools
Roads & Trails
0 20 40 60 miles
0 50 100 kilometres
RUPUNUNI DISTRICT
Lethem
Shea
Essequibo R.
New R.
Raad
Lumidpau
Bahamas
Cuba
Jamaica
British Honduras
GUYANA
Venezuela
Colombia
Ecuador
Brazil
BRAZIL
N

INTRODUCTION

'The main thing about marrying a civil engineer,' a director of my husband's firm told me just before my wedding day, 'is never to worry about where you'll be this time next year. And, if you must worry, don't bother your husband about it because he doesn't know either, poor chap.'

It was sound advice and I tried hard to follow it. The real test came about two years later; it had been settled that my husband would be working in London for the next eighteen months and, on the strength of this information, we had extended and redecorated our cottage in Surrey. I was, in fact, painting the last bit of skirting board in the kitchen when he came home one bitterly cold December evening, looking, I thought, rather guilty. He took off his duffel coat and stared at the half-painted skirting board.

'What do you think about going to Guyana?' he enquired abruptly.

'When?'

'Oh, not for at least three weeks,' he said, as if that somehow made it all perfectly easy.

In the short silence that followed I knew that this was my great opportunity. Other wives, on such occasions, might fuss about the short notice, packing, Christmas or not having any tropical clothes but I would rise above such trivial considerations and show that I had the vision to recognize a challenge and accept it calmly and intelligently. In short, I would show what brave-little-woman stuff I was made of, for this was my finest hour and I was determined not to muff it. I put down the paint brush carefully and said, 'I think it would be wonderful—I've always wanted to go to Africa.'

There seems something a trifle immoral in writing a book about a country which one so recently located in the wrong continent. On the other hand, I can at least claim to have approached my subject with no preconceived ideas; my ignorance was total and unimpeachable.

A more serious deterrent has been the fact that a large number of books have already been written about the only British colony ever to have existed in South America. It has been a happy literary hunting-ground for explorers, animal-catchers, professional travellers and official chroniclers. Yet the country they describe sometimes is scarcely recognizable as the one in which we lived. For example, the life of the ninety-eight per cent of the population who live on the coastal strip is very different from that of the two per cent who live in the bush and anyone who reads a bush explorer's account of life in Guyana would have a very distorted view of the country as a whole. Moreover, even when an attempt to describe the country in its entirety is made—and it has been done most successfully—the official writer and the famous traveller suffer from one serious disadvantage; things are arranged for them. Their readers might be forgiven for imagining that if they themselves arrived in Georgetown they too would find invitations for confidential chats with the Prime Minister awaiting them and amphibious planes all ready to take them to any part of the Interior they wanted to see. In reality, unless they were very determined they would see very little of the country apart from the coastal strip; many Europeans have worked all their lives in Georgetown and never been into the Interior. Knowing that we had only two years there, we made perhaps a rather more than average effort to see as much as we could, but certainly we did not do anything particularly hazardous or too uncomfortable—at least not intentionally. An account of what we did manage to do will perhaps give a more realistic picture of life out there to anyone contemplating making a similar journey, even if only from the armchair.

The real deterrent, I must confess, has been the memory of many scornful remarks by knowledgeable locals about the writings of 'visitors'. 'He came here for three months,' a District Commissioner would say, 'and goes home and writes a book about it.' 'Three months!' somebody else would exclaim. 'What about that newspaper chap who came for two weeks? I've never read such muck.' Then, inevitably, somebody will remember the famous adventure book, full of heroics, whose author on every second page escaped death in the bush (alas, poor ignoramus, he even called it the jungle) but in fact had never been there at all. He was attacked by crocodiles in rivers that contain nothing more deadly than alligators, he was bitten by snakes that are not found on the South American continent and he toiled up mountains that do not exist.

It is not surprising that local experts are sceptical about the writings of visiting publicists. The Commissioner of the Interior once put the whole thing in a nutshell when he remarked that whenever he picked up a certain famous American magazine he was very much impressed by the excellence of its articles on Peru or Mexico or any other places he had not been to, but when they had one on British Guiana they always got everything wrong.

To such potential critics I can only offer two feeble excuses: one is that the outsider can sometimes get a more general view of the country than the residents can; he is struck by things which, through long familiarity, they no longer find striking, but which are nonetheless vital characteristics of the country. His perspective is different, but it may be the perspective in which the reader who does not know the place can most easily envisage it. Secondly, while admitting that those who have spent their lives in practical administration are the ones—the only ones, perhaps—who can speak with real authority, it often happens that they are not writers, though usually great talkers.

This is not much of a defence, I know, so perhaps it would be wiser to ask their forbearance and leave it at that.

I should like to thank Anthony Tasker for reading the MS and for his help in checking facts and dates which has been invaluable.

I hope that those readers who are as ignorant as I was about the whereabouts of the country will enjoy the voyage of discovery as much as we did. Those who were inclined to confuse British Guiana and Guyana will perhaps be relieved to know that they were quite right to do so: in May 1966 British Guiana became independent and changed its name to Guyana. The Guianese became the Guyanese. For the sake of simplicity I have throughout referred to the country as GUYANA.

CHAPTER ONE

Getting There

We left London Airport at seven o'clock one icy cold night in early January. It was hard to believe, as we shivered in our thin clothes, that tropical heat really did await us at the end of a two-day journey. Whenever I have gone to some reputedly sun-baked country in Europe it has always turned out to be cold and wet, though it has always been very hot the week before. I still in fact had the European's feeling that sunshine is something desirable. In the intervals between packing and having injections I had read the current Government Report on Guyana and was disappointed to find it contained no statistics on temperature: a long list of the diseases we were most likely to die of in descending order of probability provided small compensation.

This was my first long flight and I found the luxury of it rather unnerving. It is, after all, unnatural enough to be hurtling through the air at several hundred miles an hour without all that champagne, too. What, I found myself wondering, were we all celebrating? Hardly the fact that we were encased in a brightly-lit metal cylinder, half-sitting, half-lying, in rows, one behind the other (how extraordinary we must look in cross-section) suspended three or four miles above the earth. Fortunately we do not really believe it; if we did we should certainly want to get out.

The powder room was also disconcertingly luxurious, with its range of creams and powders and rouge and lipsticks, presumably provided for women who absent-mindedly set off for the Caribbean without their handbags. All the same I liked the powder room with its little jars and bottles and would have spent more time in it if it had not always been full of hostesses washing their blouses.

Towards midnight the pilot told us that the next stop would be Gander in Newfoundland and that we were now travelling at four hundred miles per hour at a height of twenty thousand feet. The male travellers listened to this information and nodded knowledgeably as if to imply that that was just about what they themselves had calculated.

Most of the passengers were men and seemed to be habitués. Some seemed almost to have been built into the plane like the drivers of children's model cars. There was also A Personality on board, a political peeress I think. She seemed to spend a lot of time shaking hands with the crew whenever we stopped or started. When we reached Trinidad she thanked them loudly and at length as if they had done it for her alone and the rest of us were just hitch-hikers.

The pilot bade us goodnight and the lights were dimmed. Those who had bunks began to climb into them, rather surreptitiously, as if they had just decided to sleep on the luggage rack. I noticed that the man who was going to sleep above our heads made one concession to the conventions of going to bed; he took off his shoes and put on a pair of sandals before climbing into his bunk.

It now became incredibly hot. The plane must have been heated to a temperature of well over eighty degrees and the ventilator by our seats did not work. We tried to sleep but were too conscious that our mouths were dry, our tongues like old leather and our eyes felt as if they had been the victims of a recent sand-storm. We asked the air hostess if our ventilator might be mended and she smiled sweetly and said that that was a job for the engineer really and the engineer was busy. Dick asked if she could bring a screwdriver so that he could fix it but the hostess clearly did not take kindly to the idea of providing passengers with the wherewithal to unpick the plane.

As we approached Gander the pilot told us that the airport was icebound and the ground temperature was seven degrees below zero. There followed one of those conversations which must be quite common between civil engineers and their wives. It went roughly like this.

'Why,' I asked, 'is it safe for an aeroplane to land on solid ice, when a car skids even if it drives quite slowly on just a little patch of it?'

'Well, you see, it's really an altogether different principle. A car is propelled by a self-motivating and autodynamic mechanism of inter-relating gyrometrics, while in the air the metabolic rate of the carbo-diesel, being predominantly volatile and in suspension, isn't subject to the same pretensile stresses. To put it simply, the microplastics operate by centrifugal force in a series of iso-efficiency curves and the relative specific speed is calibrated empirically so of course you don't have the same inertia pressures operating that you have with non-integrating centripetal mechanisms.'

'Yes.'

The air hostess brought us our butterscotch to suck and we fastened our safety belts ready to land. As we touched down the plane seemed to lurch and sway about for rather a long time and then we stopped with a great jerk and a lot of noise. We were glad of our safety belts, but nobody panicked except the air hostess, but as it was her first trip that was understandable. The pilot explained rather breathlessly that we had skidded on the ice and would have to stop at Gander for repairs.

To step out of the overheated aeroplane into the sharp night air of Gander was to return to reality. All around us were huge walls of ice and snow and above us the polished black glass of the sky was filled with hard and brilliant stars. It was very still. Suddenly the cruel reality of seven degrees below freezing struck and we began to run awkwardly across the ice to the bus which was to take us to the waiting-room. The Personality found time for only the briefest handshake and broke into a slithering jog trot. She had very flimsy shoes but sensible legs and made quite good time.

We sat on benches in the big, bare waiting-room for about an hour before we were told that the plane would take some time to repair so we must go and queue in a corridor for sleeping tickets so that bedrooms could be allocated to us. We trailed into a queue and thence to rough little rooms which were as hot as the aeroplane and unventilated. But the relief of stretching full length on a bed more than compensated. My last waking thought was a hope that the plane was badly enough damaged to need eight hours to be repaired.

Two hours later we were called to await take-off. My watch now registered four o'clock, but any hope that we had disposed of a sizable chunk of the night was ill-founded. One of the most dismal things about flying westwards is that you are constantly putting your watch back. You work heroically hard to get rid of a few hours only to have them given back to you; this is as frustrating as running up a downward escalator.

We waited over an hour, hunched up on benches, bewildered and crumpled. The passengers were looking less and less like blasé world-travellers and more and more like displaced persons. Any one of them would have exchanged all last night's champagne for a cup of tea this early morning. Here again was the disconcerting incongruity of air travel; one minute it is gala dinners and free cocktails and the next a simple cup of tea is an unobtainable luxury. One minute there are speeches of welcome and friendly little announcements of statistics and the next you are being herded about, into buses, down corridors, given no information and subjected to violent changes in temperature. The whole thing is inappropriate; one expects to rough it on a camping holiday or travelling on a third class train across Europe, but not in the middle of a weekend at the Savoy. Psychologically people might react better to the discomforts if they had had rather less of the artificial luxury treatment beforehand.

The rest of the journey was uneventful. Dawn came at last, or more accurately, we caught up with dawn and in the early morning we landed at Bermuda, where a fine drizzle greased the tarmacadam. When, towards the autumn, English newspapers come out in a rash of advertisements about Coming to Sunny Bermuda, I feel sad, for to me the name conjures up no golden memories but only a vision of scrubby bushes and abandoned oil drums around the airstrip, of weariness and tepid coffee with tinned milk and swollen ankles and the fine drizzle making the tarmac shiny.

Flying by day was much pleasanter than flying by night had been. It was cool enough to sleep and this is what I did as we flew over the Caribbean, resisting all injunctions to look out of the window. If I look out of an aeroplane window I never see anything but the wing; my husband on the other hand, being blessed with a double-jointed neck, can see round and under the plane. In the same way if he looks at something through binoculars it immediately appears larger and clearer, but when he persuades me to look through them I cannot see anything at all except a thick fog. It used to worry me; now I just accept that some people have a way with inanimate objects like binoculars and aeroplane wings and some people have not.

We landed at Trinidad in the afternoon and any doubts that I had had about tropical heat were instantly dispelled. Stepping out of the plane into the outside atmosphere was like entering one of those excessively hot and damp tropical plant houses at Kew, when the heat hits you like a solid object, so that you back out and shut the door, with only a passing regret for the glimpsed palms within. But now there was no backing out and shutting the door and we set off across the long stretch of the airstrip, the sun beating down on our bent heads and reflecting up into our faces from the tarmacadam. We had, in fact, arrived on a particularly hot day and soon the thunder began and the rain started to sluice down. By then we had made our way to the airport hotel and had been shown into an air-conditioned bedroom in which, we soon realized, the air-conditioner did not work. Since air-conditioning necessitates blocking all the windows the room was a kind of well-sealed oven. But we were novices and did not complain.

The other disadvantage was that our room overlooked the air strip and jet planes seemed to take off at hourly intervals throughout the night from under my bed.

Since then, I must in fairness add, we have stayed several times at this same hotel, in wonderfully cool rooms, fully air-conditioned, quiet and overlooking the swimming pool. It seems to be something of a Jekyll and Hyde establishment. Fortunately that first night was short for our plane for Guyana left soon after six which meant rising before five.

Now we were on the last leg of our journey: a mere 350 miles separates Guyana from Trinidad. As we flew, Dick reported on what was going on below the plane: we were flying over the sea, we were over the line where the blue of the Caribbean gives way to the brown waters brought down by the Orinoco, we were flying over land, over dense forests, over a great estuary, which must be the Essequibo, the widest river in Guyana, over more forests, over another river which must be the Demerara, and now, here we were fastening our safety belts and sucking our butterscotch, landing at Atkinson Airport, Guyana.

CHAPTER TWO

Arriving in Georgetown

Although only a handful of people alighted from our plane and a very few were waiting to get on it, there seemed to be several hundreds of human beings in and around the airport buildings waiting to welcome them or speed them on their way. It is always so, I discovered later, at Atkinson Field. The Guyanese are a hospitable and very warm-hearted people and nobody is ever allowed to leave their country or to arrive there without a sizable escort. Besides, the amusements in Georgetown are limited and roads even more so, and a drive out to the airport provides one of the few outings there are.

The official business of being allowed into Guyana and the checking of customs may be slow, but they are pleasantly informal. It is usually possible to go and have a chat with friends over the flimsy barrier before going into Customs and I have occasionally seen people wisely availing themselves of this opportunity to hand to their friends those baskets and parcels that they do not want to trouble the customs with.

My main preoccupation that first day was to find some shade while Dick queued up with our passports. I found a bench with strips of shade where the shadow from the window slats fell on it. I lowered myself gingerly on to one of them and tried to remember what it felt like to be cool. A little stream of sweat was trickling down my spine and the general stickiness of my body seemed to be beginning to concentrate at strategic points, like behind my knees and the back of my neck.

A large white lady came towards the bench and as I squeezed nearer the wall so she could have the next strip of shade, she told me not to bother because really it was so cool today. I looked at her suspiciously, but she was evidently not joking, so I could only deduce that there were hotter seasons. I had already noticed that she was American and she now told me that she was a missionary and that she and her husband were returning from Trinidad. I was pleased by the encounter. I knew that in the next few days we should be meeting a great many business people but was not sure if we should meet many who were here for the sake of the people rather than for the commerce of Guyana.

I asked her where her Mission was and she told me, but at that stage all local names still sounded like something out of Hiawatha, so I did not remember it. Certainly it was an Amerindian Mission somewhere deep in the Interior for she had a long journey ahead of her. I was eager to know more about the people she lived among and what kind of work she was doing. I asked her about their life and she told me it was bad, but with the Lord's help it would improve.

'How have you altered their lives?' I asked.

'We have clothed them,' she said simply.

I was so astonished by this reply that I suppose I must have shown it. It seemed so extraordinary that someone should have come all this way, especially someone whose mission was spiritual, and have been most impressed by whether people wore clothes or not, surely an accident of climate rather than a matter of religious principle.

'You see,' she explained, 'when we arrived they were just naked savages.'

I did not know at the time that the whole question of the influence of missionaries on the Amerindians is one of the most controversial in the country. Later I was to hear it discussed frequently but now I just thought I had come across a lady who converted naked savages into clothed savages. She had, it seemed, reinterpreted the story of Adam and Eve in such a way that their donning of clothes was a sign not of their fall from grace but rather of their achievement of it.

'Of course,' she was saying, 'they often relapse and take them off. It's tempting, of course, for them when they're so much in the water and their skins do get irritated by clothes, but we persist and we are bringing out a skin specialist next tour.'

She went on to tell me that the natives were very susceptible to the infectious diseases which affected the missionaries' own children and that a whole Amerindian village could be wiped out by an attack of the measles. She sounded just a little bit peeved by this, as if she felt that they would not have succumbed to such childish ailments if they had had greater moral stamina.

Altogether I was relieved when Dick called over to say that we were free to go.

We were met now by one of the directors of the Booker Company with which my husband's work would be most concerned. Then and often later he was to provide us with much useful information about the country. But now, as we drove from the airport to Georgetown, I was not tuned in for the reception of useful information. I think that when one arrives somewhere totally strange it is better at first not to rationalize, but just to wonder. It is more important to feel than to think. Later one starts to think, to classify and compare, but at first it is enough just to be there and enjoy the curious knowledge that in a few days it will seem quite familiar and normal. Strangeness is a fleeting quality; it should be savoured.

The land was cleared of trees on each side of the road for a depth of a few hundred yards and there were poor shacks by the wayside, stuck lopsidedly on stilts, looking as if the sound of the horn would be enough to topple them over. Our companion looked at them with distaste and said that it was a pity that new arrivals should have to pass them and that there were far better houses built of concrete in Georgetown and Dick remarked that even these compared favourably with many he had seen in India. Their voices formed a kind of background of normality and yet just out there, only a few feet away, sometimes separated from us by not much more than the thickness of the steel body of the car, people were carrying on lives as different from ours as one could imagine, separated by centuries of different ways of living, separated by poverty, by education, by colour and race. And yet so near.

Children stood by the roadside and stared at us with huge brown eyes; there were solemn-faced little boys wearing a single vest-like garment that reached just above their genitals. There were little girls who peered at us above the hands which they kept over their mouths and cheeks. An old woman was sitting under a house pulling the feathers out of a chicken, her knees widespread. Unlike the others she wore shoes; they must have been many sizes too big, and stuck up in front of her like milestones.

Some of the houses had long poles stuck into the ground outside with brightly coloured rags tied to the ends. These, I learned later, were prayer flags which the Hindus erect with great ceremony on special occasions or at the making of a vow.

We were bumping along very slowly now. The road which had been a smooth tarmacadam one for the first mile, had deteriorated suddenly as we passed through a gate out of the airport grounds.

Thereafter the road was made of burnt earth, a fine red powder made by cooking mud very slowly in great mounds, rather as the old brick kilns used to bake bricks in England. When the heavy rains fall, this surface is, of course, easily washed away and more has to be put on. Things were improving, however, for until recently nobody had attempted to drive to the airport without a shovel in the boot to dig the car out of the holes. During the time we were in Guyana it improved still further, until most of the road had been properly surfaced. It has since been completed and extended much further up country to Mackenzie.

Sometimes, through the undergrowth on our left, we caught a glimpse of the Demerara river as it flowed grey and muddy out to a mud-laden sea. Sometimes we saw 'kokers' or sluices between us and the river as we bumped over wooden bridges that crossed the canals which carried the flood waters down to the estuary, for the coastal area of Guyana lies some four feet below sea level. I used to wonder if that was what originally attracted the Dutch to settle here; perhaps, three thousand miles from home, they felt reassured by tackling a familiar problem with time-proven methods. They built a system of canals through which at low tide the flood waters could be drained into the estuary. At high tide the canals were shut off by 'kokers' which held the sea water back. In the nineteenth century the British, having taken the colony from the Dutch in the Napoleonic Wars, built the sea wall, which is today the main defence against the Atlantic Ocean.

On the outskirts of Georgetown, we now approached La Penitence, a poor district with a very colourful market. Stall after stall on the roadside was piled up with fruit and vegetables. I saw bananas and pineapples and looked at the rest with wonder; they would soon be as familiar as apples and oranges, but now I did not even know their names. It was Saturday morning and there was a tremendous air of bustle along the pavements; people called out to each other, gesticulated, laughed and pushed. The women who were selling—and they were nearly all women—wore huge and exotic hats and everyone wore bright colours, for they dress for the strong sunshine in bright reds and blues, as we dress for our grey skies in muted pastel shades.

The road was as crowded as the pavement and we nosed our way cautiously between pedestrians and donkey carts and bicycles. There is a noticeable lack of any road sense in Georgetown, despite the number of modern cars. For the motor car is a recent arrival and as a result people still tend to think in terms of the donkey cart. Moreover, on the bad roads, they naturally drive where there are fewer bumps and holes, which may mean keeping to the right or, more probably, dictates a zig-zag course.

After this approach, the centre of Georgetown came as a great surprise. It is a beautiful one, far more gracious, I later realized, than that of any of the lovelier West Indian Islands with which Guyana is often unflatteringly compared. Its spaciousness derives from the way in which the Dutch laid out their roads. They built very wide streets with a canal down the centre. More recently a system of pipes has been installed and it was, therefore, possible to fill in many of the canals and as a result the main streets of Georgetown are very wide with an expanse of grass running down the centre which is often planted with trees.

Never very good at finding my way about, I was much confused at first by the fact that the roads are reckoned wide enough to be called by one name on one side and a different one on the other. Further confusion is caused by the fact that the streets are numbered not according to houses, but according to the lots into which the land was originally divided. There may be three or four houses on the lots and they will all have the same numbers. A final complication is that the lot numbers are repeated in the same road, so the section of the road has to be known as well as its name and the lot number of the house. Altogether it is perhaps not surprising that letters have a way of going astray.

From what I had had time to read about Guyana, I had deduced that shops would be practically non-existent and had spent precious hours trying to work out impossible sums like how much toothpaste we would need for two years. It was something of a let-down, therefore, to see, as we drove into the centre of Georgetown, large modern stores, such as Bookers, a department store and a supermarket as well stocked as any in England. I thought of the trunkful of soap and talcum powder and all that toothpaste and felt rather foolish.

Of course, the majority of shops are very different from these modern concrete stores; they are little, wooden buildings, owned by East Indians and Chinese and located in the smaller side streets. I was always aware of this sense of contrast in Georgetown; just by turning a corner one could move from the primitive to the modern, in a few minutes go to a rough and busy Indian grocery, next to a stuffy Victorian family business and then to an American-style emporium where even the curtains were called drapes.

Up country too, I later realized, there could often be a startling intrusion of mid-twentieth century urban civilization. The leader of an expedition into the Interior once told me how he travelled in the bush with an Amerindian guide who one night shot, with his bow and arrow, a trumpet bird which he cooked in an improvised pot over a wood fire. It was very good, the European told his guide. 'Would have been less tough with pressure cooker,' the Amerindian replied nonchalantly.

The car drew up outside a big, white-painted wooden hotel where it had been arranged for us that we should stay until we had found a house. It had a spacious air about it and one sensed that the staff outnumbered the guests. Leaving the men on the verandah to talk, I made my way to our room, or rather joined the little procession to it. First there was a little East Indian boy, about ten years old, who was all strung about with our hand luggage. Cases swung from straps over his shoulders and boxes and little parcels seemed to be attached to different parts of his small person with lengths of thick string. Behind him came an old and very fat African woman carrying a pile of towels. I brought up the rear, following them up steps and down long, narrow corridors lined with coconut matting. Finally we stopped outside a door; the old woman fumbled with a great bunch of keys and the little boy fixed his huge brown eyes on her and stared. Suddenly she rounded on him. 'You got him key, man?' she demanded. He took it silently out of his pocket. She snatched it from him and gave me one of those 'Oh, these children, they're all the same nowadays' looks, which are to be seen on the faces of ageing adults the world over. Then she pushed the key emphatically into the keyhole and opened the door with a flourish.

The change was scarcely credible, for this really was an air-conditioned room, and by crossing the threshold one entered a different world. All the everyday noises were excluded; there was no sound of voices, of distant doors slamming or of cars blowing their horns in the streets outside. The room was completely sealed off. It had its own peculiar atmosphere, which consisted of a kind of cool stuffiness, thickened with the whirr of the air-conditioner and the smell of Flit. It is a most evocative atmosphere and whenever we have come across it since in other parts of the world it has always brought me back in an instant to the day we arrived in Georgetown.

The old woman was scolding the boy for standing in the doorway, 'You gonna let in all dem mosquitoes, man?' she grumbled, pushing him out of the door, so that he scarcely had time to disentangle himself from the mesh of luggage which entwined him.

Having sent him packing, she bustled about the room proprietorially. She was one of those big African women, whom I later used always to enjoy watching, who do everything with great aplomb. Their movements are free and dramatic and they have a great sense of style. I sensed, as she stood smiling and nodding and hoping that I would be comfortable, that she pictured herself as the great lady welcoming the guest. She had chosen to be proprietress rather than chambermaid and played her part with enjoyment, even relish.

'Here den is de bathroom,' she said, throwing open one of the doors off our room. As she did so something black scuttled across the tiled floor. It stood quite high, like a small mouse. Her foot shot out and there was a loud crack. Then she picked up the cockroach, grumbled at it and dropped it down the lavatory which she flushed ceremoniously.

When she had taken her leave, I lay down on the nearest bed, my shoes clattering to the floor. It seemed almost miraculous to be cool again and to relax without having to tense oneself against the heat. I let myself drift. I seemed to have escaped from a sun-grilled hillside into a cold silent cave or to have stepped out of a hot Italian cloisters at noon into a cool and hushed cathedral. As I dozed the air-conditioner played its distant organ music and the smell of Flit spiced the air like incense. Sleep crept down the hot and tired corridors of my brain. Just before I slept, I noticed that the thermometer hanging by the bed registered 80 degrees. Years ago, I thought, years and years ago, in England, wouldn't that have been considered rather hot?

CHAPTER THREE

Moving In

The next day was a Sunday and was to be devoted entirely to deciding where to live. I knew that we must settle the matter immediately for once Dick started work on Monday all domestic problems would be dismissed with an air of slightly irritated abstraction.

Houses, our friend from Bookers told us as he drove us from the hotel, were in very short supply; there were only five possibilities for us to look at. Having once hunted for a cottage in Surrey, this seemed to me to constitute an almost embarrassingly wide choice.

There were two basic types of house to choose between; in Georgetown itself there are big, wooden 'colonial-style' houses. Painted white, raised on pillars, with an outside staircase leading up to the front door, they are charming and full of character. Further out, there are modern houses, built of concrete, which are no doubt easier to run and less likely to harbour horrors like cockroaches, but have much less character and charm. Their rooms are smaller and although the material of which they are built might be expected to be cooler, they seem stuffier. The older houses seem better designed to catch the breeze and avoid the sun.

By the end of the day the choice had dwindled to two alternatives: there was a big wooden house in Georgetown, near the Botanical Gardens and a recently finished concrete one outside the town in a development area called Campbellville. 'Finished' is perhaps too strong a word, for the walls were still unplastered and the outside a mess of builders' rubble, while the only way into the property was over a little plank precariously balanced over the wide ditch which surrounded the plot.

It was hard to choose between them, especially for one who has a horror of taking even the smallest decisions. Dick left me to decide which it should be and allowed me Monday morning to make up my mind. The next morning I went out alone to Campbellville and stood in the concrete house totting up the advantages of a modern building, but not feeling any affection for it. Then I went back to Georgetown and let myself in through the heavy wooden gate of the other house, climbed up its outside stairs and unlocked the front door. It was dark and had a friendly musty smell, it felt established and had a garden and an atmosphere of its own. Feeling as I did about the house, it was not hard to discover advantages; it would be easier to get to the shops, for example, and be much nearer for Dick to get to work, for Campbellville was on the far side of the town from the site.

I locked the door, pocketed the key and felt as if I had lived here for a long time. Back at the hotel, I sat on the verandah and enjoyed that lightness of spirit which comes from a decision wisely taken.

When Dick came in for luncheon, I noticed that the preoccupied air had already settled upon him. 'Had a good day?' he enquired automatically.

'Yes, very. I've decided about the house.'

'Good, good,' he said, sipping lime juice. Then came the familiar words; 'I'm afraid I'll be a bit late tonight. I've some things to run through with my chief clerk. By the way, I think he'd rather like to live in that house we saw yesterday near the Botanical Gardens when his wife comes out. They've got a little boy and there's a school near and the gardens would be convenient too. You don't mind, do you? There was another one outside, wasn't there?'

I did not mind; at least not more than I always mind taking a decision unnecessarily, with all the waste of nervous energy that that involves. I was already telling myself that it would be quieter out of Georgetown and I loathe shopping anyway.

I spent the afternoon buying equipment for our new house; it was all very simple compared with setting up a home in England. There was no need for carpets or proper curtains—the 'drapes' were mere pretence strips hanging at the side of the windows and could be put up any time. The kitchen was already provided with an oil stove. Beds, tables and chairs were lent to us by Bookers, those generous all-providers. We kept other furnishings to a minimum, for a room quickly feels stuffy and cluttered in a hot and humid climate.

Like practically all houses in Guyana, our house was really a bungalow built up high on stilts, in this case concrete pillars. This was in order that the rooms should catch as much breeze as possible and be well above flood level in the rainy season. It meant that there was a large covered area under the house which was useful for all kinds of activities, functioning as a kind of open-sided workshop and greenhouse. It allowed room, too, for a garage, maid's room and washroom.

Unlike the older houses, our stairs were inside so that the front door was on ground level, which turned out to be a not very sensible idea as the floods came under the front door and ruined the covering which we had foolishly put on the hall floor. The stairs led up into the living room, one end of which was a sitting room and the other a dining room. Beyond that was the kitchen. It was the only part of the house which was not protected from the glare of the sun by an overhang, it was very small, had tiny windows and faced due south. Clearly it was not anticipated that the lady of the house should spend much time in the kitchen. Future occupants will feel about the architect as many English householders do about those Victorian builders who designed their houses on the assumption that cheap coal and cheaper servants were part of the natural and eternal order of things.

On the north side of the house were three bedrooms, one of which we made into a study, and a shower and a lavatory. Houses in Guyana do not usually have baths and only very rarely have hot water. Of course, the tap water was always warm and for drinking we used to boil it, cool it in the refrigerator and then disguise it with limes and sugar.

The internal walls of the house did not reach the ceiling; they were built up to a height of about seven feet and then there was a great gap between the top of the wall and the steep roof. This allowed the free circulation of air throughout the house; it also allowed the free circulation of cooking smells, the sounds of guests cleaning their teeth and the creaking of their bedsprings. This kind of open-plan living struck us oddly at first. Indeed, we did not feel we were going to bed at all when it only involved going round to the other side of the partition wall, but we soon grew accustomed to the idea that keeping as cool as possible is the one overriding consideration. Perhaps our enclosed rooms in England suit our more enclosed, reserved natures, just as their open living suits the more gregarious and noise-loving character of most tropical people. Both character and way of life must originally have been moulded by the climate.

The day we moved into our house the temperature dropped to

eighty-two degrees and everyone said how lucky we were to have it so cool. The humidity stayed at a steady ninety-seven.

The fact that a house is built on stilts may be useful in time of flood, but it is something of a handicap in time of removal. All that Saturday afternoon a long line of men carried tables and beds and crates of china up the stairs while Dick tried to direct them into appropriate rooms and I stirred up the tissue paper in a crate of kitchen things I could not remember having ordered. Suddenly at the end of the line appeared a man who was not carrying anything. He was a passer-by, we supposed, just interested in the proceedings. I said, 'Good afternoon,' and he said, 'Here der is a teef-man.'

We had only been in the country for a week and were not yet much good at interpreting.

'A chief man,' I murmured hopefully. 'A chief man lived here?' Then Dick said confidently, 'Ah yes, a dentist.'

He nodded politely at both these suggestions, as if he thought them excellent if irrelevant. 'Teef-man,' he repeated. Then more excitedly, 'Teef-man, teef-man.'

Suddenly he ran downstairs and reappeared a few minutes later via the drainpipe and lavatory window. He repeated this performance three or four times before we realized he was warning us against house-breakers.

'Ah, THIEF-man,' we sighed.

'Dat's right, Burglar,' he said.

By this time all our goods had been delivered and we sat on crates and asked his advice on keeping out thieves.

'Big dog,' he said. 'I've got plenty with long teef.'

We did not particularly want to get involved in any more teef conversations so explained that we had to unpack now but would think about the dog. 'Right, den I sees you Monday,' he said and left us.

In the days that followed, neighbours, tradesmen and passers-by all warned us about teef-men. Apparently they were quite fearless, usually came at night, naked and covered with grease, so that they were too slippery to catch, and armed with a cutlass. The occupant of the house was always at something of a disadvantage as he was encumbered by the mosquito net and likely to get entangled in it if he tried to attack a thief who appeared in the bedroom. Everyone recommended keeping a watch-dog and most, it turned out, had one to sell.

In the nights that followed, however, we turned very anti-dog. The nights were long and hot and sleep difficult. The wild dogs made it impossible. They roamed the area after nightfall, howling and barking as they hunted in packs. Sometimes there would be a short silence and then a distant howl would be taken up by another and another, weaving a pattern of sound that inevitably ended up under the bedroom window. By the time we had leapt angrily out of bed, been brought up short by the mosquito net, fumbled our way through it, found something to throw and removed the wire mesh from the window, the dogs would have retreated out of reach round the corner, whence they continued to bay their defiance.

During the day they slept peacefully under houses, in ditches or in the perilous shade under a parked car. They were a dirty yellow colour, had wild, mad eyes and were as quick and cunning as rats.

It was clear that if we were to have a watch dog it would have to be a well-trained one that would not answer back the insults that the wild dogs would no doubt hurl at it throughout the night. Dick decided on a bulldog and we let it be known that that was what we wanted, and that we would see any that were for sale the next Saturday afternoon. Since we had never seen a bulldog in the country we did not expect the response to be great. It was overwhelming. That evening the garden and the road outside swarmed with dogs, some chained to trees, some on pieces of string brought by children so small that it almost looked as if the dog had brought the baby along to sell.

They were all wild dogs and were enjoying the garden. The more energetic ones were beginning to fight and howl in readiness for the night, some slept among the young plants we had just put in, others fought over the contents of the dustbin. Not one made the slightest effort to look like a bulldog. One or two, perhaps, had a touch of the terrier, but most were the usual dusty yellow colour, like world-weary pancakes. All gave themselves away by the mad gleam in their wild eyes.

'But, they're WILD dogs,' I heard Dick objecting. 'They're no good for house dogs. I said BULLdogs.'

'Day is all bulldogs,' one owner explained patiently, hanging on to his mangy cur as it strained to reach the dustbin. 'You did say bulldog. Day is everyone bulldog. All is good. Mine is best.'

'I said Bulldog—'

'Der is no bitch here, day is all bulldogs.'

So it was. A bulldog is any male dog. We had as many wild dogs snarling and cringing in our garden as if we had asked for male curs.

When our first visitor had said he would see us on Mondays, I had taken this as a polite form of words of farewell, for he had not thought to tell us that he was the Kerosene man who would come every week with fuel for the evil oil stove in the kitchen which was our only means of cooking. He thought everyone knew that.

He had heard about the bulldog episode and was very sorry about it.

'You right,' he assured me the next Monday. 'You don't want no wild dog. Day is no good watch dogs. You want good dog.'

'That's right,' I agreed. 'We need a specially bred dog.'

He laughed, a confident, even triumphant, laugh. 'I fix it,' he said. 'You leave it to Kerosene Joe.'

'How?' I asked suspiciously, for I had been disappointed too many times to be easily excited by such a promise.

'My uncle breeds best dogs in whole country,' he said.

'What breed are they?'

He beamed, confident of approval, 'Lady,' he said, with pride beyond that of a man whose pet has just taken a first prize at Crufts. 'Lady, day is every one a bastard!'

In the three weeks we had had to prepare ourselves before leaving England, I had picked up a pamphlet at a tourist office which offered advice to those about to set up home in Guyana. Under the heading of domestic help, it stated that most Europeans managed with a cook and a butler-chambermaid. I had spent many idle minutes since wondering what kind of bi-sexual institution a butler-chambermaid could possibly be. Arriving in Guyana I was very disappointed to find that the species appeared not to exist or has anyway become extinct at some time before living memory might recall. I was, however, provided with a great deal of information about domestic help. All servants, I was told, were awkward, obstinate and dishonest. Those who did the washing refused to iron, those who ironed would not work near a refrigerator for fear of catching cold, they all left just when it suited them without any warning, but had recently taken to sueing any employer who sacked them without notice. Above all they were unreliable and never turned up on time. This I was told by practically every woman who employed local servants and none of it, I found by experience, was true.

Lucille was sent to me by the wife of our friend in Bookers who had already been so helpful to us. She was an African with a smooth, unlined face and a slim girlish figure. I took her for perhaps twenty years old. It was some time before I discovered that she was nearly forty, had six children and had lost her husband two years earlier when she was expecting her last baby.

She was shy to the point of seeming, at first, sullen. She answered my questions with a short yes or no and there was none of the easy exchange of domesticities that one associates with such an appointment in England. Clearly I was expected to make all the arrangements and she would agree to anything I proposed. It did not strike me as a particularly good way of doing things; I should have preferred to know what suited her, for arrangements that suit both parties have a way of lasting longer.

Here, I realized later, was one cause of the complaints of employers about their maids. The level of unemployment is so high that a girl will agree to practically any conditions or times to get a job, even though she knows she will not be able to keep to them. When she gets home and thinks it over she may realize she cannot manage it and, frightened to go back and face the wrath, she takes the easy way of just not turning up. She may try for a while, always being late and making excuses until she is sacked. The underlying cause is the false relationship which past colonial attitudes foist on to both sides, making the one too subservient and too afraid to say directly what its requirements are, and the other too domineering. I say that these attitudes are foisted upon people today by the colonial past because it is very difficult to avoid them. If the maid refuses to say what suits her, the mistress is forced to be more dictatorial than she would otherwise be. We did not choose the appellations 'Master' or 'Boss' or 'Mistress', indeed they grated horribly on our ears at first, but were obliged to accept them from those who worked for us. It was their choice, not ours.

I found it more difficult to communicate with Lucille than I had expected in what was, after all, an English-speaking country. True Creolese, which is the language of the less educated people, is practically impossible for an English person to understand without years of practice. Education often complicates things by encouraging the speaker to introduce a tremendous number of unnecessary abstract nouns and high-falutin turns of phrase which completely obscure the meaning. The letters in the local papers used to provide some impressive examples. Lucille, however, spoke to

h commemorating the
ependence of Guyana.

Georgetown cathedral. One of the largest wooden buildings in the world.

A 'koker' or sluice which shuts off the canals at high tide and so holds the sea water back. This is an unusually elegant one.

Victoria regia lily. The leaves, which float like trays of cork, are about four feet across.

me at least very simply, unless she was excited and broke into Creolese. She had more difficulty at first in understanding me than I had of her. I did not realize why this was until one day after we had been in Guyana for a few weeks, and I came home from the school where I was doing some part-time teaching, bringing a colleague back with me. When Lucille opened the door I asked her if she would go and put the kettle on. She looked blank and as usual I repeated the request several times before her face lightened and she went to do what I had asked. My friend was also an African so I asked her if she had any idea why I had this difficulty in getting Lucille to understand. 'You make it all too elaborate,' she explained. 'All this "I wonder if you'd mind" and "perhaps you could go and" business in front of an order confuses her and she's trying so hard to think what it means that she doesn't hear the important part at the end.'

Of course it was so; Lucille, now I came to think about it, always came to me with very abrupt requests like, 'Please for de soap.' Henceforward I tried to put things as succinctly as she did, but some deep-rooted horror of sounding like a mem-sahib usually inhibited me.

Lucille had the African's love of clothes and was an expert washer and ironer. She took over the care of the linen with great gusto and our limp and dispirited English clothes were soon unrecognizable. Even if they had only been worn for an hour or two they disappeared in the morning and reappeared at night, washed, starched, ironed and aired. I had expected to send sheets to the laundry, but they were whipped off the beds, washed, blued and starched and stretched out on the grass before I had had time to make any other arrangements for them. She washed everything by hand and in cold water, but they looked cleaner than they did in England after the ministrations of the laundry. I did try to persuade her that she would find it easier to boil water, but she preferred to do it her way. Later I tried—and failed—to persuade cooks to use boiling water for washing up; they preferred to use cold water and plenty of elbow grease, even for pans and baking dishes. Yet the plates were never even smeared.

Lucille was a great improviser; indeed all the Guyanese are fond of 'fixin' things', often with more enthusiasm than finesse. On Lucille's first morning with us I heard sounds of activity in the wash room and went to tell her not to wash for a day or two as I had not got the clothes line yet. I found that not only had she done

Our house in Campbellville.
Colonial-style house in Georgetown.
Cows grazing in a suburban road.

most of the washing, but had found a roll of wire under the house and festooned it from every nail or piece of wood that she could find: it zig-zagged under the house, between the verandah and the garden fence and wove its way about the plot like a huge spider's web and was already lively with washing.

After a melting week in the tiny kitchen with the oil cooker, I asked Lucille if she could find us a cook. 'I'll bring me friend Myra,' she said. 'She come see you dis evening.'

Later in the day there was a knock at the door and I found a stout lady on the door step. 'You must be Myra,' I said. 'Lucille told me about you. Would you like to come and be cook?' She said she was and she would and we arranged that she should start the next day.

An hour or so later there was another knock at the back door and another African stood there. 'I'm Myra,' she said cheerfully. 'Lucille she say you wantin' cook.'

I began to wonder how many more Myras would be applying for the job. I had not yet realized that so great is the unemployment in the country that women go from door to door looking for jobs and are so anxious to get work that they would not dream of letting a slight obstacle like not being Myra stand in their way. This one, however, had brought Lucille with her for moral support and Lucille and I now jointly appointed her.

Myra had been a nanny in an English family who had taught her, she told me, a little cooking. Pressed further on the extent of her culinary knowledge, she told me, 'I knows scrambled egg and Bird's custard.' She added that she was very willing to learn. She was indeed very willing, but she was also unfortunately unteachable. Desperately eager to oblige, she could never bring herself to say she did not understand, which made it difficult to teach her even the simplest things. Boiled eggs seemed a good starting point. Morning after morning they appeared either raw or hard-boiled despite repeated instructions. And morning after morning I asked her if she was sure the water had been boiling, and she assured me that it had, and I asked how long they had been in that same boiling water and she told me for four minutes by the kitchen clock. She was always sure that the next morning they would be just right, but they never were. At last I realized the truth; she could not tell the time. 'Four minutes by the kitchen clock,' was just another way of saying that she had guessed. She was not a very good guesser. After a few attempts at teaching Myra to tell the time I decided it would be easier to buy her an egg-timer. A friend coming out from England kindly brought one with her and I presented it to Myra who greeted it joyfully. I began explaining to her how it worked, but she interrupted with, 'Oh, I know egg-timer,' so I left her with the new toy. The next morning I went into the kitchen before breakfast to find, boiling away in the pan together, the eggs and the new egg-timer.

She tried very hard, but since she was not used to thinking and so unable to grasp the reasons for doing things and since she could not read or write and so could not write down instructions for constant reference, she had to try to commit everything to her unpractised memory. She took all instructions absolutely literally, sometimes with unfortunate results. The first time we had a visitor staying in the house, I asked her to make the tea much stronger, as we drank ours milkless and very weak. 'Three teaspoons,' I said several times, 'three teaspoons in the pot.' At breakfast time I noticed a curious clinking sound and looked into the teapot to find three teaspoons rattling around in the tea.

Milk was always a problem. We had only been in the house a few days when an old East Indian woman appeared on the doorstep with a wooden tub of milk on her arm. 'Lovely good milk, mistress,' she croaked, spitting, and missing the tub more by good luck than good management. 'Look, lovely and clean and no roaches,' and she proved her point by stirring the milk with her grimy hand. I knew about these tubs already. When they sprang a leak they were repaired with donkey dung which dried nice and hard like plastic wood.

Later a pasteurization plant was set up but while we were there it was having what are politely known as teething troubles, and the milk was often sour. I told the milkman this and he replied cheerfully that it was good when he brought it but no doubt I sent it bad myself. I persuaded him to wait while I poured some of the milk he was delivering into a pan and boiled it; it separated. 'Look,' I said, showing him the lumps, 'it is sour when you bring it.'

'It's you spoils it, mistress, like I said. It was good, good until you boils it.'

Myra was a bit puzzled by the whole proceeding but I could see that she agreed with the milkman and that she was sorry that I had lost face by proving myself so patently wrong.

Thenceforward we had tinned milk. Even so we were constantly plagued by gastric troubles and had to be very careful over the preparation of food. There were all kinds of difficulties; Myra regarded the refrigerator as a kind of magic box that could cure any form of decay by freezing it better. She exposed us and herself to more dramatic dangers too. The working of the oil cooker required an ability to distinguish between methylated spirit and paraffin. It was the kind of thing that Myra found a bit confusing. Stirred on by the thought that she might blow us all up and also by medical instructions to live on grilled food, we decided to part with the oil cooker and replace it with one of the new calor gas ones that were being imported into the country. What we had not realized was that bottled gas has no smell and that Myra did not distinguish between tiresome little monosyllables like 'Off' and 'On.' Regularly each evening she carefully turned on all the knobs before she said goodnight to us. During the day she just left on one or two. I began to be haunted by a vision of Myra entering a gas-filled kitchen, smiling her willing smile as for the last time she reached for the match box.

Parting with her was a sad business and I could not have done it if she had not been well provided for by the return of her only son to her home. I knew she would be happier in a job looking after children, whose demands and thought processes she could understand and that we should be safer without her attempts to learn to cook in our kitchen.

Myra's successor won her place mainly on the strength of her name. Names in Guyana were a source of constant joy to me. Our driver, Jubraj, told me that the Chinese chose the names for their children by ringing a bell and seeing what sound it said. It is a nice thought, albeit an unlikely one. Indians consult their priests when a child is born to see how it should be named and their family names remain a strong tradition, but Africans are gloriously free to look about and choose the most flowery or impressive that history, current politics or glossy magazines can offer. Sometimes they simply consulted the labels of bottles or tins of imported goods; we came across a Dettolin and a Silver Dip and an Aerosol. The surname was usually either English or Scottish and often denoted the father's occupation, which suggests that that was sometimes all that the unfortunate mother knew about him. Just as many English surnames have derived from crafts giving us such names as Carpenter or Hooper so in Guyana they are derived from more modern occupations such as Surveyor or Contractor.

The cook who presented herself after Myra's departure was a diminutive figure, quite round and about four foot ten inches tall. Her face seemed, of necessity, to be constantly upturned and her features were slightly Mongolian as if she might have had some Amerindian blood. She had a big slow smile. Like Myra, she did not know much about cooking but said she was willing to learn, at which optimistic forecast my heart sank. Nothing is so disheartening as somebody promising to do their best. As she was going I asked her name.

'Mable Adonis,' she said and I engaged her on the spot.

Mable—for that is how Mabel is rendered in Guyana—was not a practical person. Had her circumstances only been different she would have been a scholar. The very reverse of Myra, she always wanted to learn and know the reasons for things. She was widely read and loved nothing better than to discuss with me at length books and politics. She was very dreamy and slow and undoubtedly in the wrong job, but her country could offer her nothing else, so I set about teaching her what I could.

She was very thorough and logical, though even that sometimes proved a disadvantage. Once when we were having a dinner party I managed to get hold of some tinned Blue Danish cheese, newly imported and something of a novelty, as cheese was not much eaten. When I went into the kitchen just before the guests arrived, Mable greeted me sadly. 'That cheese,' she said, 'was of very poor quality. I had to cut out most of it and what is left is scarcely worth keeping.' There remained on the board, after her cleansing operation, a few yellow crumbs. It was hard to give her any convincing explanation of the fact that while I insisted on throwing away any bad bits of pawpaws or mangoes, I should offer guests a lump of bad cheese.

Fortunately Lucille and Mable got on as well together as Lucille and Myra had done, and both regarded our East Indian garden boy with a kind of tolerant and motherly affection. Of Jubraj our driver, they were at first slightly in awe, for his management of that costly and complicated machine, the car, cast upon him the mantle of a superior being.

Jubraj was an East Indian and acted as chauffeur throughout our stay. At first he used to spend part of two mornings each week taking me shopping, but soon I found it easier to entrust him with lists of commissions which he fitted in while waiting for Dick, whom he drove to meetings. He was very reliable, solid and extremely slow-moving. He was not over-impressed by the virtues of work and did not, as other drivers did, rush about opening car doors and carrying shopping baskets. On the other hand, he never, as some other drivers did, made off with the car for his own purposes nor made a profit for himself on the commissions he was entrusted with. Indeed he could not have been more meticulous in his rendering of accounts and took great pride in delivering up the change correct to the last cent.

His appearance was misleading; there was something warlike about it. He had long, thick hair, swept back and up from his forehead and perhaps it was this Stalinesque touch which gave him a slight air of the assassin. In fact, he was eminently peace-loving and gentle, if not actually timid. On our first drive through Georgetown he pointed out to me a little park and said it sometimes had lovely flowers for sale. I asked if we might stop and have a look, but he told me that a woman had once been murdered in the gardens and he thought it would be better if the boss took me instead.

He had a horror of getting involved in any kind of dispute or even friendly argument. The only kind of altercation he would risk was one carried on with a cyclist through the window of the car and even then he would hurl his abuse and accelerate before we had time to hear the answer.

He loved children and animals and jokes. He kept chickens not because it was profitable, but because he liked having them around. He was fond of Lucille and would spend any time he had to wait at the house mending the well-patched tyres of her bicycle. He did quite a lot of waiting at the house, because he always arrived early, for he was utterly dependable about time as he was about everything else. The only occasions upon which plans went awry occurred when he decided as he put it, 'to act on me initiative.' That was fatal, but it was fortunately extremely rare.

It was rare because he was by nature disinclined to be active in any way. He seemed to live under the influence of a mild soporific. His walk was that of a somnambulist and, if he was not driving, he settled himself in the seat of the car like one settling down to hibernate. He needed a great deal of sleep. If ever I asked him what he had done at the weekend, he would seem surprised that I needed to ask and the reply would invariably be, 'Spent it sleeping, mistress.'

He was abundantly blessed with the one gift essential to a chauffeur, patience. He was able to sit for hours in the car, just letting time pass. Other drivers might get out and gossip together, or read or amuse themselves in one way or another as they waited for their employers to come out of a meeting, but Jubraj preferred just to sit and wait in a kind of semi-trance. Once Dick asked him what he thought about as he sat in the car doing nothing. 'Ladies,' Jubraj replied simply.

I noticed no signs in our household of that discord between African and East Indian that I had been warned about. They all talked about each other and acted towards each other in the friendliest possible way. They identified themselves, too, with our home-making activities, Jubraj with a kind of avuncular tolerance of such frenetic efforts, the others with great interest and gusto, offering advice and suggestions with apparently no resentment at the overwhelming difference between our standard of living and their own.

It took a little time to get used to the unfinished look of the house, for the walls which we had thought were awaiting plaster were in fact complete. They are usually left with their rough concrete surfaces exposed. The woodwork was very badly finished too by European standards. The standard of workmanship is on the whole very low and the work crude for there are very few craftsmen in Guyana, as in most underdeveloped countries. It seemed to me that this was partly the result of poor living conditions in their own homes. They were not accustomed, as British workmen are, to doing things well in their own houses, and there was little finesse in the way they set about doing something even as simple as putting up a shelf. So long as it stayed up for a while at least, they were not concerned that they had made a huge hole in the wall, plugged with an ugly protrusion of wood. Since there were several jobs still being done in the house we had to suffer the sight of some very bad work going on around us. We resolved that we would do any other jobs ourselves, which turned out to be just what our landlord wanted.

One might imagine that houses in Guyana would be very cheap compared with those in England, for they do not have to be well insulated, require no heating system, chimney or fireplaces or hot water, and the fittings are very simple. Really a house is no more than a concrete shell with a few internal partitions. Yet, we soon realized, they were no cheaper than houses in England. This is partly the result of the price of land which is expensive as it has to be drained for building, but largely of the curious manner in which the building of houses is undertaken. Speculative building is carried on at an alarming rate by private individuals with very small means, for it is made easy to build a house for anyone who can raise a small deposit. I imagine that this was originally done so that a man could build his own house even if he had no capital, which seems a good theory. In practice, too many of the optimistic Guyanese seem to have decided to build a house as a piece of speculation. Most have no idea of the difficulties involved and find themselves getting shorter and shorter of money as time goes on and so tend to economize on building materials. They are very much in the hands of the building contractor, who may not be over scrupulous. It all makes for shoddy building. The speculator aims above all at finding a tenant for his house in order to start getting a return, and with luck, somebody who will finish the house for him. Best of all, he hopes to let it to Bookers, who pay well and will not quibble about finishing off the odd jobs undone in the house.

We watched, at first with professional interest, then with fascinated horror, a house being built near ours, soon after we moved in. The speculator was a shop assistant with no capital and less knowledge of building. He began with immense enthusiasm and gradually grew more depressed as difficulties arose which he could not deal with. He was dreadfully bullied by his builder. As his financial position worsened his one hope was to attract a good tenant to pay an extortionate rent. He therefore spent what money he had on eye-catching gimmicks which would interest the passer-by. For example, he employed a team of men to paint bricks on the front side of the house, which did succeed in arousing interest, but would-be tenants who walked round to the back then noticed that huge cracks were already appearing in the other walls, as the house had such poor foundations that it was already beginning to sink. So he painted bricks over the cracked walls too. This meant that he could not afford anything but the roughest wood inside the house and had not enough money to make proper drains. He went bankrupt before he had managed to let the house.

There was another house which we used to pass on our way into Georgetown which was being slowly unbuilt. The man who had started it had been very ambitious and tried to build a kind of little Gothic castle, with turrets and all kinds of conceits. He managed one storey before going to prison for debt and people were now helping themselves to the property which had shrunk almost to its foundations by the time we left.

There were many facts about the housing system which we did not, of course, realize, when we arrived in Guyana. We simply thought we had a very helpful landlord who was kindly allowing us to move into his house before he had quite finished it and who was just about to complete the drains, concrete under the house, make paths and do various other things, which he was most careful to point out needed to be done. When after a month none of these things had been done, we wrote rather apologetically to ask him when he would be arranging for the work to be carried out. He did not reply to that or several other letters. Finally we went to see him, but he had, his wife told us, just gone out. After several more abortive calls we did manage to see him and he quite disarmed us by his astonishment that the work had not been done long ago. He had instructed the builders to see to it weeks ago, he assured us, and could scarcely believe that they had been so wicked as not to carry out his orders. He was most dreadfully sorry that we had had this trouble and with the rainy season almost upon us too. He promised that he would go and see the builder the next day and instruct him to come to the house without fail to complete the work within the week.

Two weeks later the work had still not been started. We went back to our landlord who looked at me reproachfully and said the builders had indeed been to see us but had been sent away. The maid had told them she had orders to admit nobody when the mistress was out. When I got back home I asked Lucille when this had happened and she said never. Confronted with this the landlord explained that the builder must have gone to the wrong house and been turned away by the wrong maid. It seemed a little strange that the builders could not even find the house which they themselves had built. We were, at last, beginning to get suspicious.

A foretaste of the rains now showed what would happen when the real floods came. Water poured into the front door, for what little levelling had been done to the land had been in the wrong direction so that the water drained towards the house instead of away from it. The land all around became a swamp and it was difficult to get in and out of the house. What we had so far achieved in the garden was ruined. Time, we now realized, was on the side of our plausible, apologetic and ever-helpful landlord. Now that we were settled in our new home, he knew it was unlikely that we would move out; he could afford to wait and we could not. In the end we did everything ourselves, levelling the land, making paths, drains and concreting the whole area under the house. When all was finished, just in time before the rains came, our landlord came to inspect it. He was a religious man and, as he looked lovingly around his now much improved estate, he told us he was always giving thanks to the good Lord, for sending such a great blessing in the form of wonderful tenants. Truly, he told us devoutly, he believed we had been sent by Providence. It seemed an opportune moment to tell him about the vagaries of the septic tank, but when I began he suddenly remembered an urgent appointment. He dashed away, down his new concrete drive, waving his hat triumphantly and calling down blessings on our heads.

CHAPTER FOUR

The Garden

The Civil Engineer is necessarily a nomad. He builds a dam, a pier, a tunnel, and when it is finished there is nothing to keep him near his creation. This does not seem to worry him. Usually before one job is done, he is studying the drawings for the next.

Not so his wife; she develops a kind of love-hate relationship with the site, suffering with it in its difficulties with the weather, with its labour problems, with the tribulations caused by the vagaries of the clients. She knows that when the job starts her husband will spend weekends with it and stay with it late into the evening. Confronted with the charred remains of his dinner, he will explain that things are always a bit rushed at the start of a job. After a month or two he will be late because of the piling, and then he will be late because of the concreting, and so until he is late because things are always a bit rushed at the end of a job. His faith in the exceptional nature of his lateness is rather touching. Nothing seems to shake his belief that the need to overwork is a temporary one, due to quite exceptional causes. His wife, meanwhile, since women are less inclined to cherish illusions, has come to realize that the site holds him captive and that their lives are as much bound by the engineering contract as the marriage contract. She may become so disillusioned that the site sometimes seems no more than an amalgam of reasons for ruined meals.

Domestically, it is her lot to move from house to house more frequently than most. There are two alternatives: either to have a settled home for a settled wife while the husband travels alone living in hotels or digs for short jobs, or to travel about together, even if it sometimes means renting a house for only a few months. This had always been our policy and it had one inevitable consequence: we were continually pouring light paint over other people's brown woodwork and making gardens.

The Campbellville garden posed a new difficulty; we had never before had to provide our own soil. Guyana is a land of mud. The natural ground in the 'yard' (the unlovely name given locally to a garden) was mud baked by the sun to the consistency of a brick. It supported a kind of tough, creeping grass, but that was all. To make soil we had to mix up equal parts of donkey dung, fibre dust (from the coconut palm) and sand. This home-made soil was expensive and could not therefore be used to cover expanses of land; it had to be contained.

I often wondered what would happen to life in Guyana if some other means of transporting oil was discovered. Oil drums play a vital part not only in the economic life of the country but also in its cultural activities, in its sanitary arrangements and in its horticulture. We had already heard the steel bands whose drums are made from oil drums cut in two and beaten into hollows which provide different notes. We had already acquired an outsize oil drum to do office as a dustbin. Soon we were to set about equipping the garden with oil drums, which, cut in two and punctured with holes, were filled with the home-made soil and painted white or left their original red and planted with cuttings or seeds.

Our latest garden was small, like most gardens in and around Georgetown. For a garden there does not serve the same purpose as it does in England. Since the houses are raised up high on stilts, the garden is not visible as a long view from the house. It is too hot to sit out in it during the day or to enjoy working in it. Night falls swiftly in the tropics; there is no twilight as there is no slow dawn and no change of seasons. The evenings are short and not very cool and it is always dark by half past six. Moreover, it is as well not to walk on the grass, which is alive with bête rouge, a tiny red insect which burrows beneath the skin. Furthermore, in the evenings the mosquitoes like nothing better than to have a meal of blood sucked from the feet and ankles of unwary gardeners.

However, it was at this uncomfortable time of day that we toured our new domain on the evening we moved into our house. The plot was only about one-sixth of an acre with the house almost in the centre. This was a standard-sized plot for a new house, for although Guyana is eighty-three thousand square miles in area and has a population of less than a million, all but two per cent of that population is concentrated on the coastal strip where there is a shortage of drained land. Great stretches of land disappear under water in the rainy season and land which is fit for house-building is therefore expensive; it is made more so by the activities of speculators.

Even those plots which have been drained and sold as building land are liable to some flooding and the first move of anyone going into a new house is to raise up the level of the yard by bringing in rubble, 'dirt' or fill of any kind so that when the rains come they will drain away on to their neighbour's land.

Our landlord had therefore tipped huge quantities of sawdust into the garden to raise the level. It presented us with many problems for even the creeping grass refused to grow on it. That had been the extent of his gardening. He also promised to make concrete drains. At the moment the waste from the house ran out into little open grass ditches which led into a larger ditch running round the perimeter of the plot. This in turn joined the ditch by the side of the road outside the house and eventually all these road ditches gathered together and entered the canal which emptied itself into the sea.

It was all right in theory, I suppose. In practice there was something wrong with the levels; ours were lower than the ones outside and consequently water from the main ditches flowed back into our garden. I was never quite sure what stopped the Atlantic Ocean from finding its way into our Campbellville yard. The position was made worse after the visit of a Government Inspector who told us that the government was going to clear its drains so we must do ours at once. We did so, making them somewhat deeper in consequence, but when we left the public ones had still not been touched and were now at an even higher level than our own.

Another feature of the arrangement which did not appeal to me was that the ditches harboured frogs; they were outsize things, about six times as big as the British variety. Utterly gross, they peered out from their drains and sometimes roused themselves to move slowly, with a horrible flopping sound, across the concrete. If we came in late at night there would be dozens of them splodging along the path and I moved in horror of stepping on one. The little tree frogs that appeared on the walls were much more lovable and ours never developed the distressing habit of climbing up the pipes and popping out of the taps or plug hole as they did in some houses.

Apart from the frogs we saw nothing in the garden on that first reconnaissance, except the septic tank, about whose appalling smell we complained regularly to the landlord for two years. Once he sent a man to cure it; he was a big African and brought with him a donkey with a load of manure which he proceeded to tip into the tank. 'Dat,' he said with satisfaction, 'dat will get it activatin'.' It made no difference; perhaps the septic tank was active enough already.

Since it was such a little garden, easily the smallest we had ever had to subdue, we thought we should be able to manage it ourselves. One evening's toil in stifling heat, with blisters rising almost instantly on the soft moist skins of our hands, with bêtes rouges starting their long under-skin journey up to our waists, where they raised blisters, and mosquitoes feeding off our legs and ankles, was enough to change our minds.

East Indians form the gardening corps in Guyana; they are either women, usually fairly old ones, called Grannies, or boys. We knew that with work so much in demand it would not be hard to find someone, but we wanted someone who really knew about gardening, since our own knowledge of local conditions was nil, so we asked Lucille to make careful enquiries.

On Sunday morning, an old man appeared on the doorstep. He was an East Indian, very ragged but with a shrewd and knowing expression. Yes, he would clear the yard, he said as we walked around the garden. He would want forty cents an hour and it would take him a day. That was more than most gardeners charged but since he was going to do it so extraordinarily quickly, we did not quibble.

We showed him the tools; here was a pair of shears, there a spade, and a fork, but he interrupted us. 'I bring me cutlass,' he said simply.

A cutlass is the universal tool in Guyana. Like the oil drum, it is impossible to imagine life there without it. A ferocious-looking implement, it is used for cutting crops, particularly sugar cane, for hacking up meat in the market, for cutting grass, for digging and even, in times of stress, for chopping up wives.

There is also a shovel-like instrument for digging. A dinosaur among spades, it has a very long handle about six feet in length and a tiny little head fashioned like a scoop. It is said by some Europeans to represent the Guyanese attitude to work; a thing to be kept as far away from one as possible and to be done in as small amounts as one can.

Our newly-appointed gardener set about chopping at the coarse grass with his cutlass, oblivious of the morning sun, which soon drove us inside. When we looked out a little later he had disappeared. The next time we looked he had not returned, but the garden was full of people. They were all busy. A woman, a bandana round her head, her dress tucked modestly between her knees, squatted on the ground chipping away at the brick-like mud with her cutlass. A boy had begun to dig the grass out of the ditches and a great many little girls were occupied in various ways about the garden.

We went downstairs and approached the woman. She looked up and smiled radiantly. From the distance I had thought she must be very old, but she can only have been about thirty-five. 'Me, his wife, mistress,' she said. 'He send me to work. These me children,' she added, waving towards the girls. 'He, me son,' she said looking towards the boy. 'When all is cleared, he will work for you.'

'But,' I objected, 'we arranged with your husband that he should come. We want a real gardener.'

'I tell the boy,' she said. 'Sometimes I come myself and see how he make out.'

They had evidently arranged it all and we could only fit in with their plans. It made an interesting contrast with Lucille's appointment. At the end of the day, Father came back to collect the money. He explained to us that there had been eight of them working for us for six hours and that would come to twenty dollars. We protested that we had taken him to mean that he would do the work himself in six hours and that anyway they were only children. He laughed and said he would call it fifteen.

Father was a rogue, but his son, Singh, was a delight to us throughout our stay. He did not know very much about gardening, but his mother kept to her word and told him what to do and visited us quite often to see how he was getting on. He had her quick smile and winning manner. He was immensely enthusiastic and very sensitive.

We soon realized that Singh's conception of gardening was very different from ours. To us, here was a piece of land to be made into a garden; to Singh a yard was a place to grow things. How or where they were grown was quite unimportant. We tried hard to explain to him that we wanted to plan the lay-out of the garden. He would seem to understand and then the next day I would go to a patch we had cleared and levelled for a lawn and find Singh had made a kind of rough barricade in the middle, heaped some soil into it and planted vegetables.

Vegetables are not grown in oil drums. Singh told us how to make beds on top of the ground by setting out boards of wood into a long box about six feet by four. The rectangle was then filled with the mixture of sand, donkey dung and fibre dust. What he actually made were four beds of different sizes, every side a different length and no right angles to be seeen. The boards sloped outwards and soil dribbled out at the corners. They did not last long; the next weekend Dick set about them with hammer and saw, with measuring tape and spirit level. Singh did not partake in this foolishness; he went off and planted radishes in a tub of African marigolds.

The carpentry was, however, watched by a little East Indian boy who used to stand outside our gate and stare. He often came and stood in the road, watching; I used to ask him if he would like to come in, but he was too shy and preferred to stand and stare at the queer white people who worked in their garden. Slowly he gained more confidence and came nearer and when one day Dick called to him to come and hold the other end of the measuring tape, he was in the gate like a flash. For the rest of our stay, Basdeo was always to appear whenever there was a tape to be held, wood to be measured, points to be lined in or any other garden engineering to be shared. Since Singh's talents in this direction were non-existent there was no clash between them.

We could make symmetrical beds for Singh, but we could not make him plant things in them in rows, or even plant the same things in each bed. A seed shop which sold imported seeds packaged in tin foil and stored in an air-conditioned room, had recently been opened by an enterprising Guyanese, so we were able to grow some familiar vegetables. At least they were familiar in name though their development was often very different from what it was in England. We grew lettuces that consisted of a handful of flat and floppy leaves. We planted radishes and they grew huge tubers, like turnips. Parsley was very satisfactory for it came up almost overnight and grew into a thick bush. We planted celery and though it tasted just the same, it grew like a coarse parsley. Everything grew very quickly which suited me for I find nature very tedious and slow in England.

The local vegetables grew even more quickly and seeded themselves readily. It was difficult to be sure of their names for the Guyanese are not very particular about botanical labels. Most climbing things were vines, most strange flowers were called lilies and it seemed at first as if green vegetables mostly went by the name of Calaloo. 'What's this?' I asked Singh on one of his first evenings with us, picking up a long stringy stem with small, dull green leaves. 'Calaloo,' he said promptly. 'Good to eat.' Next I picked up a big fleshy plant with thick, shiny leaves, 'And this?' I asked

Campbellville in the rainy season; a view from our verandah.

Basdeo unloading donkey dung for the garden.

Dick and Mable Adonis with a home-grown pumpkin.

Singh, Myra, Lucille and author on our back steps

Singh planting Calaloo with a cutlass in beds he has made out of planks and filled with soil he has made out of coconut fibre, donkey dung and sand.

him. 'Calaloo,' he said again. 'Good to eat. You boils it.' Nearly everything seemed to be Calaloo. There was broad leaved and fine leaved, there was Caterpillar Calaloo and a spade-leaved one, rather like spinach. Calaloo cropped up all over the garden. It seeded itself unasked and grew unaided. If I asked Singh to root it out of a flower tub or a bed of lettuces or to unravel it from the tender little tomato plants which would eventually bear little red marbles, he would agree willingly and appear to rush away to do it, but I would later find the work untouched. It was not that he meant to be disobedient; he simply could not take seriously any order to destroy something that could be eaten if left alone. Finally we made beds of the stuff and Singh moved all the plants into them, but it continued to seed itself prolifically and Singh sabotaged all my efforts to control it.

This was but one of the many ways in which I came to realize the major difference in outlook between those who have known hunger and those who have not. Once we showed Basdeo a picture of Trafalgar Square. He looked at the pigeons in amazement and then pointed at them. 'But they walks about free,' he said. 'Yes,' I agreed, 'they're very tame.' 'But why doesn't the people kill them to eat?'

I was reminded of this conversation later when a friend of ours who was a doctor from Britain told us how he had found an East Indian boy holding a little bird, about the size of a small sparrow, that he had killed. 'Whatever made you do that?' he asked, horrified at the wanton cruelty. 'Why did you have to kill it?' The boy looked bewildered, 'To eat,' he said, surprised that anyone should need to ask.

A deep abyss separates the lives of those who have known hunger from those who have not; there is a great gap fixed between those for whom a little bird is a charming creature and those for whom it is a meal.

I was often struck by the difference between Guyanese children and English. They seemed so old and worldly-wise for their age. East Indian children who used to come to our door selling baskets of fruit and vegetables were of an age at which one felt that their English equivalents would have been still shaking the bars of the playpen. One tiny pair, both girls, used to come regularly. About four or five years old, wearing curious old trilby hats, they laboured up the steps, like old women, dragging heavy baskets. Huge, serious brown eyes gazed out from under the trilby hats as they quoted their prices like experienced saleswomen. The first time I bought from them the one who was in charge of the money took the coins I gave her and bit them each in turn. Then she nodded her satisfaction and remarked, 'Last week we mudder got passed a bad coin in de market.' I said that if she liked to bring it to the house I would change it for a good one for her. She shook her head confidently. 'Dat's all right, mistress,' she said. 'Next week she take it to de market and pass it on.'

From the beginning, Singh used to bring little bundles of plants, obviously grown in seed boxs, for planting out in our tubs and beds. Later, when we had our own array of seed boxes decorating the top of the septic tank, our seedlings would often disappear with him in the evening. For he had two gardening jobs—presumably arranged for him by his enterprising father—and so was able to rationalize our garden supplies. Once he must have been managing three gardens, for I came out into the yard to hear him say to an astonished guest, newly-arrived from England, 'I have three mistresses—but this here is my favourite mistress.'

The distribution of plants from garden to garden worked quite well, though there were times when I was grieved to miss plants I had had my eye on for some particular purpose. There were surprises too; once I found a little bed we had made near the path neatly planted with cow parsley. Singh, no doubt, was just as amused when I told him about the struggling coxcomb plant we had grown in a little pot in our English drawing room. Here they grew wild to a height of several feet, dropping seeds which sprang up like weeds. Growing difficult and non-indigenous plants seems to be a challenge that gardeners the world over cannot resist. I would have been quite content to have filled our Campbellville garden with bougainvillaeas, hibiscus, ixora, oleander, plumbago or coralita, but Singh's pride and joy was a pathetic rose which trailed wearily up the side of the sun-scorched house and bore scentless flowers of anaemic pink, measuring about half an inch across when fully open. I suppose it gave him that sense of achievement which the possession of a washed-out bougainvillaea in the greenhouse gives to an English gardener.

Singh delighted in all living things; he belonged to a sect that would not take life and I knew that he did not take kindly to my ways of massacring garden pests. 'Oh, we torments them,' he would say piteously, as I got busy with spray gun and insecticide on a line of marching ants.

Religion was something joyful in his life. He talked of God with a friendly ease and assurance which fell strangely and refreshingly on English ears, accustomed to His name being used with embarrassment or unctuousness. Whenever I now hear missionaries telling captive congregations of the fear in which people of non-Christian religions hold their God, I remember Singh's cheerful confidence in the goodness of his Lord, to whose hand he most generously attributed all good works. He would look around the garden on an evening when the grass was freshly chopped, the tubs newly-painted and everything bright after the evening's watering and exclaim, 'God has made everything lovely, lovely.' He was so pleased with life and the garden and so abundantly grateful, that I could not bring myself to remind him what it looked like when God had it to Himself.

In the time he was not gardening—and most gardening could only be done in the early morning or the evening—Singh minded his father's cows. When he spoke of the cows his face was radiant and he sang their praises lyrically. One evening he ran in to the garden, gasped that he could not stay as he had a cow that was sick and ran off again before I had time to reply. We did not see him for two days and then I scarcely recognized the forlorn little figure that trailed wearily in the gate. 'I just come to tell you,' he said, 'that the cow she die,' and he sat down on the back steps and began to cry.

Later he said, 'She was the most beautiful of all. All the cows are beautiful and all are good. They don't hurt each other like the other creatures do. They don't kill, they want only grass. They are always giving us milk and butter and they are gentle in all their ways.' He did not seem able to stop talking; he told me about all the other cows his father had had, describing them and repeating their names lovingly. He told me how he had stayed with this one when she had had her twin calves and how it had been bad with her and how he had stayed and suffered with her day and night, and how another had been stolen and he had gone about seeking her until he had found her. He told me of one that had been struck by a train at the level crossing, but had recovered. He told me how this last had been the most special of all; he had persuaded his father to buy her. He had seen her for sale and loved her, but his father had said it was too hard to keep cows now, but in the end he had given in and Singh had been sent to bring her home and had cared for her ever since. It was for her that he always took the grass when he chopped our lawn with the cutlass. She had been the most beautiful of all cows with her big gentle brown eyes and soft skin. She had slipped into a ditch and a sharp stick had punctured her stomach. She could not be moved and he had stayed with her all night and in the morning she had seemed better and his mother had taken money to the vet and he had given her expensive medicine and said she might live. He had stayed with her all the time and stroked her and she had been so patient. Then this morning she had grown weaker and begun to moan and at noon she had died and now they were moving her away from the ditch to bury her.

He sat and stared unseeing, or rather seeing only his Goddess, 'All her silken flanks with garlands dressed.' And I sat and marvelled, for cows in Guyana are scraggy beasts, skeletal caricatures of their lush English sisters. As they bend their stringy necks to seek for dried patches of unnutritious grass by the roadside their bones seem likely at any moment to poke their way through the tight and sore skin. Sometimes they collapse in the middle of the road, too weary to respond to the impatient hoots of the horn.

The draining of the land for building in the countryside outside Georgetown has deprived many a poor East Indian farmer of his former grazing rights. Where once there were rice fields or open spaces where the cows could wander freely, there are now houses or plots held by speculators who refuse to let the cows on to their land. The position of the farmer is reminiscent of that of the eighteenth century English peasant deprived of his pasturing rights by the enclosure movement. Like him, he has no redress.

It was a common sight, therefore, to see little East Indian boys and girls moving their father's cows from place to place, seeking doubtful nourishment from the parched and dusty grass by the roadside. Once in a while, of course, they found their way into a flourishing garden and had a Gargantuan feast. They were then at the mercy of the impounder. If the cows were found in the wrong place they were 'pounded' and the owner had to pay a fine in order to get them out of the pound. The bane of the farmer's life was the impounder and Singh would speak of him as a kind of East Indian bogey man, the arch enemy of all cows.

But these trials and tribulations would no longer beset Singh's cow; she had gone to free and happier pastures where there was no impounder to harass her. And a part of Singh had gone with her too.

CHAPTER FIVE

The Six Peoples

I had hoped to be able to give an impression of the six races which make up the Guyanese nation simply by describing individuals; it is, after all, by such individual encounters that general impressions are formed. But in the interests of clarity and brevity it seems necessary now to give a brief summary of those races and of how they come to be in Guyana for without it even their nomenclature can be confusing. Besides, there comes a time, when one is living in a strange country, when one does begin to catalogue impressions of people and to realize that the ways and manners one had attributed to an individual may be a manifestation of a racial personality.

The first European settlers who came to the land which is now Guyana decimated the local population. Known collectively as Amerindians, the remnants of these indigenous people now live in the bush, far away from Georgetown. They are made up of different tribes with widely divergent customs. Like all primitive people, they present even an enlightened government with a real problem; if they are left alone they will most probably be eliminated by the encroachment of so-called civilization. If they are protected, their customs guarded against outside influences, they will tend to become museum pieces. The Amerindians are represented in the administration of Guyana and in 1965 a Department of Amerindian Affairs was set up to try to help Amerindians to participate in Guyanese society, but they are seldom seen in Georgetown and a description of them and their way of life properly belongs to the Interior.

When European settlers needed labour for their plantations they were obliged to import it from Africa. The descendants of these early African slaves now form one of the two main racial groups in Guyana. To a stranger arriving in Georgetown it seems that Africans must easily make up the majority of the population, but this is a false impression given by the fact that the Africans have tended to congregate in the town.

When slavery was abolished in 1833 the Africans left the plantations en masse, following some deep instinct to escape from the scene of the humiliation of their race. After this exodus Europeans had, perforce, to find substitutes for their African slaves. They brought over indentured labour from the East Indies and from India itself. Although they were free men, the lot of these East Indians was little better than that of the Africans had been. They could rarely afford to return home, as many had hoped to do when they had raised sufficient money, and so were obliged to settle. Their descendants now form the largest single racial group in the land and their numbers are increasing more rapidly than those of the Africans. They are still known as East Indians to distinguish them from that ethnic amalgam, the West Indian, and also from the Indian, a term often used to describe the native people of America, whom I find it less confusing to remember by the more cumbersome term Amerindian.

Their different backgrounds still exert a profound influence upon the outlook of these two races and create problems for the country. The stigma of slavery still marks the African. As a rule,* he will not work on the land and speaks with contempt of the 'coolie-man' who does. Instead he lives in the urban areas where Africans man the Civil Service, work as clerks in offices, as policemen and postmen. The women do all the domestic work as maids and cooks and washers, but the men are never gardeners.

Arriving as slaves, having been snatched from their homes and tribes, they brought with them no skills, no crafts, no traditions or culture. Like magpies they have picked up European habits of dress and speech and all kinds of Western sectarian religions. Living as slaves on plantations where the basic needs of life were provided, they lost any habits they might once have had of fending for themselves. This has left them with a reputation for fecklessness which contrasts strongly with the East Indians' renowned thrift. Not allowed as slaves to marry and live a family life, they were nevertheless forced to breed in order to increase their owners' stock of human capital. Consequently they have not taken easily to settled married life and a large proportion of African children are born outside wedlock. The women frequently seem to prefer this to saddling themselves with a man who might be something of an encumbrance. Illegitimacy, despite the efforts of the preacher, does not

*African farmers on the East Coast, for example at Buxton, provide an exception to this rule.

seem to carry with it that sense of shame that it does in England. After all, the slave owners who enforced it were Christians too. Indeed they were often indefatigable in giving the slaves the Gospel, for this was, after all, one of the main justifications for slave-owning.

The East Indians kept, for the most part, to the land and now predominate in the country districts. Since the staple food of these people from the East was rice, they soon began to grow their own supplies when they came to work on the plantations. Now rice is the country's second crop and the East Indian rice farmers of the coast lands are among the richest men in Guyana. Any money these farmers saved was invested in more land and slowly the East Indians have acquired most of the land in the country. In recent times they have invested some of their money in education for their children and one gets the impression that soon they will oust the Africans from their position of supremacy in the professions.

In some ways this preference of the two races for a different way of life has prevented clashes between them. Now, however, there may sometimes be a clash between the interests of the town and country dweller. In the budget which sparked off the 1962 riots, for example, the Government had imposed compulsory savings on salaries of a certain size. It so happened that this mainly affected office workers in the towns. It was not hard, therefore, for those who sought to further their ends by disorder, to convince the town mob that this was an attack by an East Indian administration, upon the interests of Africans.

No two races could be more dissimilar than the African and East Indian. Generalizations are misleading, but I think that most people who have lived in Guyana would agree that the African is much the easier person for the European to understand. Even those in the most needy and difficult circumstances seem to preserve an endearing, child-like and slap-stick sense of humour. God, one of them told me, had given knowledge to the British and wealth to the East Indian, but to the African he had given a big smile to enable him to bear all his troubles. Sometimes I would remember this as I walked through Georgetown, observing the strained and harassed faces of the English and the happy, carefree expressions of even the poorest Africans; it would seem that the Almighty is less biased in his dispensation than sometimes appears.

The East Indian is much more reserved and less boisterous. One senses in him much deeper resources and a much more complicated attitude to life. Even the wealthy seem poor and ragged, as if the East Indian thus showed his contempt for the outward things. By contrast even the poorest African families turn out their children beautifully dressed and on Sundays especially they are a magnificent sight in their gleaming white frocks with lace and ribbons, and petticoats so starched that they would stand up by themselves.

Of course, among better educated East Indians and Africans these differences are less noticeable. Their education is predominantly a Western one and they tend to absorb with it Western ways and manners. The distinguishing features are still there but they are toned down. To the English, the East Indian's reserved manner and rather more devious ways of going about things can make him seem sly and untrustworthy. He finds the African easier to deal with because, lacking any background or culture of his own, the latter is more ready to welcome new ways, more amenable, more eager to fit in.

I noticed these differences slowly, at first mistaking them for merely individual characteristics. The first time I paid Singh his wages, for example, I did as I had done with Lucille and Myra, counting the money out into his hands. They had always followed the transaction carefully and pocketed their money cheerfully and openly. Singh clearly could not bear it. He seemed to blush for my crudity. Seeing how appalled he was at my brashness, I slipped the rest as unobtrusively as possible into his hand and he put it away without looking at it or me. It was always so; each week I either slid it surreptitiously into his pocket or handed it to him nonchalantly while talking about something else. He never looked at the money or acknowledged its presence by thanking me.

Similarly at Christmas time when we gathered around the tree for presents Lucille and Myra and their children opened theirs with the interest and enjoyment that is customary when presents are being opened. Singh and Basdeo accepted theirs glumly with murmured thanks and sat with the unopened parcels on their knees. We suggested that they might like to open them, but they wriggled and looked very uncomfortable at such a suggestion and were quite clearly very relieved to be able to go away still holding their parcels intact. In the weeks that followed it was obvious that both the penknife and fountain pen had been a huge success, but there was no outward sign that they had given pleasure at the time. Basdeo did manage a word of gratitude the next day and added, 'We do not open them; it is not our custom.'

It was moments of awkwardness such as these that made me realize the difficulty of these East Indian children. Unlike their parents they were living in much closer contact with other races, with different ways from their own and they had no idea how to adapt themselves or how to fit in comfortably with these different ways without feeling disloyal to their own people. Unlike the Africans, the East Indians have preserved their customs and religion even in an alien land and their traditions are still guarded by an influential priesthood. I frequently noticed in Singh a sense of conflict between modern ways of thought and methods prescribed by the family priest. He seemed to move in two worlds. One day he would tell me I must go to the drug store and buy sulphate of ammonia to make the green vegetables grow and the next, when asked why a plant was languishing, would explain with as much assurance that, 'Someone must have looked at it too hard last evening.' When he had earache he went to hospital and the trouble was put right and yet when his sister was taken ill she was left to the mercy of the priest, who diagnosed evil spirits. It was as if part of the soul was still in the bush while part inhabited the concrete ways of Georgetown. There is bound to be conflict for one who has recently emerged into a world of schools and hospitals leaving a part of himself loyal to age-old beliefs still strictly adhered to by his elders. If ever I found myself becoming impatient with this ambivalence, I would remind myself that even those of us who have been brought up in modern scientific ways of thought need only spend a few nights in the jungle to come to believe that evil spirits are more credible than germs. Much of our rational ways of viewing things depends upon a good strong electric light bulb.

When the slave trade was abolished, indentured labour was obtained not only from the East Indies, but also from China and Madeira. The descendants of these labourers, the Chinese and Portuguese, now form sizable minorities. The Chinese were joined by others who came for trade, as do the Chinese the world over. They are a close-knit community, keeping themselves very much to themselves and preserving many of them their ways and language. This tendency is strengthened by the fact that they are constantly bringing out members of their family from home or from Hong Kong. We were told that if they needed another assistant in their shop they would send home for one rather than employ a local of a different race. I noticed, when I was teaching, that the Chinese girls, though often among the most intelligent, had more difficulty in writing English than those of other races. I imagine that in many homes it was not spoken and had to be learned like a foreign language. Good business people, the Chinese seem not to interest themselves greatly in politics but to concentrate upon their trade and their domestic affairs.

The Portuguese who came to work as indentured labour did not stay long on the land. Lacking the physical strength of the African and the reserves of toughness of the East Indian, they soon drifted to the towns, where their descendants live on as business people and shopkeepers. They have not maintained their ways as the East Indians and Chinese have done, nor have they the vivacity and good humour of the Africans. Nor yet are they truly European. Although they might form a nucleus of a Guyanese society, they do not seem to have the breadth of vision to fulfil such a role.

They and the descendants of mixed marriages between early English settlers and other races, form a local white population. I noticed a tendency to refer to such people as 'Guyanese' as if Guyanese is what is left over when the African, Amerindian, Chinese and East Indians and British have been removed. So long as the other races are so easily distinguishable, I suppose this is to a certain extent inevitable, but it does not facilitate that movement towards unity and nationhood which is so urgently advocated by all who have the interests of the country at heart.

Guyana is fortunate in not having to face the problem of reconciling the interests of a group of European settlers with those of local native peoples, for this is something which has embittered political relations in former African colonies such as Kenya. The English who went to Guyana went only to work; they did not buy land or settle there and so did not have a permanent vested interest in British supremacy. The local white population is a Guyanese one that has lived there for generations and is as native to the land as any other group, be it African, Indian or Chinese. Yet it struck me that this group of local white people had arrogated to themselves the attitudes which in other colonies had been taken up by some English settlers. They were more inclined than most British people to speak disparagingly of people of darker colour than themselves, they were more belligerently loyal to Great Britain and they were more politically reactionary.

Perhaps this stems in a large extent from the colour snobbishness which undoubtedly exists in a country whose people's skins, as a result of mixed marriages between six races, cover the whole range from white to deepest black. In *A Morning at the Office,* Edgar Mittelholzer admirably describes this hierarchy in which the paler the skin the higher is the social status of its wearer. This attitude springs from British example, but it is an example from the past. The white Guyanese often seemed to me to be emulating middle class society in Victorian England. There is a kind of gentility and, among the wives, a preoccupation with an empty social round. One wanted to try to tell them that they would do better to try to catch up with modern British life, if they must look in that direction for their pattern, that women actually do work in England and that membership of a profession can be more satisfying than spending one's time arranging bridge parties, coffee parties and an endless procession of dress shows.

Like the other five races, the British have undergone great changes in their customs and attitudes. These result not so much from government policy, as from that of Bookers, the virtual controllers of the sugar industry. The influence of this company, as the largest employer of labour, both Guyanese and European, and the greatest owner of capital, is akin to that of a government, in that its decisions vitally affect the life and future of the people of the country.

In the past Bookers enjoyed the kind of reputation which most companies operating in the colonies shared. British commerce since the Industrial Revolution depended on cheap raw materials from the colonies. Since sugar commanded a very low price indeed, wages paid in the colony were particularly low and conditions of work particularly bad. These circumstances lay behind the troubles which broke out in the early 1950's which were an outburst of feeling against an extremely unpopular firm. Out of those troubles a new policy emerged. Bookers were fortunate to have at that time as their new chairman that rarity in the commercial world, a man of vision. Sir Jock Campbell* seemed able to view the position more dispassionately than others who have found themselves in similar predicaments have been able to do and to conclude that if the company was so universally execrated, something must be radically wrong with the way it was organized. He set about reorganizing it; indeed by the work of this one man the company and its relationship with the country was transformed. It would scarcely be an exaggeration to say that he transformed the country itself.

The policy of 'Guyanization' which Sir Jock introduced meant that for the first time local people could have the chance of rising

*Now Lord Campbell of Eskan.

to important positions in the firm. Grants and scholarships were made available to young Guyanese to enable them to study in England at Bookers' expense. Great emphasis was placed on the work of personnel managers who helped, in ways too numerous and personal to mention, many local people to fulfil themselves and develop their talents. As a result (an incidental result, for the policy was one of conviction and not mere opportunism) the public image of the company has completely changed. The general attitude towards it is now very different from what it must have been in the angry days of the early 1950's.

I have said that the help given by Bookers to individual Guyanese in ways not connected with work were too numerous to mention, but cannot refrain from giving one example. We became interested during our stay in the work of a young African artist called Patrick Barrington, and bought two of his pictures at an exhibition arranged for him by Bookers. Quite untrained, he had one day had pointed out to him in an old copy of *The Observer* which had found its way to Guyana, an advertisement for a scholarship to a famous art school in London. It was open to anybody and he sent off pictures and drawing books and won the scholarship. The day before he sailed he came to lunch with us and we asked him about how all this had been achieved. How, we wanted to know, did he send off so many pictures? Bookers had arranged the shipping. Bookers photographers had taken photographs in colour of the ones that were too big to send. How had he got hold of money for his passage? Bookers had arranged the exhibition and he had sold enough pictures to pay his fare. We were anxious about his arriving alone in England, he who had never been out of Georgetown. Somebody from Bookers would meet him at the airport, he told us, and they would help to pay for his digs. Naturally his praise for Bookers knew no bounds. I give this example among many because it shows not only the breadth of Bookers activities but their disinterestedness. After all, helping artists is not and never has been an easy occupation or a tangibly rewarding one.

Of course, there were faults in the system; one heard bitter criticisms and rumours of internecine disagreements, but these are inevitable in any organization where men have to work out the details together. When one stood back and took a long view one saw unmistakably a great company trying honestly to do its best for the local population, not simply to create a good impression in order to maximize its profits, but because it was seeking to serve the community as an end in itself. The obstacles must have been great, for the problems of such a company operating overseas are enormous compared with those at home. The work had to be carried out in an atmosphere of political uncertainty and an awareness that time was short and memories long. In such circumstances Sir Jock maintained the principle that only idealism is practical.

It was all the more startling, therefore, to find some English people disapproving of the relatively happy relationship between the British and the other five races. The explanation seems to lie outside the boundaries of the country itself. As the frontiers of the former British Empire contracted British ex-colonials naturally tended to concentrate in the areas that remained. British Guiana was such an area and these people, unlike Charles II, did not learn from their travels.

Contractors are made particularly aware of this problem as, in order to staff jobs abroad, it is often necessary to draw on that pool of men who prefer to work out of England. One has to admit that, while there are some adventurous spirits who seek to widen their experience in this way, there are also many who, for various psychological reasons, cannot settle down in their home country and have found from experience that if they try they do not command there a job equivalent in responsibility and salary to the one they can command abroad. Some enjoy the status that being British in a British colony inevitably carried with it. For them a white skin was the perfect status symbol; it draws attention to itself and its acquisition requires no skill or effort on the part of its owner. Its only disadvantage is that it is of no economic use at home.

During its colonial past, Guyana naturally did not easily attract able administrators. Poor, backward, and with a humid climate, unimportant on the world stage, it was not the kind of place to which the Colonial Office as a rule sent its ablest men. On the one hand it was, as a result of its natural disadvantages and lack of resources, a country which needed the services of men of exceptional ability, but on the other hand it was hardly a posting which such men would regard as promotion.*

Bookers, too, have a similar personnel problem. Like all com-

* Another reason why the ablest colonial administrators did not find their way to Guyana was because each colony was responsible for the cost of its own administration. Hence the unattractive salaries in Guyana compared with those in richer colonies like Nigeria.

panies operating abroad it has somehow to tempt men who have, or could have, successful careers at home in England, to give them up and work abroad risking a great disruption of their family life. Money and good living conditions are the usual bait, but may attract exactly the people the firm leasts wants if its work for Guyana is to thrive. It says much for the new deal in Bookers and the persuasive power of the Chairman's idealism, that so many talented and enlightened people have been attracted there in the hope of finding the kind of work that was worth devoting their lives to.

Such people tend to congregate at the top of a firm's hierarchy; its lower branches are less noticeably laden with the highly trained or the social idealists. It is here, however, that improved salaries and conditions will play the largest part; it is here that one finds the greatest prejudice and the greatest boredom of the greatest number of wives.

Men, after all, have their work, but their womenfolk, many of whose interests were at home confined to their housework, have not even that. Insufficiently occupied, they devote much of their time to gossip and grumbling. It was for their sakes presumably that the doctrine of Guyanese hospitality has been evolved, and now operates to such an extent that cocktail parties, at least in the high season, are practically nightly affairs. The idea of having to spend an evening at home together seems to be a prospect which some English couples abroad find quite terrifying. Night after night the same people meet in each other's houses. Official entertaining seems to be an essential part of modern commercial life, but in excess it soon ceases to be in any way entertaining.

There was among this group of women a constant harking on the superiority of all things British. They stressed always what they missed; there was nowhere to meet for coffee, there was no television. If it was useless to point out the surprising number of amenities that did exist in Georgetown—for example the very modern library and museum, which formed a lively centre of activities of all kinds—it was even more useless to point to the teeming interests of the Interior, for they really did not want to be interested in anything in the country. Their enjoyment consisted in musing on the things they were missing at home. Instead of regarding themselves as lucky in having the chance to widen their experience, they seemed determined to limit it. Instead of exploring and enjoying those things which were different in South America, they seemed to want to create a bit of suburban England in its midst.

Prisoners in an unfamiliar land, these expatriates sought to find comfort by creating a pattern of life as similar as possible to the one they had left behind at home.

It was sad and yet, I suppose natural, for they did not want to be there in the first place. Unlike those women who came out to work in the hospitals or schools, or to study the flora and fauna of the Interior, or those whose hearts were with their husbands in their work for the country and its people, they had nothing to keep their interest or their sense of wonder alive. Without these, boredom is inevitable.

Sir Hugh Casson, writing in a *Times* Supplement on Design in November, 1961, wrote of passengers in a ship, 'Every passenger is a prisoner, however willingly he has paid for his captivity. He will therefore, be wayward, critical, greedy and easily bored.' Passengers in a colony can also develop such symptoms.

Independence is everything and nothing; it creates some problems and, of itself, solves none. But it is an essential condition of national unity in a country made up of people of different races. For undoubtedly the existence of these six races, some of them with very distinct cultures and all tending to have separate interests, enormously complicates the development of Guyana.

This is not to say that the present political problems are inherently racial or that any responsible Guyanese would consciously promote racial intolerance. We saw very little evidence of bitter feeling between individuals of different races and much evidence of friendliness and co-operation. True, one did sometimes hear not very flattering remarks made about one race by a member of another but they were not much more forcible than the kind one might hear an Englishman make about a Scot or a Welshman. The danger in Guyana, however, is that the political and economic stresses may bring out latent ill will between races. Loyalty to one's race is a deep human instinct and its power has to be recognized in a country such as Guyana which has not yet had time to develop a larger instinctive loyalty to the country as such, within which racial loyalty can safely express itself. This kind of patriotism cannot perhaps develop in a colony, owing loyalty as it must to an alien land. This is why it seems to me that independence was a *conditio sine qua non* of national unity.

In the past the different races have gradually entrenched themselves in positions taken up for various economic and historical reasons. Without going into too much detail, it is possible to trace the development of modern political parties from these attitudes and to see how they have in turn shaped the course of recent political events. For example, it was in reaction to the sugar industry's former domination of the colony that Dr. Cheddi Jagan formed the Political Affairs Committee in 1947 which in 1950 became the left wing People's Progressive Party, and the first political party to be formed in the country. When in 1953 elections were held under a new constitution, Dr. Jagan's party won a tremendous victory at the polls. The consequent measures of reform and demands for more complete independence alarmed the British Government, who feared Communist influence in the P.P.P, and the constitution was suspended and a state of emergency declared. The interruption of normal constitutional government and consequent political frustration combined with Burnham's dislike of being in a party which might be labelled 'Communist', led to a split in the P.P.P., which had formerly embraced all races. Now, in 1955, Mr. L. F. S. Burnham, the leading African in the party, led his African following out of it to form the People's National Congress and the alignment of political parties was henceforward on racial grounds. It need not have been so and was due as much to differences of occupation and habitation, between urban Africans and rural Indians, as it was to racial feeling.

In 1957 elections were allowed at which the P.P.P. won nine seats and the P.N.C. won three in the single chamber legislature. The two parties were agreed in seeking independence and limited internal self-government was promised for 1961.

A third party now emerged; the white Guyanese were violently anti-Jagan and to express this view Mr. Peter D'Aguiar now formed a political party, the United Force, which was made up mainly of right wing business men with some middle class support. It aimed at encouraging private enterprise and attracting foreign capital, and its main object was to get rid of Dr. Jagan's government. Their crusade against the supposed Communists of the government was strengthened by the fact that the Portuguese form the backbone of the Roman Catholic Church in Guyana.

The attitude of the U.F. towards the Government differed from that of the British, many of whom conceded that Dr. Jagan was a man of real calibre who bore the stamp of leadership and while disagreeing with some of his proposed methods, had no quarrel with his aim, which was the devoted pursuit of his country's welfare. There were of course those in both groups for whom it sufficed to stigmatize the Prime Minister as a Communist and therefore an ogre and leave it at that.

Those who felt like that had of course little compunction about the methods they used to unseat the government. In January 1962 a sudden alliance was patched up between Mr. Burnham and Mr. D'Aguiar, who incited the mob to protest against Dr. Jagan's budget whose measures happened to press hardest on the Georgetown business class who supported U.F. and the lower middle class urban Africans who supported Mr. Burnham. In the subsequent riots a few people were killed, many injured and much damage done to property.

This seems to me to illustrate one of the main difficulties of trying to introduce methods of Western democracy into British colonies. The forms can be introduced but the restraints and assumptions that control their use cannot be implanted. In their enthusiasm to get rid of the party in power, the opposition do not always make the necessary distinction between defeating the government and overthrowing the constitution.

The commission of enquiry into these disturbances supported the view that the riots were not racial in origin, but that they had the effect of emphasizing racial differences. Internally, racial discord, once roused, would not easily be quitened. Externally, the riots increased mistrust of Dr. Jagan's government. The United States was already concerned; after the elections of 1961, Senator Dodds of the Foreign Relations Committee had already pronounced that, 'international Communism has established its first bridgehead on the South American continent.' The United States had consistently refused aid, although by so doing they contributed to the financial crisis which necessitated the budget.

At the Constitutional Conference convened in London in October 1962 the P.P.P. sought immediate independence while the opposition parties demanded proportional representation, for by now they could assume that since the East Indians commanded a numerical majority it followed that they would win any election based on direct voting. Understandably the conference failed.

Racial strife increased when, fearing that the Trade Unions were being used by the opposition to further their own political aim of overthrowing his government, Dr. Jagan introduced his Labour Relations Bill to allow the government to choose which unions should be recognized by employers. The unions went on strike and demonstrations against the bill led once again to violence. The government survived the crisis though the strike lasted for three months.

It is significant that while the government was sustained by oil and flour sent by Cuba, the unions were helped by American dollars. Already burdened with problems enough, Guyana now had the added complication of being regarded as a pawn in the cold war; the United States even went so far as to advise that the constitution be suspended and direct colonial rule by Britain restored.

Although the letter of this advice was not followed its spirit prevailed. In October 1963, Mr. Duncan Sandys introduced a plan which delayed independence and provided for elections under proportional representation which was what the P.N.C. and U.F. had been demanding and now welcomed, while Dr. Jagan called it a 'dastardly and unprincipled decision'. Many of his party, however, were bitterly critical of him for inviting the 'Sandys solution'.*

Despite a wave of strikes on the sugar estates accompanied by sabotage and violence which led almost to civil war, elections were held without incident at the end of 1964. The P.P.P. won 24 seats, the P.N.C. won 22 and the U.F. won 7 and a coalition government of the P.N.C. and U.F. was formed. Cheated of what he regarded as his victory at the polls, Dr. Jagan refused to resign and the constitution had to be altered in order to ensure his removal and replacement by Mr. Burnham as Prime Minister.

Britain and the United States were now evidently satisfied that their scheme to debar Dr. Jagan from office was successful and in November 1965 promised that the colony should have independence. This was granted on May 26th, 1966. Until becoming a republic in February 1970, Guyana recognized the Queen, represented by a Governor-General as Head of State. The coalition government led by Mr. Burnham was supported by American aid which has enabled greater development of the newly independent country than would otherwise have been possible; for example a new road from Atkinson to Mackenzie has been built and planning of its continuation to the Rupununi is well advanced. The East Coast road has been hard-topped as far as New Amsterdam and the Corentyne road begun.

*When the 1963 conference reached deadlock (as the 1962 conference had done) Mr. Sandys offered to impose a solution, if so invited in writing by Dr. Jagan, Mr. Burnham and Mr. D'Aguiar. To everyone's surprise, Dr. Jagan did just that, because he thought that Mr. Sandys would produce a 'British' compromise on the issues that divided them. Burnham and D'Aguiar readily agreed. The three leaders specifically undertook to abide by such a solution. In the event Mr. Sandys ruled against Dr. Jagan on all the issues and so paved the way for the Burnham/D'Aguiar coalition in 1964.

These material benefits and the fact that future development largely depends on foreign capital which in turn depends on political stability were not lost on the P.P.P. supporters. Although they felt cheated by the election results which, by denying them an overall majority, thrust them into opposition, they saw little profit in sacrificing to party loyalty their share of the relative economic prosperity. They were therefore more inclined to live peaceably under Mr. Burnham than were the supporters of the P.N.C. and U.F. under Dr. Jagan.

This, combined with the government's firm handling of the enforcement of law and order, has ensured that since the coalition took office communal violence has been suppressed and racial tension has eased. Mr. Burnham's government continued in office despite the departure of Mr. D'Aguiar from the coalition in 1968.

Dr. Jagan expects to be cheated at the next elections which he claims will be rigged to keep Mr. Burnham in power. Since the rate of growth of the East Indian population is much greater than that of the other races, however, even the present system of proportional representation cannot for ever keep the P.P.P. in opposition. On the other hand past events have made it clear that a P.P.P. government cannot survive the combined racial opposition of the U.F. and P.N.C. Everyone hopes that ultimately a long period of peaceful development and increased prosperity will enable the parties to develop on non-racial grounds; even now Mr. Burnham strives to identify the East Indians with his administration and Dr. Jagan claims an increasing African element in the P.P.P. It will be a very long time, however, before race ceases to play an integral part in the politics of Guyana.

It is often remarked that the constitutions of newly independent colonies do not survive for long. We should surely not be too surprised if a way of government evolved in Britain slowly over five or six centuries should fail to establish itself overnight in a foreign land. We might perhaps learn from the gardener; seeds may be taken from England but in a different climate the plants which grow from them may well surprise us. We should not be too censorious if the constitutions we choose to transplant should wilt, like Singh's rose, among the more exotic local blooms.

Note to Chapter Five

The government of the country was in fact radically altered in 1980 when a new constitution was promulgated which created the office of Executive President. Mr. Forbes Burnham, who had remained in power as Prime Minister since Independence, now took over as Executive President with Mr. Ptolemy Reid as his Prime Minister. On Mr. Burnham's death, in 1985, he was succeeded by Mr. H. Desmond Hoyte who is the Executive President at the time of writing. Mr. Hamilton Green is the first Vice-President and Prime Minister.

The centralisation of power, which marked the new constitution is, however, to some extent balanced by the increased autonomy given to the regions. This is reflected in practical ways: the national service scheme, by which young people are trained in mining and agricultural skills, is based in Georgetown but organized from small and scattered centres in the country.

The more settled political climate has encouraged the flow of capital into Guyana and there has been steady, if slow, economic progress. Gold and diamond mining has become more industrialized: both are now exported in much larger quantities than before. Fortunately this has not squeezed out the Pork Knockers who still maintain their colourful and independent way of life (see Chapter Ten). Timber too now contributes much more to the export trade and a wider range of species is exploited. All this has enabled the economy to withstand the dramatic decline in the profits of the sugar industry, caused by the greater use of artificial sweeteners, particularly the use, by the soft drinks trade, of corn-based syrups, and by the increased productivity of European sugar beet farmers. Both these factors have hit the Guyanese sugar industry, always perilously dependent on the world price of sugar, very hard indeed. The rice farmers, on the other hand, have the opposite problem: despite increased mechanisation, they are hard-pressed to produce enough to satisfy the foreign demand for rice.

Thus the Guyanese economy, though still beset with problems of under-capitalisation and shortages of such basic resources as water and electricity, now rests on a much broader and firmer base than it did.

CHAPTER SIX

Monkey Jump

The coastal strip of Guyana consists of mud. Had it not been so, we should probably not have been there.

Bookers had decided to build a Bulk Sugar Terminal, where the sugar from their various factories could be delivered, stored and then automatically fed into sugar tankers that would come up the Demerara. This necessitated a great deal of heavy building on the river bank, the erection of much heavy machinery and the construction of a new jetty.

The difficulty of building on such a site is obvious. Even houses tend to sink into the mud; heavier buildings would very soon start to subside and do so unevenly so that not only would the walls crack but the machinery would not function properly. The store was to hold forty thousand tons of sugar.

Called in to advise on what kind of foundations would support such a construction, Dick's firm designed a kind of floating raft, made up of a series of concrete squares or caissons, rather like egg boxes, which would be allowed to sink right down into the mud to a depth of twelve feet, where it would stop and the superstructure could then be built on top. The terminal would thus be built on a kind of raft floating in the mud and if it began to sink the sinking would be uniform, as the raft would always find its own new level and so right itself.

It was, of course, rather more complicated than this wife's-eye view suggests. Frankly, I never understood how they knew it would stop sinking at twelve feet and not just go on until the whole building disappeared into the mud.

For all this a great deal of concrete was needed and an immediate problem was to find, in this land of mud, stone to make it with. Dick was told about a quarry in the Interior and thought, from samples, that the stone might be suitable. He decided that he must go and see and I decided that I should go too.

The outing to this quarry was our first expedition into the Interior and worth describing in some detail, for we were struck by

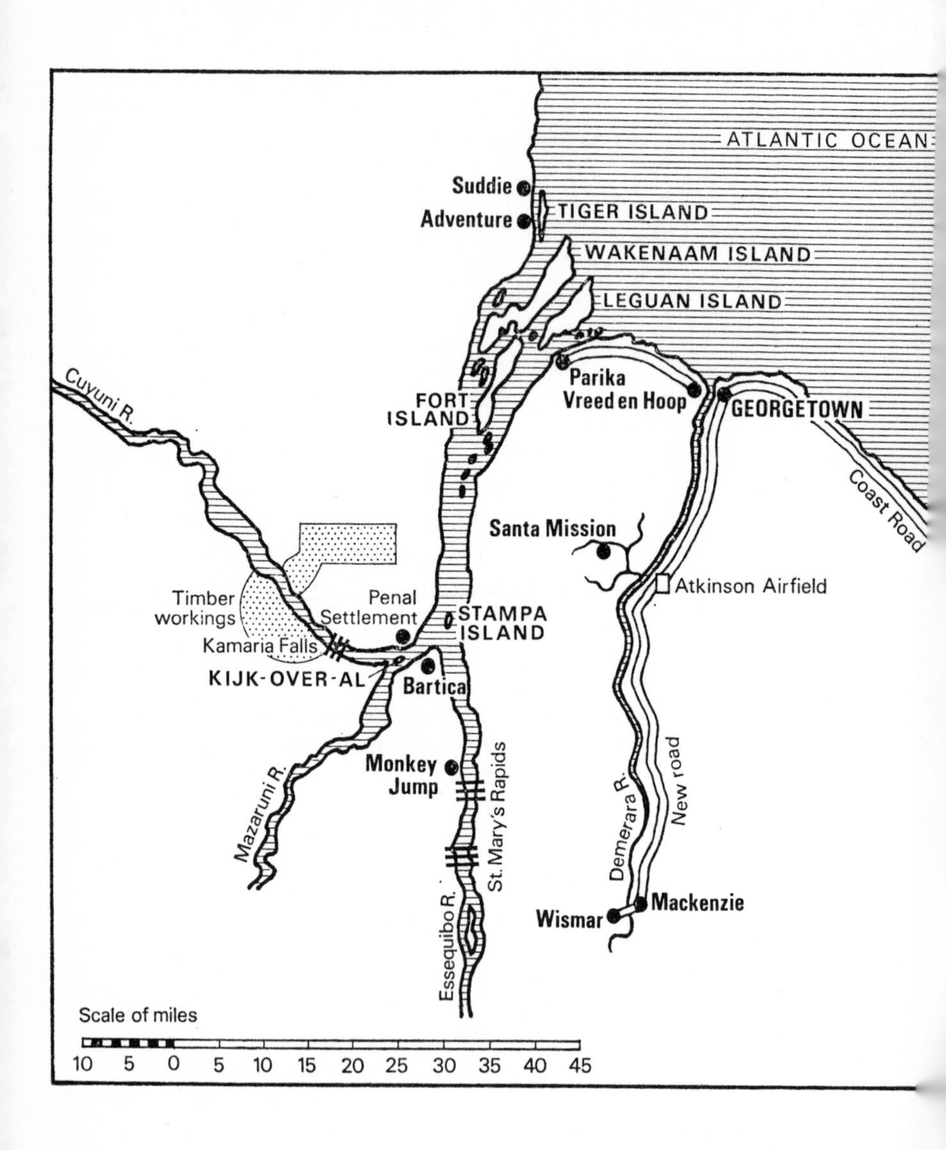
ATLANTIC OCEAN
Suddie
Adventure
TIGER ISLAND
WAKENAAM ISLAND
LEGUAN ISLAND
Parika
Vreed en Hoop
GEORGETOWN
Cuyuni R.
FORT ISLAND
Coast Road
Santa Mission
Atkinson Airfield
Timber workings
Penal Settlement
STAMPA ISLAND
Kamaria Falls
KIJK-OVER-AL
Bartica
Mazaruni R.
Monkey Jump
St. Mary's Rapids
Demerara R.
New road
Essequibo R.
Mackenzie
Wismar
Scale of miles
10 5 0 5 10 15 20 25 30 35 40 45

many things then which, on later expeditions, we tended to take for granted. This was the first time, for example, that I really understood the vital part that rivers play in a country with few roads or railways. Of course, one reads that our forebears used rivers as the main means of communication, but somehow it is hard to feel the truth of this in England; one still feels that a river is an obstacle to be crossed by bridge or ferry rather than a way of getting somewhere.

We looked at maps and found that the quarry was up the Essequibo river, above the point at which it forks from the Mazaruni. At the fork is the town of Bartica where we could stay the night and also hire a boat to go up to Monkey Jump, where the quarry was situated. We could get to Bartica from Georgetown in one day by the steamer which sailed twice a week from Parika, on the mouth of the Essequibo. The journey to Parika seemed quite straight forward: we had to cross the Demerara by ferry and drive along the short stretch of road which traverses the twenty miles of land between the Demerara and Essequibo estuaries.

Jubraj, we decided, should cross with us by the ferry and drive us to Parika. There he would leave us and return home, but would be back at Parika to meet us off the home-coming steamer three days later. It all seemed quite simple; we had not yet learned that journeys in Guyana never are simple.

It was always difficult to get a definite reply to enquiries about times and distances; rightly so for there are all kinds of imponderables to be considered. However, we did not realize that and hopefully asked Jubraj, who had been before to Parika, how long it would take us to get there from Georgetown.

'Not long, mistress,' he replied, cheerfully.

'But how long?'

'Well, sometimes it long time coming, sometimes short.'

'What is the road like from the Demerara to Parika?'

'So-so, boss. Sometimes worse than other times.'

'Well, it seems to be about twenty miles. Would it take us about an hour—or more?'

'Anything you say, boss.'

The Demerara ferry is a very modern affair. Just before seven thirty in the morning we joined the queue of cars outside the gates of the quay and drove slowly through as the ferry approached. Crossing regularly from Georgetown to Vreed-en-Hoop on the other side, it provides an essential service, for it is the only means of crossing the mile-wide Demerara river. It came alongside the landing stage now and its automatic gang-planks were lowered, one for passengers and one for cars.

Crowds of people streamed off on their way into Georgetown for a day's work or shopping. Since the ferry is the only way for the public to cross the river, it is the best place for seeing a cross-section of the Guyanese population. There were old East Indian women with baskets of fruit, young boys with bicycles, African commuters in bowler hats and city suits, highly-dressed girls off for a day's shopping or visiting. An official report states that the ferry holds a thousand passengers, '25 cars or 15 lorries, 100 cyclists with cycles and 25 hucksters with baskets.' They seemed to be all there that day, down to the last huckster with basket.

We left Jubraj to drive the car on and made our way on to the passenger deck. For the five or ten minutes of the crossing we watched the muddy waters of the Demerara divide before the bows of the boat and so reached Vreed-en-Hoop without incident.

Jubraj was a peace-loving man and did not join in the battle of the drivers to be first off the ferry. We were not surprised when our car emerged last of the twenty-five on to the road.

This road was surfaced with burnt earth with two parallel lines of concrete, one for each wheel. It was not designed for overtaking. We crawled along, through villages and over bumpy wooden bridges, the last of a long procession of cars. It was only when the concrete strips petered out, leaving us on a plain burnt earth road, that we realized what their advantages had been. The burnt earth had been eroded into hollows and piled up into hillocks. Like the surface of the world itself, it had been worked upon by wind and water to form many and varied contours. We bumped and jerked our way along in a cloud of red dust thrown up by the car in front; it filled our eyes and noses and covered us all over until we looked like Thomas Hardy's reddleman. Finally we closed the windows and sat and grilled in our little metal box.

There is great skill in driving along these roads; the driver must leave sufficient space in front to allow the dust from the car ahead to settle a little, otherwise he can see nothing at all. On the other hand, if he leaves too much space, an adventurous car will appear from behind and overtake him. Jubraj, a cautious driver, was constantly being put back a place in the queue.

The villages provided other obstacles; children played in the roads, a mother goose held up the traffic while her long line of goslings waddled slowly across from one ditch to the other. At one point a donkey cart swung out into the road from nowhere and without heeding or showing any gratitude for Jubraj's thoughtfulness in swerving so violently that we nearly toppled over the bank, proceeded to roll along in front of us with extreme slowness in the centre of the road. We followed at about two miles an hour.

It was half past nine. If we missed this steamer, there was not another for a week for the next one had been cancelled as a result of some rearrangement of timetables.

'Are we half way there, Jubraj?'

'Maybe, mistress.'

'There's only half an hour, Jubraj. Are we going to catch the steamer?'

'Is very doubtful, boss. But then the steamer she is most times late.'

At a quarter to ten, Dick leant forward. 'Jubraj,' he said. 'I want you to drive as fast as you can.'

The transformation was astonishing. We learned later that Jubraj was not one to take the initiative. He would not drive fast of his own accord, even if he knew we were late, but under orders, there was no beating him. He leant forward now, gripped the wheel tightly, scowled hard and put his full weight on to the accelerator. We roared along, shrouded in pink dust like a divine chariot racing through the evening clouds. We rushed through villages, glimpsing startled faces—possibly no more startled than our own—as people leapt off the verges. We zig-zagged wildly down the road, weaving our way between potholes and around bumps. Chickens squawked out of our way, their feet scurrying frantically and their wings outspread in a hopeless attempt to get themselves airborne. The human and animal world alike treated us with a new respect, we who had clearly no intention of stopping for anything. Even donkey carts kept miraculously out of the way. And so we dashed into Parika, our wheels scarcely touching the ground, with about five minutes to spare before the steamer left. The first half of the drive had taken us well over an hour and the second about ten minutes.

We thanked Jubraj, in rather quavery voices, as we drove in a more leisurely way towards the river bank. He was once again his slow and diffident self, as we parked the car and walked towards the jetty or stelling, which is the name used locally for these piers since the days of Dutch possession of the colony. Here we saw an African with PIER MASTER written on his cap.

'No sign of the steamer yet, then,' Dick remarked looking down the river.

'She's gone,' the pier master replied proudly. 'Dis time she leave nice an' early: to make up for times she leaves nice an' late.'

He laughed and pointed upstream in the direction where the steamer had gone so nice and early.

Incredulity, acceptance and determination to get there some other way; our reactions followed the usual course. Jubraj's reaction also was his usual one of simple resignation. He ambled slowly towards the car, 'We come back next week then,' he remarked casually.

'No, we go today, somehow.'

'No other way, boss.'

We asked the pier master if he knew of any one who had a boat who might take us or let us hire it.

He thought and then said, 'Only one way, the Police Launch.'

He pointed out the Police House to us and we made our way towards it, walking slowly for the sun was very hot and penetrated even our thick protective layer of red dust.

The Sergeant was most obliging. Yes, of course we could go to Bartica in the Police Launch. There were things to be seen to in Bartica, he added darkly, which made a visit necessary anyway.

We said we were ready to go straight away and asked if we could wait here until the launch was ready.

'Well,' he said slowly, 'the launch, actually, she is not exactly quite ready. She is under repair and it will be some little time before she is quite fit for to go to Bartica.'

'How long?'

'We should say perhaps a week.'

Even more slowly we walked back to the pier. Jubraj stood, as we had left him, leaning against the car.

'No luck, boss?'

'No luck, Jubraj.'

The pier master listened to what we told him and summed it up neatly for us, 'Either you waits a week for Police Launch or you waits a week for steamer,' he said.

'No, we go today. Can you think of any other launch or boat of any kind that could get from here to Bartica?'

He thought. He shook his head. He thought some more. Then he said, 'There is Temptress.'

'Temptress?'

'Temptress. You like to see Temptress? Then I calls she.'

If Temptress was someone who could get us to Bartica then certainly we should like to see her.

He leant over the side of the pier. 'Temptress,' he bellowed down into the water. 'Temptress,' he roared, his voice swelling like an organ. 'Temptress,' he roared again, pulling out all the stops.

We waited, half expecting to see some siren rise from the waves of the Essequibo.

Something crept out from the side of the river. It was a little box of a boat with a rim all round, very sharp at the front and square at the back. It shook compulsively as it moved towards us and suddenly stopped itself by bumping against the pier. On its unlovely side was written in huge letters the single word 'TEMPTRESS.'

'You there?' the pier master shouted at it.

The top of the little box popped open and an old man's head appeared. It grinned at us cheerfully.

'Is Dan,' the pier master told us. 'He own *Temptress*. He make she. Dat is he son,' he added as another head squeezed through the box. Then he raised his voice again and shouted down at them, 'You go to Bartica? You take dis lady and dis gentleman?'

'We do it,' Dan replied instantly. 'You walks down dem steps and in you jumps.'

Temptress proved to be an even more extraordinary boat when viewed from within. There was just room for the four of us to squeeze on to the narrow bench that skirted the square end of her. Right in the centre was the engine. It was uncovered and its whirring belts and knobs exposed themselves to our gaze while the noise was tremendous. At first the sun beat down on us, but after we got going Dan closed down the hatch on our heads and his son went forward and held the steering wheel, peeping out of the open end of the box at the front.

Before we were battened down, we just had time to wave goodbye to Jubraj, who was too dumbfounded to wave back. He just looked at us with total disbelief. Then he turned and walked slowly back to the safety of the car, shaking his head sadly, his disapproval tempered with his usual resignation.

Dan had a gnarled and wizened face and both his thumbs were missing. This is a characteristic of many men who work in Guyanese waters, which are infested with pirai. The pirai, or piranha, although small, are the most deadly of fish. Extremely ferocious, they descend in their hundreds on their prey and tear its flesh from the bones with their razor-sharp teeth. They are said to be able to reduce a man to a skeleton in five minutes. We never saw one in action but once saw one, as it died, slice through a steel fish hook as if it had been the tenderest piece of steak.

Both of his thumbs, Dan told us, had been taken off so smoothly that he had not felt even a little tug. He had known nothing, he said admiringly, until he saw the blood. 'Pirai very well equipped,' he said with a roar of laughter. 'So is we too,' he added pointing to the engine.

'It would be safer covered up,' Dick told him, but Dan just took that as another joke and laughed again.

Dan and his son, like the *Temptress* herself, were unusual characters, very endearing and inspiring absolutely no confidence. It was somehow impossible to imagine that we should ever reach Bartica, if doing so depended on this trio. The engine spluttered and roared and produced appalling fumes, the atmosphere now that the boat was covered, was stifling and the noise horrific. Dan's son steered with much bravado and evident enjoyment, but little skill. Dan himself jumped about with great agility and shouted cheerful if inaudible comments at us, roaring with laughter as he did so.

The throbbing vibrations of the engine jerked us up and down and we soon began to ache and sweat. It was a relief to realize that the series of croaking sounds in my ear was Dick saying that we would stop at Fort Island on the way and give ourselves half an hour to recover.

Fort Island is about a third of the way up to Bartica from Parika. It was once the centre of the Dutch defences and the settlement there had a commanding view of the river. We had been told that there were on the island the ruins of the old Dutch fort. Dick managed to convey the message to Dan who said he was stopping there anyway to buy Coca-Cola. We had not realized that the island was inhabited and were immensely cheered by the news. For the next two hours being jerked and deafened by *Temptress* we were sustained by the thought of food and drink, but mainly drink, on dry land.

Towards one o'clock we felt *Temptress* slow down. Dan lifted up the lid and we peered out, screwing up our eyes against the sun, despite our dark glasses. The river here must be about six miles wide, but it seemed narrower, since Fort Island is very long and appeared as the right bank of the river. Dan's son had only slowed down in order to give the small population of the island time to gather on the stelling to watch us land and admire his flamboyant seamanship. He now accelerated and rushed at the stelling, aiming straight at a huge greenheart bollard, which, by twisting the wheel sharply at the last possible moment, he missed by a couple of inches. He then stopped the engine by stalling it and we bumped to a halt against the side of the pier.

For the first few moments on Fort Island we continued to jerk and tremble as if we were still being tormented by *Temptress.* Slowly we relaxed and found a little shop on the stelling which sold us bottles of lime juice, ice cold, and packets of biscuits. As we set off for the fort we saw Dan and his son disappear into an adjoining rum parlour.

Walking to the fort, it was hard to realize that the island was inhabited, it was so quiet and still. Even the birds and insects were silenced by the intense heat of the midday sun. We walked, heads down, under the beating sun, along a little path through tall grass. I was in front and was approaching a low wall when suddenly there leapt over it a huge African, in a tattered shirt, waving a cutlass. It was the only time in Guyana when my mind flew to some fantasy world implanted by childhood reading where missionaries are boiled in pots and black men chop up white. 'The natives have done for me,' I thought sadly and wondered about screaming and so on, but, before I had made up my mind, he was saying that he was the groundsman in charge of the fort and were we not pleased to be on this nice island and since the boss had a camera and would probably soon be taking a snap, he very much regretted not putting on his best shirt this morning.

The most startling thing about the fort, of which only an archway and some outer walls remained, was the fact that it was made of brick, a unique sight in Guyana. All the buildings we had seen in the months we had been there had been made of wood or of concrete. We had seen no brick buildings since we arrived. Apparently the Dutch used to bring bricks as ballast in their ships when they came from Europe to South America and it was from that ballast that the fort was built. It was lovely old brick, pink and mellow and just to look at the crumbling broken remains of those walls brought back the feeling of home, of European streets and houses.

The fort was very high and there was a sheer drop to the Essequibo. It was perfectly placed for bombarding trespassers sailing up the river. Our guide pointed this out to us and the holes through which the Dutch could fire. It was a pleasant place to linger, the grass green and more luscious than most and the old brick restful and serene. Unwillingly, we made ourselves return to the stelling, remembering the miles we had still to cover and that the longer we delayed the longer our crew would have to spend in the rum shop.

The same small crowd had gathered to watch our departure. We had hardly time to settle ourselves in the boat before Dan's son took off with a flourish, turning downstream in order, I suppose, to be able to do another impressive turn in front of the stelling, as he swung the boat upstream again. Down stream we went and then he swung the boat round and rushed towards the greenheart bollard again at tremendous speed. I watched him as he approached it, his head thrown gallantly back, his mouth in a wide grin. Then his expression changed and, following his appalled gaze to the wheel, I saw that he was turning it round and round in circles with absolutely no effect on the direction that the boat was taking, which was, at that moment straight towards the bollard. It was too late even to try to attract Dick's attention in the hope that he might be able to stall the engine. Dan's son did not even seem to think of putting it out of gear; he was mesmerized by the wheel that turned in such swift circles between his hands.

There was a terrific, shuddering crash. I saw Dan lifted high in the air and dropped overboard and I felt myself rise and land I was not sure where, except that it was somewhere noisy and not very comfortable. I was not there long anyway for Dick and Dan's son swooped down and hauled me out before I had had time to decide where I was: in *Temptress*'s engine.

'I told you that engine ought to be covered,' I heard Dick saying angrily. 'It's extremely dangerous to have it exposed: it might have been ruined having my wife fall in it like that.'

Hardly comforted by this remark, I sat somewhat stunned and watched Dan heave himself back into the boat. I could not understand why we did not sink. Neither could Dan's son apparently, for he was leaning over the side to make sure and looked delighted as he reported that the water did not seem to be getting any nearer.

The front of the boat was flattened. She had hit the bollard right on the point so that now we were as square at the front as the back, but for some reason only a little water was trickling in at present. The engine, despite the crash and my descent, was still running.

We prepared to return to the stelling for repairs, and were astonished when we realized that Dan and his son meant to set off again as if nothing had happened. Dick told them we must stop and overhaul the boat and her engine.

'But nothin' wrong, boss,' Dan objected cheerfully, as one might reassure an unreasonable child raising unreasonable difficulties.

'Just de little pin he come outa de steering wheel,' his son amplified. 'I found he and fix he nice an' safe. Look she steer well now.'

'But the engine—it might be damaged and far better mend it here than have it break down when we're half way to Bartica. How do you know there's no harm done?'

'Because,' Dan explained patiently, 'she still running. You can't hear she? Listen!'

It was useless to explain that just because the engine was running now it did not follow that it would necessarily be running in half an hour. There was too much optimistic African in Dan's mixed blood. If the engine was running now, he simply could not imagine that it would ever cease to run. We set off.

We kept fairly close to the right bank, which I found comforting for although always told that a boat is safest in open water, I feel a landlubber's consolation in being able to see terra firma close at hand.

Temptress's engine had been in no way subdued by her encounter with the bollard. It still roared and spluttered and vibrated and shook us up and down on our little wooden bench. When, suddenly, silence broke out, the immediate reaction was a sense of wonderful release. Then came the realization of the implications of the fact that the engine had stopped. Now, as often later, we were reminded of the extent to which man owes his superiority in the natural world to the machine. A few seconds before, we had dominated the river with our speed and noise. Now she could toss us about as she chose; we were no more than four helpless beings on a piece of wood that bobbed up and down on the waves like a cork and then began to spin around in circles. Suddenly we were much more aware of the depth of the water and the density of the jungle, of pirai and alligators and electric eels. Without machinery, we were, in water or bush, no more than animals less well equipped than most others to survive in nature's kingdom.

I was thinking these thoughts while Dick, who is more practical, was asking Dan where he kept the paddles—not that being practical proved very advantageous for Dan had left the paddles in Parika.

We now suddenly stopped revolving, for a long overhanging

branch had caught the boat and pushed it towards the bank. As we bumped among the mangrove a swarm of mosquitoes arose to welcome us. However, this respite did give us time to look at the engine and discuss what to do. It seemed that there was nothing wrong with the engine but that in the crash a hole had been made in the petrol tank and the fuel oil had slowly emptied itself into the Essequibo.

'Is all right,' Dan said. 'We drift back on de tide. We back in Parika tonight.'

'But we are not going back to Parika. We're going to Bartica.'

'How, boss?'

'Well, you tell us.'

'No way, boss.'

There was a pause while we digested this and slapped at the mosquitoes. Dick hacked down some lengths of wood to make something between a paddle and a punting pole.

'Are there any little settlements where we might find someone with a boat?'

'No, boss. No such t'ing at all.'

'Well, we'll go back to Fort Island and see if we can find a boat there.'

We were now so deeply entangled in the undergrowth that it took us a while to push off. From now on, however, our luck changed. We were caught up in a current which took us rapidly in a diagonal path right across the river, and held us firmly against the far bank. As we struggled to push off, a man in a canoe with an outboard engine appeared around the corner. Not very hopefully we asked this *deus ex machina* if he could take us in his canoe to Bartica. He showed no surprise, and said that if we cared to come now to his house we could wait there until the tide turned in about half an hour and then he would take us.

We looked at the solid, uncompromising green of the bush. 'Your house?' we queried.

'In there,' he said, waving his hand towards the bank a little downstream. 'You follow.'

He swung his boat round and the little dug-out canoe, fashioned out of a trunk of a tree, moved straight and purposefully down the river. *Temptress* lurched and bumped and swayed behind her in her own ungainly way. The current pushed us against the bank, we pushed away, the current pushed us again and so we tacked our way down the Essequibo.

An old watchman on the Abary talks to the superintendent.
East Indian boy fishing in a sugar canal.
Pork-knockers diving for gold and diamonds above the Peiama falls on the Mazaruni river.

The canoe stopped at a little clearing and *Temptress* ran aground not far behind. The canoe's owner jumped out, secured his boat, transferred our luggage from *Temptress* to the canoe and helped me out into the water which was a foot or so deep. Before we waded to the shore we had to say a sad farewell to Dan and his son and give them some money for their trouble, their lost petrol and their repairs to the boat. Far from feeling abandoned by them as they left us in the middle of nowhere, we felt guilty at leaving them to manage on their own; they seemed so childlike and so full of trust that things would work out somehow without any efforts or planning from them. However, they seemed not in the least bit worried as they set off to drift back home on any current that would take them and when Dick warned them not to forget to stop at Parika or they would go on drifting out to the Atlantic they roared with delight as if such a fate would be the greatest imaginable joke.

'I am Nimmo,' our new boatman told us as we walked behind him up a narrow path through the bush to a little clearing in the centre of which stood his house. All around were banana trees, one or two pawpaws and several mangoes. At the back, he told us, he grew pineapples, cassavas and some other vegetables which he sold up and down the river from Parika to Bartica. His house was quite invisible from the river and we realized now that there were several such homesteads hidden away whose existence we had not even guessed at as we sailed up the Essequibo.

He took us up to the steps to his house and his wife came out to welcome us. She was very shy, but proudly showed us her children, a little girl of about two, in a very short cotton frock which she modestly raised to hide her face, and a baby of only a few months old. We sat together under the house and drank warm Coca-Cola and talked babies while her husband made sure the canoe was in good shape for the journey.

The heat was intense even in the shade under the house and the prospect of several hours exposed in a dug-out canoe low in the water was a little daunting. Fortune, however, continued to smile on us, and as we entered the canoe thick clouds covered the sun and rain began to fall.

Our new skipper could not have been more different from our last. A tall, lithe, silent man, his every movement and expression inspired confidence. Of course the canoe was much more fragile than *Temptress,* much smaller and more likely to capsize if we

Amerindian family.
Partly built house of Akawaio Indians near the Mazaruni river.
Akawaio Indians at home. Water keeps very cool in gourds.

moved too energetically, yet we felt considerably safer in it and sure, for the first time, that in this vessel in the charge of this man, we could not fail to reach Bartica.

After a very few minutes in the canoe one could not but feel his complete mastery of his craft and of the water. The river was his road; it was as familiar to him as the electric railway is to the London commuter. He knew its tides, its currents, its moods. He was quite imperturbable, as indeed his reaction to our request to be taken to Bartica had shown. He can hardly have had such a demand before, yet he had shown no glimmer of surprise and his wife had raised no objections. To Europeans accustomed to all arrangements being complicated, it seemed odd, as if she might have been expected to say, 'But you can't go tonight, darling. Surely you haven't forgotten the Joneses are coming in for drinks?'

It was very quiet and we could hear only the plopping of the rain on the river and the gentle throb of the outboard engine in the water behind us. Nimmo answered our questions but did not often volunteer information unasked. The first time he did so was when I let my hand hang over the side of the canoe and trail in the water.

'Please not to do so, mistress,' he said. 'The pirai they have very sharp teeth. Once I knew a man and he went to Bartica with some other fellers and he get very drunk in rum shop. When he comes home he lie in bottom of boat and let he hand lie in de river. Meanwhile he sleep, always still so drunk. When he reach home he find he hand still hand so far as these joints but after that he just got skeleton fingers. Pirai they cut off all he flesh which was in de water.'

Needless to say, my hand was safely out of the water before he reached this grisly conclusion.

The second time he spoke of his own accord was when we approached the island of Stampa. 'I stop here,' he announced, 'to post a parcel.'

I thought I had misheard him, but he steered towards the island, tied up the boat and we all climbed out. 'I go post me parcel,' he said, disappearing empty-handed among the trees.

'What did he say he was going to do?' Dick asked me.

'It sounded as if he said he was going to post a parcel, but there can't be anything like a post office here now, though it was once inhabited.'

'He can't have said that. Anyway I know what I'm going to do now we have stopped,' and so saying, he disappeared among the trees. I followed.

We all three met again by the side of the boat.

'I posted me parcel,' Nimmo said, 'perhaps you mistress and you boss, you gonna post you parcels too?'

So it dawned on us; the euphemism had perhaps come down to him from some far-distant forebear who had come under the influence of a very modest missionary or worked for a prudish European employer. Whatever the reason, he clearly felt he was obeying a point of English etiquette, so we thanked him kindly and told him we had already despatched our parcels and climbed back carefully into the canoe.

After Stampa there were no more large islands, which, up till now, by interposing themselves between us and the far bank, had made the river seem narrower than it really was. Now we were in the open water and the Essequibo seemed as wide as the sea. Perhaps it was reaction after claustrophobic weeks in a small community in Georgetown but the very scale of this different world gave us an unbelievable sense of release. All around us, on all sides, lay this huge expanse of water and beyond it the countless miles of bush and above us the endless sky. As we moved slowly and quietly among this vastness, a wonderful serenity and peacefulness filled us, as if a true sense of proportion had been restored to our lives.

The rain had stopped and the sky brightened, but this was evening sun, for the day was closing. The animal kingdom began to awake after the long day's drowsing. As we approached a bend in the river, we would hear the busy chattering of monkeys in the trees, but as we came level with them, there was complete silence, which lasted until we were safely past, when the excited chattering broke out again. They might have been village gossips at a street corner intrigued by the approach of a stranger, who watch sharp-eyed and silent as he passes by, only to break out into pertinent comments once his back is turned towards them.

Sometimes a tree would be black with the bodies of spider monkeys, sinister but graceful creatures who seem to glide among the branches. Black and long-haired, they look and move exactly like huge spiders and one almost imagines that they must weave great webs as they slip from branch to branch.

Brilliantly-coloured macaws flew in loyal pairs across the river, their scarlet, blue and yellow feathers shown up to perfection against the darkening water. Even more beautiful were the butterflies, as big as small birds, whose gorgeous blue wings had an unreal, papery quality. Later I saw these creatures' wings stuck on the top surface of trays as a decoration. There seems to be no limit to the hideous incongruity man is capable of when he really puts his mind to it.

We saw no alligators coming to the water's edge for an evening drink; there were few places on our side of the river that nature had designed for such a purpose, but we saw their snouts, like two black dots on the water, which submerged even as we pointed to them, leaving only a trace of bubbles.

Slowly, but quite perceptibly, for the tropical evening is very short, the sky darkened and the forests turned from green to black. The tawny water, deprived of light from the sky, thickened and grew dark. One by one the stars appeared and it was night.

It is a rare thing to be exactly the right temperature in Guyana. Indeed I think that the night of our journey to Bartica was the first time we had that experience. The air was soft but fresh against the skin, already cooled as the water evaporated from our cotton clothes, but throbbing gently from its earlier burning in the sun. Very rarely one feels thus on a soft summer evening in England after an exceptionally hot day, but here was not even a hint of that chill in the air which spoils most summer evenings in temperate climes.

The moon rose and then other lights began to appear, some on the left bank of the river and some, apparently in the middle of it. These, Nimmo told us, were the lights of Bartica which stands at the confluence of the Mazaruni and Essequibo. It was still a long way off but the lights showed for miles across the water.

All nature seemed to be sleeping as we eased our way, smooth as a needle, through the water, towards the lights of Bartica. To each side the silent forest melted down into the water and the sky pressed long fingers down into the trees and rested gently on the water. Bemused and enchanted, lost in the dominion of nature, it was something of a shock to find that we had reached Bartica and were expected to turn into active human beings again, capable of climbing up a steep ladder, while Nimmo held the canoe to the bottom rung. Only then did I realize that squatting in the little dug-out for eight hours had rendered me quite immobile. The enchantment of the night had made us oblivious of physical discomforts; now with a fearsome cracking of joints and straining of muscles we had to face horrid human reality.

The first horrid human reality we had to face was Miss Flora Macatee. Nimmo directed us to the lodging house which she ran and where we had booked to stay for two nights. Then he handed us our luggage, seemed surprised at being paid and returned to his boat, for he was going to eat and sleep for a few hours at his cousin's house a little further up the river. When the tide was right he would set off for home by the light of the moon. We watched him go, sitting erect but relaxed in the back of his canoe, gazing straight ahead, a perfectly integrated man, at one with himself and his environment.

The lodging house seemed to be shut up for the night, indeed it looked as if it was shut up for all time, so unlit and devoid of life it seemed. We banged on the door several times and it was eventually opened by an enormously fat lady who eyed us with suspicion bordering on dislike. We told her, rather apologetically, who we were.

'Cannot be,' she said in a high-pitched, plaintive and sing-song voice that seemed unworthy of her massive frame. 'Steamer come in six o'clock and you not on it.'

'But we *are* we,' I heard Dick object wearily, and I giggled rather hysterically, which did not help to alleviate her suspicions.

'How you reach Bartica then?' she asked with an air of triumph of one posing an unanswerable problem. 'No way but the steamer.'

She had addressed her question to me and I tried hard to think of how we had come. Sentences about Parika and Dan and Fort Island and the dug-out canoe and posting parcels at Stampa floated about in my mind and I began to wonder if it had not in fact taken weeks to get here. Georgetown was in a different world now; it was far too far to be only a day's journey from us. Altogether I was rather hazy about how we had done it.

'We came in a boat,' was all I could think of saying.

Eventually she let us in and when I saw the two creatures reflected in the cracked and fly-blown looking-glass in the hall I could not find it in my heart to blame her for wanting to ward us off. Our clothes had been washed in the rain and drip-dried themselves so that they were as crumpled as if they had just come out from a week at the bottom of the laundry basket. Rain and salt had turned our hair into stiff straw that stuck out wildly in all directions. Our faces were crimson and we were so tired that we looked bleary-eyed and rather drunk.

Miss Macatee led the way to our room. 'Mind on the stair,' she warned and it was as well that she did, for in our exhaustion we might not have noticed that several of the treads were missing. The whole house seemed to be made up of bits of rotting wood, heaped together like those constructions we used to make as children out of packs of cards. One walked on tip-toe for fear of going through the floor and avoided touching the walls lest they fall down.

'You can select your room,' Miss Macatee told us grandly. 'This one is a very nice double room.' So saying she opened the door by dint of lifting it practically off its hinges, easing it over the bumpy floorboards and putting it down again against the wall. Like those of our rooms at home in Campbellville, the walls did not reach the ceiling. Unlike ours they were no more than flimsy partitions of very thin plywood. In the centre of the room was a huge and concave double bed covered with the dirtiest mosquito net I had ever seen.

'Now we go and see the other room, also very nice,' Miss Macatee said. 'But first here is the toilet—very new installation.'

She opened the door next to the bedroom we had just seen to reveal a long, narrow room with The Very New Installation at the far end. There was no light in there, but the one that shone in from behind us was enough to make the cockroaches run off in all directions. Miss Macatee strode weightily through them and gave us a demonstration of how to pull the chain.

There was a tremendous clatter as if a herd of sanitation ghosts were haunting the room with appropriate balls and chains. There was a mighty rush of water, and a sluicing and crashing as of cataracts. There were prolonged reverberations and throbbings worthy of *Temptress* herself.

Evidently well pleased with these impressive sound effects, Miss Macatee stood, her weight resting on one leg and her mighty arm uplifted so that a hand rested behind her ear to act, apparently, as a quite superfluous amplifier.

Then as minutes passed and the sounds became more mournful and gradually died away, she came slowly back to reality, shook her head and led us down a long shaky corridor to another room. Once again she manoeuvred the door open and revealed a room similar to the one that we had already seen, except that its thin partitions reached right up to the ceiling.

'Here we have the honeymoon room,' she said.

'We'll take it,' Dick said instantly, almost pushing her out of the door and I knew he was prompted less by the attractions of the honeymoon room than by the warning intake of breath, similar to that which some grandfather clocks make before they break into thunderous striking, which precedes a fearsome outburst of embarrassingly loud and uncontrollable laughter by his wife.

'I'll bring the water then,' Miss Macatee remarked as she left us. Heavy creaking sounds recorded her slow progress down the corridor.

We prowled around the room taking stock. Had it not been for the entanglement of dirty mosquito net suspended from a huge hook above the bed, we should have collapsed on it despite the unwholesome linen.

Since our six o'clock breakfast, we had eaten nothing but a few biscuits, and the hunger which excitement and the glories of the river had kept at bay now began to gnaw us. We cheered ourselves with the thought that if Miss Macatee was fetching water for us to wash it must be that she wanted us to be clean before she fed us. We had ordered dinner when we booked the room, so presumably it was still hanging around somewhere.

She returned with two glasses of water, 'In case you gets thirsty in the night,' she said, putting them on the floor.

'Miss Macatee,' Dick said ingratiatingly. 'We're very hungry. Would it be possible to have just a little supper?'

Her body stiffened; she look scandalized. She was transformed into an English landlady in a not very prosperous seaside resort.

'Supper is at 6.30,' she recited. 'Breakfast 7.30. No meals can be kept. Goodnight.'

We drank our water and reflected on the European influence. Without it Nimmo followed the rhythms of nature, eating when he was hungry, sleeping when he was tired, travelling when the tide was right. With it, Miss Macatee was bound by the clock and by rules. It was very sad; we were very hungry.

But there were compensations; the air here was fresh and invigorating. After our room in Campbellville the honeymoon room was marvellously cool. Moreover although the windows were not netted there were no mosquitoes to be seen or felt. We only kept the net over the bed to keep out the cockroaches. When we leaned out of the window we realized that we looked right over the Essequibo; stars and a nearly full moon hung in its waters. Certainly there were compensations.

The next morning Dick went off early to arrange for a boat to take us to Monkey Jump. Nimmo had given him the names of several boatmen and he set off now to find them. There was unlikely to be any difficulty about this for the boatmen of Bartica are known for their skill; both the Mazaruni and Essequibo are full of rapids which demand superb seamanship and which have taken a great toll of life. My contribution to the operation was confined to shouting, 'Don't forget, breakfast 7.30 and No Meals Kept,' as he departed.

Miss Macatee had managed to fill her house with a kind of seedy boarding house atmosphere. It was very strong in the dining room with its little tables covered with grubby cloths, with bottles of sauce in the centre and nasty little imported condiment sets innocent of salt and pepper. I was in attendance on the stroke of 7.30 when she brought in tea and two bowls of a brown mucilaginous substance. It was warmish and I drenched it in tinned milk and sugar. It turned out to be a kind of curry. The tea was very strong and some coffee seemed to have leaked into it from somewhere.

She soon reappeared with two more plates on each of which there was a piece of flat pink nourishment and a few lightly fried lettuce leaves.

'Lunch is at twelve o'clock,' she said. 'Or you take sandwich.'

I told her that we should be out all day and so should take sandwich.

Dick appeared just before eight and just after I had prevented Miss Macatee from removing his breakfast. Fortunately he does not notice what he eats.

'I've got a man with a boat,' he said, shovelling pickles on to the curried glue-and-cornflakes mixture. 'He's called Rama. We're to meet him at the boat in half an hour. He says we'll get to Monkey Jump by noon. Don't you want that pink stuff? I'll eat it for you; it's all right with lots of sugar. No, I don't think it's spam—well, maybe it is.'

'Do you think,' I asked, 'that if we told Miss Macatee that we're celebrating tomorrow she might make something edible for us?'

When she reappeared Dick smiled winningly at her and said, 'It's our wedding anniversary tomorrow night, Miss Macatee, and I've brought a bottle of wine from Georgetown. Perhaps you could put it in your refrigerator for us? And it would be rather nice to have something a little special for supper if you could manage it.'

'Yes,' she said stolidly. 'I cannot remember exactly what I have made for tomorrow night's supper. I am sure it is good.'

Defeated, we said we were sure it was too.

There was a curious shanty-town atmosphere about Bartica. As we walked down its long main street between wooden shops, I felt as if we had strayed on to the set of an American Western. The sheriff and the bad man might at any moment start a shooting match across our path. It had that half-built look of a town that has never quite fulfilled the role it was planned to play and at the same time the dilapidated look of a town that has declined from what it once was. This perhaps comes about because Bartica was once the metropolis where gold diggers, or pork-knockers as they are called in Guyana, came to spend their fortunes, for their delight was in the search of gold rather than any long-term possession of it.

Stopping only to buy a straw hat apiece, we made our way directly to the river where Rama had tied his boat up. He was of mixed African and East Indian blood, a compact little man who talked all the way and told us a great deal about the efforts to exploit the timber in the Bartica region. This was something we had already heard discussed in Georgetown and had only the previous week been to a talk on the Forest Department. This trip up the river had driven home to us the fact that Guyana possesses vast quantities of timber; it had also made us realize the tremendous problems of exploiting it economically in view of the great transport difficulties. The most valuable wood is greenheart, which provides extremely hard and heavy timber used in Europe for piles and marine construction. It is practically indestructible in temperate waters and is also a popular wood for fishing rods.

Guyana is the only source of greenheart in the world. Unfortunately its stocks have been used in the past without any thought of replacement. As a result it is now necessary to go further and further into the bush to find the trees and all this adds greatly to the cost. Tremendous trees, up to one hundred and fifty feet high, their felling is no easy business. The Forest Department is therefore trying to encourage the use of other trees and overcome the strong traditional prejudice in favour of greenheart. It is trying to encourage builders to use other local timbers such as mora and wallaba. Crabwood has always been the traditional wood for making furniture.

As we went up to Monkey Jump we saw the wood being brought

down the Essequibo. The old method of transporting greenheart was to manhandle it to the edge of the river. It could not then be floated down river as greenheart is not quite buoyant; bulk for bulk it is very slightly heavier than water. Big timber barges were therefore built with outriggers cantilevered out on each side. Ropes were used to strap the greenheart trunks lying by the riverside under these outriggers, so that they were just below the level of the water when the raft set off. This method saved lifting the heavy trees and also meant that a great deal more could be taken than if they had been laid on top of the raft, which would have sunk under any undue weight.

Nowadays things are usually done by more modern methods. The trees are handled by a ropeway, loaded on to timber bolsters and hauled by heavy lorries down to the river where they are put on to steel pontoons which are towed by tugs. We saw both methods in use as we sailed up the Essequibo. Certainly the time honoured method was more peaceful and easy going; the huge rafts moved very slowly and the men with the long poles who seemed to be making leisurely steering movements that had little effect on their elephantine barques always had plenty of time to wave and shout to us.

It was a grillingly hot day and the hard sunlight reflected back harshly from the water. The straw hats maybe saved us from sunstroke but did not do much more.

The river bank now rose steeply to our right; we were approaching the quarry. All along, I had found it very hard to believe in this quarry. Now that it appeared, it did indeed seem somewhat incongruous. Out of thick forest we saw a great escarpment, bare of trees and the naked and bony side of the cliff revealed. There was a landing stage where the boats which carried the stone tied up, and there Rama steered his boat and helped us out; he himself was going to go a little further up to a cousin (all relations in Guyana seem to be cousins) but he promised us he would return in time to take us back in the early afternoon. Before leaving he found time to point out to us how narrow the river was at this point; it gains its name from the fact that it is narrow enough for a monkey to jump. Since it was some three hundred yards wide it was tempting to paraphrase Churchill and say, 'Some monkey, some jump.'

The manager of the quarry, an East Indian, had come down to the riverside to meet us and we found ourselves being given a formal welcome and generally treated as important visitors, which was a novel sensation for us.

'We have planned,' he said, 'a detonation for you. Also a tour of the quarry. Also lunch. In which order would you prefer this?'

It was arranged as I had feared; tour, detonation, lunch. My sole interest by now was to find shade. If it had been grillingly hot on the river, it had been cool by comparison with this. The heat reflected from the rock all round us and we stood in a kind of pit which no air seemed able to penetrate. Slowly we walked across to the other side to begin our tour by inspecting the staff accommodation. About forty Africans worked on the quarry, some of them married. They lived in little wooden houses in a patch of cleared land not far from the quarry. Only the manager and his wife were East Indians and they had a house set a little apart from the rest.

The Africans were dotted about the cliff face, casually handing gelignite about as if it was as harmless as soap and tossing electric cables here and there in readiness for the detonation. Suddenly the manager decided we should call in at his house for a drink. His wife gave us a gracious welcome and I noticed that rice and curry were already on the table. We drank beautifully cold iced lime juice—the oil refrigerator rightly stood in a place of honour in the middle of the small sitting room—and then the manager told his wife, 'Tour, detonation, lunch.' She, to my immense relief, replied, 'Lady stay here for entertainment. Tell us when you goin' detonate.'

The manager's wife entertained me royally, plying me with lime juice and showing me round her sitting room which was decorated with calendars of different years, pictures of the Queen cut out of illustrated magazines and photographs of her own children who, she explained, had been sent away to one of the workmen's wives to be out of the way during our visit. Then she moved two chairs to the door and we sat and looked out across the quarry and made polite conversation. We may have been in the midst of the bush but the talk was out of *Cranford*.

'Social life is very limited here,' she told me. 'There are no other ladies.'

'I think your husband said some of the men were married?'

'Yes, but I don't mix up wid dem. Day not me type at all.'

Here in the forest, spoke the voice of suburbia. I do not know why it was so startling to hear; there is no reason why one should expect human nature to vary with geography, or to be more serious or dignified in rural Gayana than in urban England. All the same, snobbishness and the affectations of gentility seem more incongruous in Monkey Jump than in Croydon.

I asked her about the children and looked again at their photographs on the wall; it was difficult to make out their features through the cracked glass. 'They fall down with de detonations,' she explained. 'So is not worth the trouble of mending them.'

'You get a lot of blast then?'

'Oh, plenty, plenty. We used to live just over there,' and she pointed to a spot a few yards away, 'but it get all shook up and everything broken, so we move house a bit, but it happens just de same again so we move to here.'

Each removal had been of a few yards.

'Wouldn't it be better to move right back there among the trees?'

'No, I likes to keep me a little apart.'

Certainly she lived up to her principles; she preferred death by detonation to life among the riff-raff.

'What happens to the children when there is blasting?'

'De men wave de flag and they all run into de bush. Look now, dey gettin' ready.'

We watched as the man walked about the quarry waving his flag and then heard a warning hooter. The other men began to move away until there was just one left with the fuse.

'Down der is our gentlemen,' the manager's wife said. They were in a boat in the Essequibo. I could just make out that Dick was getting his camera ready when the final hooter blew.

'We go lie flat,' my hostess told me as matter-of-factly as if she was offering a drink. She moved inside and lay flat on the floor. I joined her, but wanted to see what happened so raised myself up a little to peer out of the window.

Everything was very still; the one man alone on the quarry face bent down over his fuse for a moment and then ran off into the bush. Seconds passed and then the silence exploded. There was a deafening thunderclap followed by a prolonged roar as the huge stones began to pelt down. For one nasty moment I thought my head had been blown off and regretted putting it so inquisitively out of the window. The house shook and rattled, the pictures fell to the floor, where various other bits and pieces joined them. The manager's wife got up and began systematically replacing things. Nothing could be seen outside for the cloud of dust and smoke, but the rumbling was breaking up into separate sounds of distinct crashes, which gradually became less frequent and finally ceased altogether.

'Would you like to wash your hands?' she asked. I should have liked to have washed my face and hair and generally as much of me as possible and moved gratefully towards the kitchen, but this evidently was not what my hostess intended, for she led me out of the house, down a path through the trees to a tall narrow box and there she left me. This apparently, was another euphemism of the come-and-post-your-parcel variety. I pushed the door gingerly. Inside it was very dark, though a little light came, oddly enough, from the floor. I looked more closely: there was a huge wooden seat on which an elephant might comfortably have accommodated itself. It was supported on pieces of wood and below it there was nothing. Evidently it was perched right on the edge of a cliff, hundreds of feet above the river. No doubt it was an extremely ingenious and hygienic idea, but not at all the thing for one who does not like heights and has never been much good at balancing. I waited for what I hoped would be considered a reasonable amount of time and walked back up the path to the house.

The men had returned. The boat had almost submerged in the blast and another little boat, tied up nearer the bank, had sunk, but without any damage being done. We settled down to the hottest cold curry imaginable which necessitated drinking huge quantities of lime juice. The talk was all of types and sizes of stone and of transport and deliveries and prices. Now that her man was there to do the honours, his wife was silent and I decided to join her in this feudal habit, for a modest silence is just the thing when one is overfed and very sleepy.

Rama had been waiting for over an hour before we joined him. The manager and his wife came down to wave us off and we parted on the best of terms for the stone had proved suitable and all the arrangements for its purchase had gone very smoothly. There was no difficulty, the manager assured us, in getting rush orders, for the men had absolutely no amusements at Monkey Jump, where there was not even a shop, and wanted to work as long hours as possible to make the maximum amount of money. On Saturday they all went down in a big boat to Bartica where they spent their week's earnings.

To Bartica we now ourselves returned and entered Miss Macatee's dining room at six-thirty, just as she was putting our meal on the table. She always put meals on the table at the exact time and removed them half an hour later; whether anybody had attempted to eat them in the interim was not of the slightest interest to her.

All I can remember about that evening is the outsize rat who came and watched us eating from a vantage point among the rafters.

The next morning we set out once again in Rama's boat, for he had agreed to take us up to a timber reserve which Dick wanted to visit. This time we sailed in the opposite direction and turned up the Mazaruni. On the far bank we could see the Penal Settlement, which must occupy one of the greenest, choicest sites in Guyana. It is here that all the most dangerous convicts are sent as escape is impossible, for at the back is impenetrable bush and on the other sides the waters of the Essequibo and Mazaruni. Some apparently have tried to swim to freedom but none has survived the ordeal. Sometimes back in Georgetown, I used to wonder why anybody should want to escape from that idyllic spot on the Mazaruni, set between two such wide and beautiful rivers, where the nights are cool and mosquitoes almost non-existent. He must prize his freedom highly who values it above such comforts.

Soon, on the other side, we saw Katabo Point where the Cuyuni joins the Mazaruni. Here on the island of Kijk-over-Al (or See-over-All) is the Dutch fort built some two hundred years ago where there had formerly been a Portuguese one.

We had no time to stop, much as we should have liked to have landed and inspected the ruins. Instead we made our way up the Cuyuni and soon stopped by a little private landing stage where Rama shouted and grumbled until a tall youth appeared in the clearing on the bank and began to walk very slowly towards us.

'I tell him to be all ready,' Rama grumbled. 'Hurry man, hurry. You can't walk no faster dan dat?'

The youth did not reply, but began slowly to untie a much smaller boat that was tied up to the little stelling. He was big and very slow and very backward. Perhaps he was dumb for he did not speak a word throughout the time he was with us, or perhaps he thought that was his best defence against Rama's bullying.

We were at a loss to understand why we were picking up this lad and his little boat; Rama had presumably assumed we were bound to be familiar with the lore of the rivers. We set off with the little boat and its mute owner behind us and after about a mile or two stopped and Rama explained that we should transfer into the little boat, leaving the youth in our boat, which was too big to take among the rapids or up the narrower tributary of the Cuyuni which we should have to travel in order to get to the timber reserve. The transfer was a hectic business, with Rama chiding the boy for being so slow and stupid and the poor lad, who was simply not the hurrying kind, getting flustered and bewildered as instructions and some of our possessions were handed about. However, in the end the three of us, Rama and ourselves, were in the little boat and departed leaving the exhausted youth in our boat surrounded by cameras, spare clothes, papers and maps. Completely immutable, he sat and watched us go and I had a terrible feeling that if we were washed away in the rapids he would stay there for ever awaiting our return.

It was hard to believe that we were approaching the rapids. We moved slowly towards a distant white line, which as we drew nearer appeared to be a line of breaking waves. Suddenly we were in it and the boat seemed to take on a life of its own. As far as we could see, ahead and on both sides, the water seemed to be divided by tiny islands, some visible and some submerged, with rushing water of varying depths leaping and swirling between them. With incredible skill, Rama chose which course to steer, zig-zagging his way between the islands and groups of islets, at a tremendous speed. Sometimes, glimpsing to one side, we could see that had he chosen to go by an adjoining channel the boat would have been smashed to pieces on rocks which lay just below the surface of the water. I assumed at the time that he must know every current and rock in the wide river, for otherwise how could he know not to choose a channel with submerged rocks at a time when he could not yet see them. Later we learned that this is not so, for the islets, rocks and currents move and change and the boatman has to depend on his knowledge of the signs and deep instinct about the ways of the river to make instant decisions about where to turn his boat. So amazed were we by Rama's skill in knowing where to turn his boat that we scarcely thought to marvel at the fact that he was able to make it go in the direction he had decided, in such waters.

On the whole we enjoyed this hair-raising experience. It is exhilarating to be involved in something extremely dangerous when one is in no way responsible for doing anything and has complete trust in the person in charge. I think I know how the passengers in Blondin's wheelbarrow must have felt as he pushed them along the tight rope over the Niagara falls.

The rivers of Guyana, which might have provided a network of communications, are much reduced in value by the fact that great expanses of them are not navigable as a result of rapids. Human travellers by-pass those stretches which are not navigable by hauling their boats overland, or arranging to trek to another boat beyond the rapids. The expense of doing this with timber is yet another factor in making the exploitation of the forests of Guyana an extremely difficult proposition.

Many people to whom we spoke in Guyana believed that in the construction of roads lay the answer to the country's problems. Money should be poured into projects for opening up the Interior by building roads, they believed, since it is in the inaccessible forests that her wealth lies. They believe that if roads were built people would leave the coastal strip and go into the Interior where the climate and the soil are much more favourable and farming might be a paying proposition. The trouble is that the building of roads in such conditions is an extremely expensive undertaking and Guyana's great problem is the need for capital. Besides, to put money into building roads in the hope that this will lead to development is an act of faith. Yet without such an act of faith it is hard to see how the country can make any progress at all.

Problems of economics seemed remote as we sailed, calmly now, between the narrowing banks of the Cuyuni and it was hard to believe that we were in the heart of the area most discussed by the Forestry Commission. It was too remote, too quiet, too untouched by human activities. It was a shock to round a bend in the river, in the early afternoon and see a great clearing with huts and piles of tree trunks, cleaned and shaped, on the river bank. Men were moving about and boats were tied up to a little jetty. On the bank near the felled trees, there stood, red and incongruous, a Ferguson tractor.

Rama steered towards the jetty and tied up alongside the other boats. A foreman, a short fat African who wore a cloth cap, was soon found, and he and Dick began to talk wood, while I sat on one of the tree trunks. After a few minutes Dick remarked casually that they would just go up to look at the reserve for an hour or so and they disappeared out of sight up a wide track that ran between arching trees. It seemed as if they were disappearing, the long lean figure and the short fat one, into a tunnel, from which they might never emerge.

Africans are friendly people and the men soon drifted towards my log to chat. They were very difficult to understand, possibly because they were not used to talking to people other than themselves and spoke a strong Creolese. They asked me if I knew the different trees and laughed when I told them that the only one I

Main road to Parika

Blasting at the quarry at Monkey Jump

knew was the silk cotton tree. It is the fastest growing tree of all and supposed to be full of obeah or magic. Indeed it is supposed to be the dwelling place of the evil spirit and many Africans believed that it is very unlucky to cut one down and that someone will certainly die if that is done. One explanation given for this is that in days gone by when a Chinaman made a fortune he would get an African slave to dig a great hole for him in which to hide his gold. Then, for fear that the man would come back and steal it, he would kill the slave and bury him too. To cover his crime he would plant the quickest growing tree he could think of—the silk cotton. If the tree is cut down, so the superstitious believe, the spirit of the wronged slave will be free to wreak vengeance.

I knew of this, for back in Georgetown there had been a silk cotton tree on the site where the sugar terminal was to be built on the bank of the Demerara. The men had refused to cut it down. The foreman, wisely, did not try to make them, but persuaded them that the age-old method of warding off the evil spirit with more spirit made the operation quite safe. Three men were persuaded to do the work and armed with plenty of rum they set about their work at night when there was nobody about to take offence. This foreman told us afterwards that he at last understood why there so often was a death when a silk cotton tree was felled, for the men were so drunk and danced so wildly around the tree as they chopped at it that he quite expected it would crash on one of them as it fell.

The timbermen told me now of the other, less dangerous trees. There was no doubt that the greenheart was the one they held in greatest esteem, not only for its immense height and hardness, but for its international reputation and for the way it has for years been used throughout the world in marine construction. It is not going to be easy to popularize other woods in Guyana; local builders are still much influenced by the prestige-value of greenheart. A far more prolific tree is wallaba which can be grown on very poor soil. For many years some specialists have believed that a thriving industry could develop in Guyana if wallaba were pulped for paper making but this project, like so many others, has not been pursued and wallaba is still used mainly for poles and fences and fuel, chiefly in the form of charcoal. The little single-track railway which runs along the East Coast from Georgetown to Rosignol used to be fired by this wood. It is the oldest railway line in South America. Wallaba is used a little in house-building, though less so than mora,

Granny at Santa.
Kaieteur fall.
Flying over the seemingly endless bush.
Transporting heavy greenheart trees down the Essequibo river.

another tree that was pointed out to me with pride, for it is a huge and impressive tree, buttressed like a cathedral.

Suddenly a canoe appeared at the jetty and another foreman, tall and becapped, jumped out. The men melted away miraculously and began desultory chopping activities. I was left alone on the tree trunk and so began to rummage around among Dick's papers and reports to find something to read. I was lucky in finding the report on the Forest Department, setting out the facts of the forest lands of Guyana. Apparently there are seventy thousand square miles of forests in the country, almost all owned by the state, of which thirteen and a half thousand are exploitable and forty thousand potentially so. The Department are concerned to provide access to the forest areas and develop the markets for those trees hitherto regarded as unmarketable. I remembered the way in which the timbermen had spoken of the 'great' trees, an attitude shared by builders and craftsmen throughout Guyana, and thought the department was in for a difficult time.

The report mentioned also the development of the trees of the far Interior which are used mainly for the collection of balata gum and other minor forest products. I had only recently heard of balata, which is a kind of wild gum which had for many years been collected by Amerindians in the bush and used as rubber. The balata, or bullet, trees are very tall and black. They are bled by slashing the bark until the white latex flows into troughs, where it is allowed to dry and harden. When a fairly thick skin has formed, it is removed and hung up to dry, like a strip of rubber. It is exported to many countries and used for covering marine cables and making machine belts and golf balls. The only balata products I had seen were some rather nasty little rubber figures of Africans on sale in a kind of tourist shop run by the government in Georgetown.

I was not surprised to read that greenheart, in the form of sawn timber, round piling and hewn squares was the chief timber export, going mainly to the United Kingdom, the United States and Holland, nor that wallaba poles are exported to the West Indies. I was surprised, however, to read that firewood and charcoal exports made quite a contribution to the export drive. I went on to read that the sawmill in Georgetown has two bandsaw head-rigs and several band and circular re-saws. I made a mental note to ask Dick when or if he returned, what all that meant. Meanwhile I put down the report, forgot about timber and thought about trees.

In the introduction to his book, *Art and Illusion,* Professor

Gombrich illustrates an argument with a drawing, taken from a newspaper cartoon, which at first looks like a duck and then, on a second look, becomes a rabbit, facing the other way, for the beak becomes visible as two ears, and a little dark depression, unnoticed when the shape was seen as a duck, becomes important as the rabbit's mouth. The longer you look, the easier it becomes to view the shape as rabbit or as duck in rapid succession. The point the writer makes is that however hard you try you cannot see it as both simultaneously.

(*Reproduced by courtesy of Phaidon Press*)

In the same way Kenneth Clark observed that he could see a great Velázquez as brush strokes and dabs of pigment on the canvas or as a marvellous work of art, but he could not see it as both at the same time. So it is with forests; they can be viewed as timber reserves to be exploited by human beings, they can be measured in square yards and their values assessed per cubic foot of exported wood. They can be examined and marked up, worked upon, changed or discarded like any other product which man has tamed and turned to his own use. Or they can be viewed another way, these same unchanging forests. One can walk among them and feel their tremendous dominion, their soaring height dwarfing man and their vast expanse defying his attempts to penetrate them. The tracks he makes through them are overgrown immediately he departs. He clears a little space and builds there, but both clearing and building disappear without trace when the forest reclaims its own.

I think what most surprised me about the tropical rain forest was the sense of being in an enclosed space. Trees, such as greenheart, often seem to grow without any side branches for fifty or more feet and then break out with a great spread of branches and foliage. There is very little light near the ground, so the life of the forest seems to be pushed up to the tops of the trees where the sunlight can penetrate. Lower down all is cool and dark and hushed. Perhaps it is this which makes it hard to walk among such trees without a sense of awe, for one's eyes are constantly drawn upwards, as they are by great church architecture.

To walk thus is to walk humbly, aware of man's puny stature. To contemplate the forest as part of exploitable nature is to walk proudly, aware of man's superior powers. Both are aspects of reality, the vision of imagination is neither more nor less true than the vision of the mind, but they are mutually exclusive. You cannot see the duck at the same time as the rabbit.

Towards evening two figures appeared round the bend in the track, one tall, white and topped with a straw hat, the other short black and wearing a cap. At the same time Rama appeared, as if by magic, in his boat and soon we were making our way back down the Cuyuni and approaching the white line of the rapids. By the time we had danced and pirouetted our way along the current between the islets and made our dash to safety and the calm waters, the light was fading. There, motionless, as we had left him, sat the mute boy in the waiting boat. It seemed sad to disturb his mindless tranquillity. We transferred into the larger boat and made our way back to the landing stage where the boy lived. He did not reply to our polite thanks and farewells.

'You go up on top,' Rama now told us. 'Catch more breeze.'

We climbed on to the little wooden cover over the boat and lay back, carefully spreading our weight as evenly as possible over the plyboard in case we went through. It was a very still night and certainly there was more breeze up here; wafts of forest scents reached us on the sultry evening air. Soon we were back on the wide waters of the Mazaruni and as we approached its confluence with the Essequibo, the stars began to appear. It did not seem less wonderful than the first night we had come to Bartica, or less remarkable. I cannot believe that even after a lifetime of living there one would become immune to the magic of those rivers at night.

In silence we lay and watched the full moon, yellow and huge, as befitted its vast surroundings. Never, I thought as I looked across the waters of the Mazaruni and Essequibo, wide here like the sea, and gazed at the full moon and infinity of stars and smelled the soft sweet smell of frangipani and night orchids, never would there be another night like this; never, if we lived to be a joint two hundred, could we have such a perfect wedding anniversary. I turned from the stars to look instead at the profile beside me, which was also gazing intently at the sky, and breaking the silence at last, I murmured, 'What are you thinking?'

'Well,' he said slowly and thoughtfully, 'I was wondering how they got that Ferguson tractor up to the timber reserve.'

The journey back to Georgetown was very tame compared with the one to Bartica. We caught the steamer and sat in deck chairs, feeling hot and sad and quite cut off from the river by the massive bulk of the vessel. We tried hard to see the spot where Nimmo lived, but the bush presented a solid barrier and there was no sign of the little path that led to his clearing.

Back in Parika, Jubraj awaited us and standing with him was Dan, who greeted us with great affection and the news that it had taken *Temptress* more than one day and a night to reach home owing to delays at Fort Island. We deduced that the delays were in the rum parlour. They had patched up the hole in her tank, he told us, and she was all ready to take us to Bartica whenever we wanted to make the journey again. We thanked him with as much semblance of sincerity as we could muster.

In fact we never went to Bartica again, though stone and timber were delivered regularly from the quarry and the timber reserve. At least, fairly regularly, for it turned out that the promises of endless supplies of stone, like many such promises in Guyana, were easier to make than to keep. There were constant difficulties over getting transport to bring it to Georgetown and the temptation to sell available stone to more pressing customers nearer at hand was evidently too hard to resist. A postal battle was waged with Monkey Jump for the next eighteen months, but it was fortunately prevented from becoming too acrimonious by the slowness and unreliability of the mail service.

Next Christmas Eve, Dick came home carrying a bottle. The manager of the timber reserve from which he bought timber for shuttering, had, he told me, sent him presents of a bottle of rum for himself and a pair of ear-rings for me. I held out my hand. He looked quite shocked. 'You don't think I'd accept bribes?' he said. 'I sent the ear-rings back.'

CHAPTER SEVEN

Markets

Stabroek Market, a long, gabled construction of the Dutch School of Architecture, stands out among the Victorian and modern British buildings of the centre of Georgetown like an exotic stranger among a crowd of compatriots. Backing on to the Demerara river and facing down Water Street, the main shopping and business street, it dominates with its tall clock tower the busiest part of the city and is ideally placed for traders and shoppers alike. Apart from the usual fruit and vegetables, fish and meat, it sells a fine collection of the rougher type of kitchen implements, cheap materials, baskets and plant pots.

In the early days of our garden-making I used to spend a great deal of time buying plant pots in Stabroek Market, for ours seemed to enjoy an extraordinarily brief life-span. Cross-examined about this, Singh insisted that they were imported and therefore could not withstand the Guyanese sun which broke them up. He recommended that I should buy the locally made, heavy, concrete ones which cost about six times as much and did not look to me at all suitable for growing plants in. I resisted for a while, suggesting, as tactfully as I could, that ours might not be so susceptible to the rays of the sun if he did not lower their resistance by dropping them on the ground so often. Although very gentle with plants, he had the Guyanese way of treating all equipment in the most cavalier fashion: garden sprays, hose pipes, trowels, they were all sooner or later found broken up and abandoned in a corner of the garage. Only the cutlass seemed to survive misuse and neglect.

Singh did, of course, finally get his own way about the plant pots and soon I was staggering home from Stabroek with armfuls of concrete ones, at least an inch thick and coated with dusty green or red powder. Not only were they very thick but their sides curved inwards so that they held considerably less soil than their massive exteriors suggested. Nothing grew well in them, but they were themselves indestructible.

The baskets that I used to buy in Stabroek were anything but indestructible. On the contrary they began to unravel themselves very soon after being purchased, but as they only cost one or two shillings they hardly needed to be regarded as a long term investment. I used to buy mine from a blind East Indian who had constructed for himself, in a corner of the market, a little house whose walls were made of baskets of all shapes and sizes, placed one inside the other. He would run his hands lovingly along them, his fingers feeling, pausing, rejecting, until he found just the right one for my needs. It was not always the one I would have chosen myself, but I knew that it would soon start disintegrating so I should not have to put up with it for long.

Bourda market was smaller and had less variety of goods, but it lay on our side of the town so I chose to go there for our household shopping. My first visit was unfortunate: although it was officially the dry season we had had torrential rain for two days. It had stopped raining when I arrived in the late morning, but the air was heavy with humidity. The women, mainly East Indians, were sitting on newspapers on the pavement. Each had a space, sometimes not much more than a couple of square yards, covered with her sodden wares. Everyone seemed to be selling the same things and few people seemed to be buying. Babies lay beside some of the stallholders and toddlers played in the dirty gutters, picking up bits of bad mangoes and old banana skins out of the fetid water. It was very hot and steamy and as far as the eye could see the pavement seemed to be covered with mangoes, pawpaws, plantains, bolongers, oranges and grapefruit and depressed human beings.

Inside the market was even steamier and gloomier, the cries of the market women more hopeless, their outstretched hands as they sought to attract purchasers to their stalls more desperate, the babies that crawled about under the stalls more sore-covered and miserable. The whole place swarmed with flies and, it seemed to me on that first day, every second person was deformed with elephantiasis.

The roof leaked so that the ground inside was slippery with mud and the remains of rotten fruit and vegetables. As I picked my way carefully between the dirt and the puddles, a thin brown hand shot out and seized my arm, 'Mangoes, lovely mangoes,' the woman whined plaintively. I bought a pile for twenty cents and she rummaged around under the stall to find a piece of newspaper to wrap them in. Suddenly there was an angry yell from a crate by her feet. I jumped and asked whatever it was.

'Me baby,' she said simply.

A few seconds later I need not have asked, for unmistakably human cries began to come out of the box. The baby appeared to realize that someone was taking an interest in its woes and began to air them most grievously. A huge cockroach evidently did not like the noise and ran out between the bars of the crate.

'I used to keep she in open box,' the woman said defensively, 'but den she begin crawl and now der is no catchin' she. Once I servin' and when I stops I find she no der. She safer in dat box dan under de wheel of de cars in de street.'

What else could she do? And what could I do but buy from her a pawpaw, that I did not want, and walk on.

I found myself in the meat market; here the stalls were all kept by men, and dogs rather than babies crouched under the stalls. Passing down the main thoroughfare I seemed to be moving down a corridor of flesh, for the meat, which was stripped from the bone and not cut into joints, hung like portière curtains from frames above the stalls. It was like walking through an Indian bazaar in which the silks had turned into steaks. As I walked, dark hands would draw the meat drapery aside and faces peer through, like inquisitive old ladies peeping through lace curtains. 'We got fillet,' they shouted. 'Best steak, mistress,' and grinned as if they knew they were really taking part in a comic opera and that on their cue they must push their heads through the crimson curtains and say their piece. Or it was a Punch and Judy show, set in a butcher's shop, or an experimental play with curtains made of raw flesh and dogs for an audience.

Later I found that the market was really a much more cheerful place than I had thought on that first day. I learned that it was best to go at about eight in the morning when it was fresher and cleaner. It was advisable, nonetheless, to go to the meat department first, when one was feeling strongest and least squeamish. Shopping for cassava bread, materials or pots and pans could safely be left till the end. I also found that although it might be pleasant to wander around the market, looking and comparing, such aimlessness laid one open to irresistible appeals from all the stallholders, each beseeching one to buy their lovely bananas or their best steak. It was better, if less interesting, to go always to the same stalls and walk there purposefully with never a sideways glance.

My butcher was a big, jolly East Indian with huge hands. He was always on the look-out for me on Tuesdays and Fridays and his welcoming face would appear through the fleshy skeins of beef to call a greeting, the meat brushing against his cheek as he did so.

The meat was very cheap, about fifty cents (roughly two shillings) a pound. He would unhook a few lengths of it and slap them down on the scales with such force that the meat bounced up and down for a few minutes before he scooped it up in his mighty hand and lowered it delicately into a long plastic bag which I held out to receive it. He always gave good measure. Indeed I found no truth in the accusation often brought by European wives who would not go to the market because, they said, the stallholders gave poor quality and weight and charged high prices to white people. On the contrary, I found that they were much more inclined to swindle their own people. Once, when I was not well, Mable went to the market for me and the meat she brought back as five pounds looked so little that we weighed it and found it was only four. She did not seem surprised. 'You see, mistress,' she explained matter-of-factly, 'they give you ladies proper measure, but they know we folks don't have no scales, so we can't tell what's right.' This seemed a much more likely way round. Moreover, a stallholder who was lucky enough to get the custom of a European who came regularly with a large order would not be likely to risk losing it. Even on occasional visits to different stalls or markets I always found that the traders were inclined to be generous in the desire to please, either from good-will or sycophantism, according to their temperament, but either way it resulted in a tendency to treat the white better than the native. Here was yet another small example of the way in which colonialism makes difficult the path towards independence. People, not the leaders maybe, but the mass of ordinary people have been conditioned down the years to be more deferential to the foreigner than they were to each other. It does not make for self respect in a young nation. When Mable referred, as she sometimes did, to 'ladies' and 'we folks' there was no doubt whom she was putting into each category; it was a question of pigmentation.

By far the largest part of the market was taken up with fruit and vegetables. It was here that competition was fiercest, for stall after stall seemed to be trying to sell the same produce. The one I finally chose was owned by a little bright-eyed East Indian woman, whose son kept the next stall. As soon as she saw me approaching from the direction of the meat market she would call out proprietorially, 'Here's me lady,' and glare around at the other stallholders in case they should dare to try to seduce my custom. Immediately

I was within reach she would lean across her stall, seize both my baskets and hide them on the ground behind her. Only then did she feel it was safe to relax, and the long recitation of all the good things she had brought in specially for me would begin. 'Lovely mangoes, mistress, spice mangoes, some ready to eat, some to keep. Den der is dis lovely pawpaw, big and ripe.' She had Singh's way of lingering on the word 'lovely' as if she really did love it and could not bring herself to part with a syllable of it. 'And den der is dis squash, and beans and okras.' Every time I went she offered me okras and every time I refused them; they were a kind of thick green stumpy vegetable that boils into an unappetizing mess of mucilaginous pods. They are highly thought of locally.

If I asked for something she did not have, she would go off and buy it from another stall. Any suggestion that I might go myself was summarily dismissed; she had no intention of risking losing custom by letting me make direct contacts elsewhere.

I had a standing order for soursop, a curious fruit that looks as uninviting as it sounds. It is about the size and shape of a rugger ball, only green and knobbly. It is not ready for use until it has developed mouldy patches and feels quite rotten. When cut in two its inside is found to consist of squashy white pulp the colour of maggots. Dotted about in this nacrescent mass are shiny pips the exact size and colour of cockroaches. The inside pulp is then scooped out and pressed through a sieve and from this unpromising purée delicious concoctions can be made. It can either be made into a drink by adding water and sugar or turned into ice cream. Either way, the flavour is unbelievably delicate. It is soft and luxurious, yet pungent, reminiscent of the smell of strawberries, with something of the taste of ripe peaches. It was a remarkable flavour, exotic and expensive, and no less remarkable for coming from such a sordid looking object.

It was vital that the soursops should be used at exactly the right moment: if they were picked too soon they simply went bad without ever reaching the edible stage. They were rather too perishable for the market people to handle economically and I was in fact introduced to them by Kerosene Joe who presented me with one soon after we arrived, for he had a tree in his garden. I am afraid I did not receive it with the enthusiasm it deserved. I remember holding the horrid object he had deposited in my hands and trying to thank him sincerely, even as my fingers sank sickeningly through the soft and mouldy skin into the putrescent mess within.

Since she sold only locally grown fruit and vegetables my East Indian lady did allow me to go to another stall for imported potatoes and carrots. Root crops do not grow in Guyana as they do in other tropical and subtropical areas, as in order to utilize the energy absorbed from the sun during the day plants require a fall in temperature into the seventies at night. The noticeable thing about the climate in Guyana, apart from the humidity, is the lack of variation at night time. Being imported, the potatoes, carrots, cabbages were very expensive, but it took me a while to get out of the European habit of thinking of them as cheap standbys.*

All transactions in the market were done with a certain formality and the final reckoning of the account was no exception. When we were quite sure that there was no other purchase that I could possibly make, when okras had been rejected at least three times and I had explained over again that we had lettuce in our garden just now and that I was quite sure that twelve mangoes were enough for three days, and that I did not need another hand of bananas, beautiful though they undoubtedly were, now, she would concede, now we could reckon it all up.

The process was complicated by the fact that the currency had changed a few years before from pounds to dollars, the dollar being worth 4/2d. Although shop prices, wages and indeed all other transactions were made in dollars, in the market both currencies were used side by side. I could find no explanation for this. Perhaps the market people were more elderly and conservative or perhaps they had grown used to setting out their mangoes in 'shilling lots'. Whatever the reason both currencies were used. A penny or two cents piece, was legal tender and so was a halfpenny, or cent. A twenty-five cent piece was the exact size and shape of a shilling, which is in fact worth twenty-four cents. A fifty-cent piece looked like a florin, which was actually worth forty-eight cents.

My East Indian stallholder could perform the most amazing feats of mental arithmetic in mixed currencies. Laying her hand on each item in the baskets in turn she would begin a monologue which went something like this:

'Two shillings de mangoes, thirty-two cents de big pawpaw and a shilling de small pawpaw. Den a penny de parsley and a shilling de beans and thirty-six cents de soursop and fiive cents de shallot.

*The Government has recently restricted the import of such fruit and vegetables to encourage home production and keep down the costs of imports.

Dat makes,' she concluded without a pause, 'one dollar and seventy-one cents.'

I was so surprised the first time she did this that she mistook my astonishment for shock at the size of the bill and insisted on borrowing a piece of paper and a pencil from her son and writing it all down for me to see. She was right, down to the last cent—or halfpenny.

We have returned home to find that Britain too is preparing to change to a decimal system of coinage. When I hear people objecting that it will be too difficult to get used to a new coinage and different prices I often remember my little East Indian market woman adding up the bill in two different currencies with such speed and accuracy and wonder if it is not about time we quietly dropped the habit of referring to such people as 'backward'.

Sometimes we would get back from the market to find waiting for us a boy selling plants. Since they were never on sale at the market or elsewhere, I was glad to have them and used at first to buy quite frequently from these boys. They often brought me cannas, those yellow, orange and red lilies that are among the most colourful and showy of the flowers in the gardens and thoroughfares of Georgetown. I had a standing order for cannas and soon the garden boasted a very striking row of them all along the inside of the fence.

Since nobody seemed to have heard of a nursery or market garden in Georgetown I was very interested to know where the plants were grown, but their vendors were furtive-looking youths and I could never get an answer out of them when I asked whom they worked for. Furthermore the plants did not seem to have been professionally produced; indeed they usually looked as if they had been pulled up by the roots by somebody in a great hurry.

Singh never seemed happy about these transactions. When I showed him my purchases, he would turn away and talk about something else, but I put this down to his super-sensitivity and decided he did not like new plants being introduced into the garden without being consulted beforehand.

It was some time before I was told that quite a flourishing business was done in stolen plants. One heard so many accusations of this kind, that I asked Singh if it was true.

'Oh, yes,' he said, nonchalantly. 'Dese cannas day all stolen.

Day is bad boys dat sells dem. Day pulls up de plants too hard and day don't love de plants at all.' It was not so much the stealing that worried Singh as the ham-handed way in which it was done.

After this we bought no more of the tempting plants brought for sale at the back door—I felt guilty enough already about my lovely row of cannas, especially if visitors admired them and then remarked that all theirs had been stolen. However my conscience did not have to suffer long, for one morning I went down to the garden and found that they had all gone. Possibly the boy who had sold them to me had decided that they had recovered from their last move and were ready to make another.

I was less philosophical about the loss of a bougainvillaea. We had tried repeatedly to grow the rather unusual pure red one; we tried to strike cuttings and friends rooted them for us, but none survived. At last we were successful and managed one that looked as if it might take to us. We lavished donkey dung on it and watered it sedulously night and morning. When a friend brought out a packet of Plantoids from England we fed them all to the little red bougainvillaea. It was the first plant that Singh went to look at when he arrived in the evening and we all treated it with the solicitous tenderness that a garden invalid deserves. Soon it was flourishing; a neat little bush bedecked with a mass of red sprays. I stood and admired it at the end of one morning as I was on the lookout for Dick coming home for lunch. When we came into the garden after lunch there was just a big hole where it had been. It had been pulled up unceremoniously in the midday sun, our poor little red bougainvillaea, and would not have a chance of surviving, but I suppose one of the furtive youths hoped to get fifty cents for it.

In poor countries such as Guyana this kind of petty thieving abounds. So one is more aware of dishonesty in everyday life and crime is more of a personal problem than it is in England. One therefore gets the impression that the community is more dishonest, but I doubt if this is so. Without having any statistics to back it up, it seems quite probable that the total value of thefts in proportion to the population is probably much higher in the more advanced countries where crime is more highly organized and profitable. In Guyana people who were inclined that way or made desperate by circumstances seemed to be prepared to take liberties with the law in the hope of very little profit.

Mr. Hope was such a man. We had not been long in our house in Campbellville when, one Sunday, Lucille brought out to us on the verandah a personable young African who appeared to know Dick quite well. 'Good afternoon, sir,' he said. 'I'm Hope, sir. You remember me? I work at Booker's Garage and fill up de car for you often.'

Dick showed signs of remembering him and he went on to tell us that he had been out on the airport road teaching one Mr. Roberts—a local clerk on the site—to drive, when unfortunately Mr. Roberts swerved and bumped into an East Indian lady carrying a big basket. Blessedly she was not hurt but, alas, her basket and its contents were damaged. She said that for five dollars' compensation she would be content. Otherwise she would have to report the accident to the police. This would be embarrassing as Mr. Roberts was a learner but had no temporary licence.

Mr. Hope then explained to us that he had gone to one of the directors of Bookers and the director had told him to come to our house. He had kindly provided him with a map so that he could find the way. He showed us the map which sketched the route from the director's house to ours. He mentioned other people connected with the site, including the accountant whom he would have called on first, but knew that he was out for the afternoon, so had taken the liberty of coming to us instead.

Roberts was a good clerk and Dick did not hesitate to hand over the five dollars. Mr. Hope insisted on giving him a receipt with his name and address and place of work on it. He left quickly in order to reassure Mr. Roberts, who was of course very worried. Neither of them, he told us, had ever been in this kind of trouble before and took it much to heart.

The next day revealed that Mr. Roberts had never tried to drive a car in his life and did not know anybody resembling Mr. Hope, that Booker's Garage employed nobody of that name and that there was no such address as the one he had given us. He had in fact gone to the director he mentioned to us and asked him for the five dollars to square the police, but, when it had been refused on the grounds that the police should not be bribed, he had improved on the story before coming to us. We never saw the five dollars again, of course, but we treasured the receipt signed 'Ivor Hope'.

It struck us that Mr. Hope had taken many risks for a very little money and that he might perhaps have had a subsidiary interest in getting a good view of the house inside and out. We were also concerned about his intimate knowledge of the site and staff. It seemed possible that his informant might have told him that in a few days time we were going to Monkey Jump.

The house, of course, would be guarded. The watchman is an integral part of life in Guyana. Even houses that are in process of being built are not left unguarded lest the building materials should disappear in the night and empty houses have their watchman on duty to make sure that all detachable fittings are not removed by some enterprising passer-by. When the house next to ours was at last complete it was left unguarded for the night before the tenants moved in. When they arrived with their furniture next day they found that the house no longer possessed a lavatory or kitchen sink.

A lean and wily-looking watchman reported for duty the morning we left for Monkey Jump. We explained that we had reason to believe that a teef-man might come to the house and that he was no ordinary prowler to be shooed away but one who must be caught if it was at all possible. The watchman was very enthusiastic and entered with great gusto into the spirit of the thing. He would keep under the house, he said, and take any 'visitor' by surprise. He was a big, tough, muscle-and-iron kind of man and I began to feel a bit sorry for Mr. Hope and his winning ways.

When we arrived home from Monkey Jump, the watchman greeted us with great pride. 'He come, he come,' he told us excitedly. We asked for details. Dramatically he explained, 'It must have been about two o'clock, boss, in de morning. I sits on dis stool here very still.' He sat on the stool very still, his finger to his lip. 'Den I hear a little noise in de road and I looks,'—here he stretched his neck forward and peered towards the fence,—'I see dis man on dis bicycle. Softly, softly he gets off and wheels de bicycle to de side of de road and lean it up against de fence. Den he come very quiet towards de gate and very quiet he lift up de catch and open it slowly, slowly.'

We had been listening, holding our breath as we envisaged the scene. The long silence was hard to bear. 'And what happened then?' Dick prompted in a whisper.

'I step forward from de shadows. I stride towards he. I ask very sarcastic, "You got invitation, man, dat you come at dis hour of de night through dis gate?"'

Again we had to break the silence.

'And then?'

The watchman burst into life.

'Den I picks up dis big stone and den I hurls it at him and hits him on de shoulder.'

'And then?'

'Den he holler and he jump on he bicycle and pedal off pretty damn quick.'

He clearly regarded his strategy as triumphantly successful so we offered him the congratulations and tip which he obviously expected and waited rather apprehensively for Mr. Hope's next visit. But he did not strike again; perhaps the watchman's shower of sarcasm and stones was too much for him.

Bananas on the wharf at the back of Stabroek Market.
Stabroek Market.
Inside the market: the lady has a parcel of fish on her head.

Three street market scenes in Georgetown.

CHAPTER EIGHT

A Chapter of Problems

It sometimes seems that Guyana has more than its fair share of problems. Its climate is humid, particularly on the coastal strip where the majority of the people live, its timber reserves inaccessible, its mineral resources, apart from bauxite and manganese, not sufficiently abundant to make large-scale exploitation of them a commercial proposition and its huge rivers which might have provided a system of highways are, for long stretches, not navigable. Man has contributed to the difficulties by populating the country with six different races with varied interests and complicated the situation by introducing slavery and colonialism into its history.

Politically it is not part of the South American continent, yet geographically it is not part of the West Indies. In consequence it seems to be isolated, out of the main stream of events. To leave Guyana and land at Piarco, Trinidad, gives one the feeling of being back again in the outside world. To the visitor from England, going to Guyana for only a few years, this is no disadvantage: the outside world is after all quite a good place to get away from. But its effect on the country is damaging, for the more ambitious of the local population tend to set their sights on getting away; to establish oneself abroad becomes the hall-mark of success. In the past the educational arrangements made this almost inevitable. The brightest pupils of Georgetown's secondary schools went to University in Europe or U.S.A. or to the University of the West Indies in Jamaica and Trinidad.* Once away they find that these communities can offer far greater cultural interest and facilities of all kinds than they could find at home. It is natural that many should prefer to go on working there afterwards. There are of course notable exceptions; some people are drawn home by the knowledge that their country most urgently needs all the skilled and trained people it can get. Nonetheless there is a distressing tendency for such people

*The University of the West Indies has faculties in Trinidad and Jamaica. In Jamaica it has Arts, Natural Sciences, Education & Medicine. In Trinidad there are the faculties of Arts, Agriculture and Engineering.

to leave the country and for a kind of educational Gresham's Law to operate.

This creaming off of the young intelligentsia of course impoverishes the cultural life of Georgetown. As in the West Indies, writers have tended to drift to Europe where, apart from anything else, they find their publishers. It seems as if the same thing may happen in the more recent development of painting; artists may have found their first inspiration in the scenes and people of Guyana, but if they are able to go to an art school in Europe they will find, like writers, a tremendous stimulus in living in a land with great artistic traditions and being among people with interests similar to their own. Those who return must feel the lack of such traditions and such society in Guyana. One cannot blame them for wanting to escape into the wider world.

Thus in the arts as in the professions there is a strong tendency for talented people to develop and employ their skills outside the country. It is therefore difficult to find suitable Guyanese to fill some positions of responsibility and the situation is made worse by the fact that those who can choose a career have a strong prejudice in favour of the law and against the scientific professions. The Guyanese are a litigious race; whether they are so by nature or in consequence of the high proportion of barristers per head of population it is hard to say.

On the other hand, there are few local engineers. All major engineering works had therefore to be in the hands of Europeans. No doubt this does spring partly from a strong tradition that only Europeans were appointed to such posts in the past so there was not much point in trying to qualify for them if you were Guyanese, whereas you might make a living as a doctor or lawyer. Now, of course, this is no longer true, but still the prejudice remains; local engineers, chemists and scientists of all kinds fail to materialize in sufficient numbers although the situation is much better than it was. (In 1968, for example, there were twenty-seven local executives on the Booker staff holding professional posts as accountants, engineers and chemists.) Since Bookers started a cadet scheme to train Guyanese staff for such work as long ago as 1954, the lack of scientists cannot be blamed on expatriate pressure to keep them out; it seems to derive from the prejudice of the Guyanese themselves. In speaking to young people who were going away to university, or to their parents, we were often told, 'If a boy goes away to study medicine or law, he comes back with a degree. If he tries for engineering, he fails. It is too hard.' One heard it on all sides. Jubraj told me of his two cousins, one of whom went to London to study as a lawyer and came back qualified, but the other wanted to be an engineer, 'but he fail, mistress. It is always so. Day say it is de calculus.'

Apart from the traditional fear that scientific jobs are reserved for expatriates and the prejudice that it is more difficult to qualify in such subjects, other factors militate against the production of local scientists. The schools have been slow to develop scientific studies; traditionally the arts predominate. The tradition is a hangover from the nineteenth century and one gets the impression that Guyana has been even slower than England to move into the twentieth century. Finally I have the feeling—and it is only a feeling—that the Africans, who have hitherto been the mainstay of the professional classes, have a stronger natural feeling for the arts than for the sciences. They revel in the use of words, they enjoy debate and have a keen sense of the dramatic. These gifts are more useful to the barrister than to the engineer, agriculturalist, chemist or geologist. Thus while the skill and brains of too many Guyanese are devoted to the encouragement of litigation, the study of the rivers, forests and resources of their native land is too often left to foreigners.

One curious result of colonialism, which people in Guyana took for granted, but which always struck me oddly, was the universal long leave. In the days when all jobs holding any kind of responsibility were held by Englishmen, their contracts included a long leave of several months every three years. When Guyanese were appointed to such jobs they naturally had the same conditions of employment and now all government employees, teachers and so on have these prolonged absences from their work which they must spend out of the country. Those girls' schools in England who have staffing problems due to the shortage of women scientists and the early exodus from teaching to marriage should count themselves lucky in comparison with the one I taught at for a while in Georgetown, where there seemed to be about a third of the staff on leave all the time and for whom temporary replacements had somehow to be found.

There is, of course, much to be said for the system. It gives people in positions of responsibility the chance to go and study further and broaden their horizons, for those of Georgetown are undeniably narrow. It enables them to measure their work against international standards and Guyana desperately needs higher standards in all walks of life. On the other hand the cost in fares and salaries alone is enormously relative to the size of the national budget; the cost to the running of the administration is harder to calculate. I used to wonder how we should have felt at school if the members of staff in charge of our Advanced Level or University Entrance subjects had disappeared on leave the term before we were due to take our examinations. I also used to wonder if anyone in a responsible post really can be spared for months on end without its having some adverse effect on his achievement.

No doubt these arguments will be carefully weighed, for since taking office Mr. Burnham has stated that he intends to reduce long leave and combine it with approved overseas training. This is part of a major effort which the Government is making to modernize the structure and administration of the public service. (A Public Service Ministry has been established under the Prime Minister, and effective help is being given by United Nations experts in this field.)

For years Bookers and the Government have tried, by giving training grants and scholarships, to encourage the Guyanese to increase their skills and to use them at home. Some university grants are dependent upon their holders returning to teach in Guyana. In time as the country develops there will be more facilities and opportunities which will encourage professional people to stay in Guyana. There is a developing School of Agriculture at Mon Repos, and, most significantly of all, a University has been inaugurated. In 1963 Bookers donated a site of 140 acres at Turkeyen, on the outskirts of Georgetown. Building was postponed through lack of finance, but site clearance was well advanced by the time of Independence. The British and Canadian Governments jointly provided funds for the first phase of construction and the first buildings were completed by October, 1968. Meanwhile first degree courses are conducted in a limited number of subjects in the evenings at Queen's College, the boys' grammar school in Georgetown. It is envisaged that the government will arrange some kind of association with the University of the West Indies in Jamaica and Trinidad.

Clearly this is a very important step forward, and once the University has its own buildings and can provide full-time higher education it can begin to hope to provide the kind of academic centre that will attract the intellectually gifted away from the old-established universities of the United States, and, of course, the West Indies, which about two thousand Guyanese students now attend. A noticeable feature of the University courses now being conducted in the evenings in Georgetown is the high proportion of East Indians, which suggest that if the young African is still inclined to go abroad for university education, the young Indian has been quick to grasp the new opportunitities at home. It is to be hoped that the University will be given every priority, for more than anything else it will contribute to that fund of human resources which Guyana needs as urgently as capital investment.

These are problems which affect directly the private lives of only a tiny minority of Guyanese; for the majority the pressing problem is to find work of any kind. Twenty per cent of the population is unemployed and of all the difficulties which beset the country, that of mass unemployment is the most frightening in its social and political implications.

As a result of the work of Dr. Giglioli, malaria was eradicated from Guyana in 1948. The population was then 375,000. By 1970, we are told, it will be one million. One cannot but be aware of the population explosion as one walks through Georgetown, especially at the times of day when the schools are emptying into the streets. The children are far healthier and more alert than they were in the days when malaria sapped their strength, but the problem of what they will do when they leave school appears insoluble.

To find their children work is the chief anxiety of most parents, even those in comparatively comfortable circumstances. There lived near us an African family called Johnson with five boys. The eldest left school with a few O Level subjects. After nearly a year he found a job as a ticket collector on one of the ferries. His mother was overjoyed and hoped that the other four would in their turn be as fortunate. Such was the plight of a family which was well above the breadline; one can imagine the despair of a child of a poor family as he left school and began the hopeless search for work.

While the population has grown enormously the number of jobs has declined as industry has become more mechanized. The project on which my husband was working involved the bulk handling of sugar, which instead of being loaded into sacks at the factories, now goes by lorry or punt to the terminal to be loaded by conveyor belt directly on to the boats designed to take it in bulk. This process of streamlining is much more efficient and economical and better suits the needs of sugar importers, but the men who made the sacks, those who filled them and weighed them, those who loaded them on to lorries, all those and many others became redundant.

Meanwhile the work on the site temporarily raised employment, for its labour force ran into several hundreds of men. They were mainly Africans who worked as carpenters and crane drivers, who did the concreting and made up the pile-driving crew. Only the digging was left to East Indians, for Africans have been persistent in their rejection of the spade since the days of slavery.

I soon became accustomed to finding women at the back door seeking work. Mostly they seemed to know it was hopeless yet still they came; what else could they do? They were pitiful these women, their faces marked with despair and their eyes having that glazed, deep-set look that comes with hunger. They always spoke of their children; there are no child allowances here or grants to widows or the unemployed.

After a few weeks I returned from the market to find an African standing at the gate. He told me that he had been unemployed for months and was willing to do any kind of work, if I could just, 'say a little word to de boss.' I explained that he must go to the site and see the General Foreman who recruited all the labour. He had already been there he said, but had been among the many that had had to be turned away. He told me about his wife and children and his desperate need for work and I explained again that he must go to the site and see the foreman. He then gave it as his opinion that jobs were too important to be handled by the foreman. 'Dis man, mistress, he goin' appoint all he relations and he friends.' I tried to explain that the foreman came from England and had not brought out all his friends and relations. 'He goin' send home for dem,' he warned darkly, 'and not give work to we all. De boss should see to it himself.'

I had conversations similar to this many times with men who, failing to get a job at the site, decided it was worth coming right across to the other side of Georgetown to try again. They were all desperate for work, they all felt that I might 'fix' something for them and they all had this same suspicion that English workers would probably come out to Guyana if they were able to pull strings. For they belonged to a society which is quite accustomed to the idea of leaving their family behind and travelling three thousand miles if there is a chance of a job at the end of the journey. This was the only kind of life they could conceive of and their supposition that the foreman's relations and friends would make the most of this golden opportunity was quite natural to them though it fell strangely on English ears.

This turning away of men who came to seek work was a painful business and I grew to dread the sight of a disconsolate figure by the gate. They were too abject even to knock at the door, but just hung about until one of us appeared. They seemed to prefer to ask me first, 'to say a little word to de boss,' and had great faith that jobs could be found by the exercise of a little influence, particularly petticoat influence. It made one feel singularly helpless; their stories were so pitiful and their need for work so obvious and so urgent that my answers sounded like all too inadequate excuses for not helping.

The stark fact is that there is very little that individuals can do to help; there are simply not enough jobs to go round, not nearly enough. Reason certainly was on my side, but injustice was on theirs. It was all very well for me to explain about the limited number of jobs, going to the foreman and so on, but just by being in a position to reason, by being well fed and clothed and housed, I felt I was in the wrong. Who can look into the face of another human being who is hungry and not feel guilty?

There were many times such as this in Guyana when I felt this overwhelming helplessness in the face of other people's suffering and this same unreasoning but instinctive guilt. I used to remember my father telling me years ago that my generation of children should be grateful that they would never have to suffer what he did as a child; to sit in warm clothes in a carriage and watch barefooted newsboys selling newspapers in the streets in the snow outside. I felt now as he must have done then; rage at the injustice of it, helplessness and guilt.

Slowly I began to understand why so many Europeans found refuge in callousness. 'Unemployed? Of course they are! That's what they like to be. They'd rather sit under a tree and eat bananas than do a decent day's work.' It is so much easier to dismiss it all like that than to stop to think, much less feel, particularly when neither thinking nor feeling does much to help anybody. Empathy is an uncomfortable endowment. It is easier to tell yourself that other people's miseries do not exist and that if they do it is their own fault.

We knew from our own experience that these generalized accusations of laziness were ill-founded. Our firm had carried out a large engineering project in Guyana some six years before. The General Foreman had worked on both jobs. He told us that when he came back to work on the sugar terminal, he set about finding some of the best of the craftsmen he had employed before, knowing them to be reliable and skilled. He asked them where they had been working in the intervening years. Many had been unemployed part of the time, some for all of it; despite all their efforts and their skill they simply could not find a job.

There were, unfortunately, always individual examples which could be used to support these generalizations that the Guyanese temperament preferred unemployment. Prolonged unemployment —and especially never having been employed at all, which is the state in which the younger Guyanese can easily find themselves— can have the effect of making a man not appreciate a job when he has it. If to be unemployed is a temporary thing, a shocking interlude, as it is to most Europeans, then it drives home the value of a steady job. Some Guyanese, unemployed from the day they leave school, have never known the meaning of steady employment. They come to regard work as a casual, ephemeral business. Some become incapable of taking the opportunity when offered. Dick was sometimes astonished at the way in which they would risk losing a job by some petty theft or carelessness even though they knew that others were queueing up to replace them. Prolonged unemployment it seems is completely demoralizing. It is physically debilitating too: in a country where the cheapest staple food is rice, the diet of the poor saps a man's physical strength to do a day's work.

It seems ironic that so much misery should spring from the curing of malaria. Sometimes in despair one is tempted to wonder, as Professor A. V. Hill did in his Presidential address to the British Association in 1952, 'If ethical principles deny our right to do evil in order that good may come, are we justified in doing good when the foreseeable consequence is evil?'

Sometimes now that we are back in England when I hear people grumbling about the iniquities of the Welfare State and blaming it for their own boredom and lack of initiative and generally using it as a whipping boy for all their frustrations, I feel that a spell in Guyana might perhaps do them good, if only to see what the alternative can mean; in contemporary England poverty can be ignored and the places which it inhabits can be avoided. In Guyana the eye cannot escape it, nor the conscience.

Long acquaintance with poverty seems to have bred in the Guyanese a kind of resignation. It was less shocking to them than to the outsider, for it was the natural state in which many of them grew up, knowing no other life. I remember one day as we drove Singh home, for the rainy season had broken suddenly with torrential rains, he pointed to a large tree in a field opposite the sea wall.

'An East Indian woman lives under that tree,' he remarked conversationally.

'You mean she is building a house there?'

'No, she very, very poor and she has two children and she keeps them under de tree. In de day she begs and at night she gives to the children and den dey all sleep under de tree.'

I looked through the slanting rain at the tree and must have remarked that it was dreadful, or something similarly inadequate, for Singh replied cheerfully.

'It's all right now, but it will be hard for she when de leaves fall off.'

He was not being callous; poor people accepted each other's misfortunes—as they accepted their own—with resignation.

CHAPTER NINE

Amerindians

In a country where the rivers provide the main highways to the Interior, the possession of a boat is more important than that of a car. We were fortunate in being able to borrow occasionally one of the two launches used on the site where the construction of the jetty required much work to be done from the water.

It was fortunate, too, that we could in a day get to Santa Mission, an Amerindian village which lay on the Kamuni Creek which joins the Demerara just above Atkinson Field, about twenty miles from Georgetown. The first part of the journey was slow and tedious for we had to travel for about four hours on the wide, muddy and unshaded Demerara. The sun beat down and the bank provided little to distract the mind from physical discomforts. Sometimes we were able to get the Indian boatman to bring the boat up to Atkinson Field while we made the journey by car in a little over an hour.

We usually went in a party of six or eight, accompanied by a phenomenal amount of baggage. Apart from the hampers of food, crates of drink and flasks of ice, we also took everything that might conceivably be required in every possible kind of emergency. We always took and needed what appeared to be several miles of rope.

If we travelled by car to Atkinson it usually happened that the boat was delayed; it ran out of fuel, or missed the tide or the boatman was too drunk to start at the agreed hour. We would wait impatiently under the sun, surrounded by our crates and fuel oil and coils of rope, peering down stream in the hope that every distant object might prove to be the *Canje Queen*. Sometimes a fruit vendor would appear and we would buy bananas and eat them in a desultory manner until one of the black dots on the Demerara really did grow into our boat.

The *Canje Queen* was a work boat and made few concessions to comfort but she was sturdy and Dick had mastered the idiosyncrasies of her engine. As she tied up alongside I used to peer down at her, some twenty feet below, and it always seemed extraordinary to me that all of us and our luggage, which covered such a large area on the stelling, could ever fit into her small interior. Somehow it always managed to without the *Canje Queen* either bursting her seams or quietly sinking under the load.

The men spaced themselves at intervals on the ladder, which consisted of rusty metal rungs down the side of the stelling, and handed down the crates, petrol tins, kettles, paraffin stoves, sunshades, fishing rods, painting books, bottles of water and lumpy canvas bags of odds and ends, which fitted like pieces of an interlocking jigsaw into the hold. Being the least athletic, whatever the composition of the group, I was the first of the human cargo to be stowed and by some miracle never did what was expected of me—forgot that several of the rungs were missing and slipped between the stelling and the boat into the deep and muddy waters of the Demerara which lay so uninvitingly below.

After this pause, it usually took the *Canje Queen* some little time to start again, but then with a certain amount of weary sighing and grunting she would get under way and chug stolidly up river. Soon we could see, on the far side of the Demerara, the opening of the Kamuni Creek and would begin to cross the river, here about half a mile wide, to reach it. This was usually a fairly rough business and, punched by the tide and a crosswind, we sometimes bobbed about alarmingly.

To leave the unshaded river and slide into the narrow opening of the creek was to enter a new world. The creek was only a few yards wide and for most of the way the arching branches of the trees met overhead to form a cool, dark tunnel. Soon the water ceased to be a slovenly mud colour and became clear and tawny like tea. It was suddenly cool, or seemed so after the merciless glare of the sun on the Demerara.

The creek twisted and was full of currents and bends which required a great deal of skilful navigating, for the corners were sharp and the *Canje Queen* could only just take some of them. We had also to keep a sharp look-out for tacoubas, or submerged logs, which lie treacherously just below the surface. The first time we went up the creek the water was very low and progress particularly slow and difficult. Several times we had to go overboard to free the propellers after they had been snarled by tacoubas or vegetation. About half way to Santa the creek was completely blocked by a mass of floating islands which had become so tangled up with each other and the mangrove on the banks that it was impossible to shift them. We had to give up the idea of going to Santa and turn back.

Not far down stream we had passed a little landing stage at the foot of a sandy incline topped with a house. Here we tied up the *Canje Queen* and went to meet the African who was coming down to greet us. He was a charcoal burner, he told us, and invited us to come up to his work. We climbed up the slope to the clearing where the charcoal was smouldering. The area all round trembled with heat and the ground underfoot was blisteringly hot. Despite my canvas shoes I had to keep hopping about like the proverbial cat on hot bricks, but the barefooted charcoal burner seemed not to notice the heat and as he talked he sometimes absent-mindedly probed a piece of burning charcoal with his naked toe.

His wife, who came out to join us, was an Amerindian and the children took after one or the other parent, each one being either African or Amerindian in feature, but none combining the two. The two youngest had the fairer skin and flatter, Mongolian features of the Amerindians. The other two looked pure African. The wife spoke not at all and would not be drawn out even on the subject of children. We asked what happened if one of them was ill; the charcoal burner told us that they just put out a red rag on a post by the river and then the next time the Dispenser's boat passed he would stop. We asked how often the Dispenser's boat passed and he assured us that it was quite frequent—every fortnight.

He showed us how the charcoal was weighed, and later we saw the great rafts which take it down the creek. They moved very slowly these black vessels, like funeral barges under their sombre load. At the back stood an African with a very long pole with which he steered, if such an active verb can be used to describe so lethargic a movement, while the cargo moved imperceptibly forward, edging its way between the close banks of the creek and down to the Demerara. It is destined for the cooking stoves of Georgetown and the villages and some is even exported, mainly to the West Indian Islands. Indeed one can count charcoal burning as one of the industries of the country for it accounts for about a tenth of the value of the timber trade.

Always after that when we went up to Santa we would look out for the charcoal burner and make sure that there was no red rag tied to his post, but we never stopped again for we were always too impatient to get to Santa.

We came to know it so well that it is hard to recapture our first impressions, gained when we still saw the village from outside. It soon became so familiar, so welcoming, so like going home for a weekend that to describe it as we first saw it is almost as difficult as trying to give a stranger's account of one's own home. I often tried to analyse this special feeling we had for Santa and the people who lived there; I think its secret lay in the peacefulness of a group of people who belonged together, so that their way of life, real and permanent, seemed a refuge after the superficialities of Georgetown's restless community.

About a mile before the village the trees at each side of the creek began to thin and the banks became more swampy and open, then we rounded a corner and saw that the creek widened into a pool from which there swept up, on the left, a gentle slope which opened out into a sandy hill. In the centre was a huge silk cotton tree whose great gnarled roots stood up out of the ground, partitioning the sand.

We had been told to present ourselves to the Captain of the village and to the Teacher. Even as we tied up the *Canje Queen* we saw the latter coming down to meet us. We recognized him immediately, for we had been told that he was the only African in the village. He welcomed us kindly and took us to see his school and his house. On the way he told us that he had been Preacher and Teacher at Santa for twenty years, the only African in the village, but that since it was an Amerindian reserve he could not settle there permanently, but must move away when he retired. He asked us if we would henceforward call him Teach, as everybody else did.

He showed us the new schoolroom with justifiable pride, for it was big and airy and full of signs of activity. I noticed on a desk two books; one on American democracy and one on differential calculus, but despite these the children seemed to be successfully making very neat raffia mats and baskets. Teach showed us the stick which he kept in one corner, but told us that it was rarely needed even as a threat, for the Amerindians, young and old, were all peaceful and quiet, he told us, and very gentle.

He showed us his own house near the school, a compact little building whose walls, like so many others of its kind, were decorated with photographs from the *Illustrated London News* of bygone days, depicting a girlish Queen Elizabeth II and youthful Duke of Edinburgh. The houses were all built of wood and raised on stilts. Their roofs were thatched with palm leaves. No nails were used in their construction, the wood all being tied in with palm strands.

The church itself, which stood in the centre of the village, near the silk cotton tree, was built like the other houses, but was rather more spacious and had a very new corrugated iron roof. The most remarkable thing about it was its tall bell tower which stood by the door. Teach told us that he had for years wanted a bell tower and had come by this one in a remarkable way. It happened that a small American plane crashed in the bush not far from Santa. Fortunately the pilot was not killed but the plane was not worth salvaging and so was abandoned. Gradually Amerindians living nearby picked it clean of everything useful; seats, upholstery, spare parts of the engine, all these were removed until nothing remained but the steel framework of the fuselage. Nobody could think of any use for that—nobody that is, except Teach. It suddenly occurred to him that, stood up on its end, it would make a very fine bell tower. He persuaded the villagers to bring it to Santa—and it must have made a very bulky and awkward parcel to carry through the bush—and fix it up by the door of the church. We gazed at it now, astonished at finding a church with a bell tower in so remote a part of the world and even more astonished at finding that it was really the body of an aeroplane. I should think it safe to apply that much abused adjective 'unique' to the bell tower of the church at Santa.

Inside the church we found yet another example of Teach's ingenuity. Hearing that one of Georgetown's cinemas was closing and that its organ was to be thrown out he determined to salvage it for his church. He went to Georgetown, persuaded its owner to let him have it, got it split up into as many bits as possible and brought by canoe to Santa. The theatre organ was now installed in his church and he played it himself at the same time as conducting the service.

Outside the church we met the Captain of the village, a quiet Amerindian whose gentle manner was in striking contrast to the excitability of the African. They both left us to have lunch and we went back to the creek and began to unpack ours. Suddenly the sky blackened and huge drops of tropical rain began to crash down. We fled for shelter under the silk cotton tree but were sodden before we reached it. As we were trying to cover up the food and our belongings the Captain reappeared and invited us to shelter in his mother's house. She was away just now, he said, delivering a baby in another village but she would be glad for us to shelter in her kitchen. We demurred, for we were a large party and very wet, but he insisted upon taking us to her house by the church.

It was different from most of the other houses in that it had a kitchen which was a separate building. A few feet away from the house, it was a simple construction without solid sides—just a roof supported on poles. We sat gratefully under this roof now while the rain beat down on the palm thatch. The Captain insisted that we should have our lunch here; it was what his mother would wish, as she would tell us, when she came back in a very short time.

It was not long before he returned with his mother. She was old, her face deeply wrinkled and her shoulders bent, but she carried with her an air of complete authority and immense poise. She welcomed each of us in turn, shaking hands and dropping a half curtsy and there was a graciousness about her and a charm which sent one's mind back to the salons of the eighteenth century, seeking for European comparisons.

The rain had stopped and she took us across to her house and showed us round. It had two rooms, a sitting-room with a hammock slung across, which she invited us to rest in, and a bedroom where we saw, to our amazement, a four poster bed. Little had we thought, as we made our way up the Kamuni, that at the end of our journey we would find a village which had a bell tower made out of an aeroplane, a theatre organ and a four poster bed.

Our hostess now took us on a tour of the village, which turned out to be much more extensive than we had realized, for we had seen only one clearing and in fact several little paths ran off from it leading to other clearings with two or three houses each which in turn led to more. She called to several of the villagers to come and meet us, clapping her hands authoritatively to attract their attention. Everywhere she was treated with great respect and people listened deferentially to what she had to say, for she was the 'Granny' of the village, in charge of the women and responsible for delivering all the babies. Hitherto we had addressed her by her surname, but now she asked us to call her Granny, as everybody else did. We began to feel part of the community.

On that first day we were, I think, rather in awe of Granny, as she showed us round her domain. She had the advantage over us that she seemed unaware of the stifling midday sun and we panted as we tried to keep up with her. She had a remarkably youthful walk, taking long strides and looking about her with great interest, pointing out anything that she thought we might find remarkable. As a guide she was brisk and indefatigable despite her years, for she was, she told us, 'eighty and odd.' I found it rather shaming, at twenty and odd, to be able to keep up with her only with the greatest difficulty.

Since we had admired her hammock she stopped at the house of Auntie Mame who, she told us, made the best hammocks of all. She had already pointed out to us the Ité Palm from which hammocks are made and Auntie Mame now showed us how she spun the fibre and then wove the hammock on a frame against the wall, using a shuttle. The fibre was hard and string-like and this hammock is a cool one. Warmer ones are made from the cotton tree and their texture is much softer and nearer in feel to wool. Auntie Mame promised to make us a cool hammock; fortunately it was the right season for picking the palm fibre and she said she could have the hammock ready for us next time we came.

On the outskirts of the village were little streams that ran into the creek. In one of these Granny showed us her own pool where she did her washing. It was a quiet little place, quite private under its overhanging trees. In the stream lay her cassava scraper, a disc about eighteen inches in diameter with holes punched all over it to form a grater. She carried it back to the house, where she showed us how she used it and other implements to make cassava bread. Cassava is the staple food of the South American Indians, but it is puzzling to think how it was ever found to be edible, for unless treated very carefully it is poisonous. Cassava is grown by all the families in the village and its white root is scraped on a grater such as the one that Granny had just shown us. She then showed us, hanging on a wall in her kitchen, the matapi, a long, cylindrical-shaped basket, which derives its name from a snake. The grated cassava is packed into the matapi, which is then squeezed by being stretched downwards so that as the matapi becomes longer and thinner the cassava is compressed and the poisonous acid which it contains is squeezed out.

Once the poison has been extracted the cassava can be baked over the fire into big circles of bread, about the size of very large dinner plates, which look like crisp, anaemic pancakes. Some people find them delicious, but they tasted to me like well-baked blotting paper. The poisonous by-product of the squeezing process is boiled several times until it becomes casareep, a thick syrup, which the Amerindians use for preserving meat. It is especially useful in the 'pepper-pot', a kind of everlasting stew. We were told that Amerindians in the bush knew of certain places where pepper-

: Captain of the village
Santa.

: bell tower of the church,
le out of the fuselage of a
hed American aeroplane.

nbing up the steps of 'our'
se.

The charcoal burner's family.

Weighing the charcoal.

Expedition across 'The Field' opposite Santa.

An Amerindian boy gathering coconuts to quench our thirst.

pot was to be found and a man could give himself a meal from it and then find some animal to kill and add to the stew before he left it, so that the next traveller would not go hungry.

After she had shown us these things, Granny suggested that we might like to swim in the creek, while she withdrew to her house to rest. She would see us again, she said, before we left.

It is hard to convey the impression that she made upon us as it was hard to understand at the time. It was puzzling to find so strongly marked in her qualities which one normally associated with people living in modern civilizations. One might be impressed but not surprised by simplicity and dignity in forest people, but to find this kind of sophistication was astonishing. Granny possessed in their purity qualities which civilization so often debases; she was forthright yet gentle, simple yet sophisticated, authoritative yet humble. Too often among more complex modern societies forthrightness becomes rudeness, sophistication a spurious glamour and authority mere pomposity. There was a refinement about Granny which suggested that she had these qualities in their essence; she had no need of the trappings.

Her needs were few and she could provide most of them herself; it struck us that what gave the community such self-respect was this independence; they did not depend helplessly as we do on outside props. They could never find themselves hopelessly at a loss because the power has failed or the tap, or the telephone broken down or the postmen gone on strike. Civilized man may be much more comfortable with all these amenities but he forfeits some of his dignity by becoming so dependent on them.

Night falls suddenly and early in the tropics and we knew that we must be off the water before the light failed soon after six. Just before four we walked up to Granny's house to say goodbye. She came out with two pineapples. 'Next time you come,' she said, 'I show you where we grows pineapples. Come, take them.' She put them into my hands and then glanced at the sky. 'Four o'clock,' she remarked. 'Time to go.'

She had no need of a watch—I often noticed that she told the time within minutes, by the sun. I noticed too how her hearing, despite her years, was much more acute than ours. Sometimes as we were talking she would turn her head and murmur, 'Motor boat,' and a few minutes afterwards we would see the Dispenser's boat or some other craft come round the bend. Yet however hard I tried I could never hear the sound when she first heard it, even though I strained in the silence. She had heard it even in the midst of conversation.

The senses of forest people are quickened by their environment; they see a trail in the bush where we see none and signs of an animal where we would notice nothing. They hear sounds when we have only silence. In our environment our senses have become dulled, our hearing deadened by the turbulent noises of civilization and our eyes weakened by its uncoordinated sights and movement. There are so many things for us to see and hear—or to half-see and half-hear—without any effort of concentration that we lose by default the gift of really using our senses in any active way. I heard people say how lost Amerindians are if they come into a modern society, but surely they cannot be more lost than a modern European in theirs. How incomprehensibly slow and stupid he must seem to them, blundering helplessly about in the bush!

The journey back from Santa was, in many ways, the peak of the day's experiences. It was cool under the arching trees and the shadows were full of mystery. On the way up we were hot, talkative, impatient to arrive. Returning at the end of the day we were quiet, sunbaked and tired, content to lose ourselves in the peace of the surroundings. As we moved gently between the darkening banks only an occasional splash or the cry of a parrot broke the stillness; it was an enchanting time, touched with evening sadness.

We had been to Santa several times when Granny suggested that we might like to stay in a house which was unoccupied. It was old and unsafe, she told us, so the family had moved out into a new one that was just finished. We were delighted with the idea and decided to go for Easter. There were nine of us in the party, including three children, and as the luggage had to include food and drink for all of us for three days the *Canje Queen* was even lower in the water than usual.

The Captain came down to the creek to meet us as we arrived and took us up to the house which was to be ours for the weekend. It was a wobbly little house on stilts at the end of a sandy path. It was perhaps a little more dilapidated than the others but as we climbed up the wooden steps it seemed to us to be quite perfect.

The larger room, which we decided we would use as a living and dining room and bedroom for women and children, was about twelve foot square. On the other side of the partition was a room of the same length but much narrower, where the three men were to sleep. For furniture there was a bench in each room. The steps out at the back of the living room had a cover over them, under which we could cook.

As we unpacked, I was struck, as always, by the intuitive courtesy of the Amerindians. It must have been an odd spectacle to them, this long file of English people carrying a succession of strange belongings up from the boat, but even the children did not stare. The Captain and one or two neighbours came to see if we needed help, quietly showed us where to get wood for the fire, helped to get it going, brought in an extra bench or two and slipped away. Their comings and goings were hardly apparent. They were observant and attentive, but never intrusive.

After we had unpacked we set about fixing the hammocks before the light failed. We had not realized quite how much room a hammock occupies. The upright posts of Amerindian houses are made very strong so that they can take the weight of a hammock and its contents, but our choice of sites for hammocks was somewhat limited as not all the posts were still strong enough to take them. The situation in the smaller room was complicated by the fact that two of the men being unusually tall had acquired hammocks that were twelve feet long. One hammock, slung diagonally across the room just about filled it. Eventually we divided up the air space and the hammocks were slung in layers across each other, which seemed satisfactory until we went and actually got into them, when the tendency for the human body to take on a U-shape and concentrate itself in one part of the hammock meant that everybody seemed suddenly to slide into the same spot. By the time we had finished the general effect was of one large web with dark forms dotted about in it like spiders.

I had added to the difficulties by bringing a very large mosquito net designed to fit on to a hammock. Although I knew that mosquitoes were less troublesome here than in Georgetown, I thought it would protect me against cockroaches and all other creepy-crawlies from the horror of which months already spent in South America had done nothing to cure me. The net was a voluminous affair and when hung from a hook on a beam in the centre of the room it spread out like a tent, and took up rather more than its fair share of space. I was persuaded to abandon it.

We managed to get the hammocks slung and the supper cooked just before night fell. We ate our supper by lamplight which fell softly, picking out the beams and the strange looping shadows cast by the hammocks. Emboldened by the semi-darkness, spiders and one or two cockroaches began to emerge from their hiding places in the cracks and joints of the house. While the rest of the party studiously disregarded them, I began quietly to get out my net again, before the braver spirits could start on their usual They're-more-frightened-of-you-than-you-are-of-them nonsense. I have always found this statement, applied to cockroaches, spiders and indeed all creatures that scuttle or creep, to be profoundly untrue, partly because They always come straight at me instead of running away, which does not seem to indicate fear, but mainly because it just would not be possible for Them to be more afraid of me than I am of Them. The other argument—that They do not do you any harm—is not so much untrue as irrelevant, for one is not afraid of being harmed. A filarial mosquito is far more dangerous than a cockroach but I know from experience which of the two is more horrible to find sharing one's pillow in the morning. The sensation has nothing to do with the damage they might inflict, but the disgust that they cause. A lion may be dangerous but is no more dreadful to look at than a big cat. On the other hand, the imagination sickens at the idea of a spider the size of a lion.

The posts of our little house creaked and groaned as we climbed into our hammocks and they took the combined weight of nine human beings. The lamps were put out and our eyes grew accustomed to the moonlight. The room seemed to be full of contorted human shapes, looped haphazardly from walls and roof. The lamps had lit the lower part of the room, but now with the light coming from above we saw how steep the roof was. There seemed to be a surprising amount of space up there and we slowly realized that it was occupied, for we became aware of a continuous twittering and squeaking above our heads and soon black forms began to fly back and forth, which at first I mistook for birds and then realized were bats. By the light of the moon we saw that the roof was solid with their hanging bodies.

The vampire bat inhabits Guyana, but it is only to be found in the area beyond Bartica. Nonetheless in a country where they are known to exist at all, one becomes rather suspicious of all bats. The vampire loves to come by night and suck the blood of human beings or other animals as they sleep. They are said to inject a gentle soporific as they pierce the skin so that they can then suck while their host slumbers undisturbed. Some carry rabies. Even a net is not a complete protection against them for they alight on a con venient toe up against it and suck just as mosquitoes do. All the same, as the bats whirled and twittered above our heads, I found it satisfactory to be able to assure the others, from the comparative security of my net, that the bats were surely harmless and certainly more afraid of us than we were of them.

That first night was not particularly restful: nine human beings unaccustomed to sleeping in hammocks and trying to do so for the first time in a confined space involves a certain amount of groaning and twisting and heavy sighing. By the third night we had all mastered the art of sleeping flat, spread out diagonally across the hammock, and so avoiding having the spine turned into a hoop. But the first night we still lay in what was the most obvious position—lengthwise and bent. We gathered, however, that somebody was managing to sleep for soon we heard heavy snoring from the other side of the partition and began to debate in whispers whose husband it was and if it would be possible to persuade him not to lie on his back in a hammock. Then we drifted into restless sleep, only to be awakened by wild screams about an hour later. We were all instantly alert, fumbling for torches, crashing out of hammocks before we realized it was one of the children having a nightmare. 'She always does this—at two o'clock every night,' her mother said casually. 'We should have warned you. It's something to do with her bladder.'

The screams had been blood curdling and I wondered if the Amerindians had heard them and concluded that the English tribe were indulging in some kind of ritual orgy. Meanwhile the child was soothed and led off unwillingly down the steps and into the bush by the light of a torch. Soon everyone was going down the steps in turn, the torch being handed back by each returning party, as if we were having a nocturnal relay race. I got as far as putting on my sandals, which I had taken into the hammock with me in case I should find them full of beetles in the morning, but then my imagination began to conjure up a picture of the little walk into the bush and of all the creatures of the animal and insect world that I might encounter, of the snakes that would slide across the path and of the outsize spiders with hairy legs and eyes on sticks that would watch me hypnotically from their huge webs low in the branches. I took my sandals off again and slept.

I awoke with a start and an urgent awareness that I no longer had the hammock to myself. Something was flying round around it, bumping against me and the net. Feverishly I began to untie all the knots that secured the net to the sides of the hammock and finally managed to tip myself out on to the floor. The moon must have been covered by clouds now and I could not feel the torch anywhere about, so fumbled my way into the next room in the darkness.

I made for what looked like the longest body and addressed its head end, 'It's a bat, a bat in my hammock. Come quick,' I whispered before I saw that it was not Dick after all. Fortunately I was talking to its feet and it did not wake up. Dick had in fact curled himself up in a foetal position and looked deceptively tiny in the middle of his long hammock. He was not particularly pleased at being woken, but after a certain amount of groaning uncurled himself and alighted on the floor. We picked our way among the sleeping forms back to my hammock. The bat had by now extricated itself and Dick suggested, predictably, that I had only dreamed that it was there. However, he spent about twenty minutes securing me in again, tying the net to the hammock with so many knots at such frequent intervals that it seemed unlikely that I would ever get out again, I was so well trussed.

I listened to him moving back into the other room, stubbing his toes against boxes and crates, tripping over piles of clothes. It was pitch black now and I hoped he would be able to find his own hammock, but evidently he was not too successful for the snoring stopped suddenly and I heard a grumpy male voice exclaim, 'Really you two! For goodness sake get Auntie Mame to knit you a double hammock next time.'

The next morning we woke at dawn and peered at each other over the sides of our hammocks, somewhat pale and hollow-eyed after the previous night's activities. The news that I, who had been the only one to lie beneath the luxury of a net, had also been the only one to be beset by bats was greeted with unfeeling hilarity. The hammocks which in the night had seemed like an Amerindian equivalent of the Mediaeval Little Ease, a peine forte et dure, had now suddenly become wonderfully comfortable and relaxing. They have this in common with beds: that they are at their most comfortable just when it is time to leave them.

The sky looked stormy, but we decided nonetheless to set out to explore a branch of the creek. As we went the sun appeared and all along the bank between the branches of the trees we could see wonderful sparkling patterns made by dew-laden spider-webs.

Some of them must have been several yards across and lovely though they were to look at I did not feel inclined to stay to meet the spider that had made them.

One tree had been taken over by hangnests. These birds choose their site carefully for nests placed just anywhere in the trees are likely to be raided by monkeys. The tree we saw was well away from any others which might provide a jumping off place and hung over the water. From every branch were suspended what looked like brown bags, elongated to a kind of urn shape. They were beautifully made, each one practically identical with the next. Their owner-occupiers were big black and yellow birds. By contrast we saw soon afterwards Guyana's smallest bird, the humming bird. This was one of the first birds we had seen in Georgetown. I remembered sitting on the hotel balcony on the day we arrived in Guyana watching this tiny little bright green bird dart about among the hibiscus. It moved so quickly that I could not follow it; it could move sideways and suddenly dart backwards when it was moving forwards, in a disconcerting manner. No other bird, as far as I know, is endowed with a reverse gear. As this one darted now among the trees it flashed and sparkled in the sun and looked as if it was on fire. We stopped to see if it had a nest near, but could not find one. It would not be easy to find anyway for the humming bird only requires a nest about two inches in diameter to hold its two eggs, each not much bigger than the tip of one's little finger.

Apart from the birds there was not much colour to be seen. One of the things that surprised us was the lack of brilliant flowers in tropical forests. The trees are at least a hundred feet tall and there is no light at their roots so that flowers flourish only on the top layer of the forests out of sight of the human eye. Sometimes we saw wild orchids and a spray of purple or mauve flowers, but for the most part there were only an infinite variety of shades and shapes of green foliage, with an occasional mass of gold where bamboo arched across the water.

We followed the creek until it opened out into a big pool, beyond which it became too shallow for the *Canje Queen*. The water was clear and we could see the pebbly bottom, something which seemed strangely English after seeing for so long only the water of muddy rivers or of creeks dyed brown by their vegetation. We had been told that there was a house nearby and we saw it now standing a little way off the creek up a sandy incline. The owner, a very silent

African, came down to meet us and insisted that we should go back with him to meet his wife. She was an extremely lively and intelligent woman, very eager for news of Georgetown where she had once lived. She was obviously very glad to have visitors from the outside world and I realized why her silent husband had led us up to the house with such pride and presented us to her like some unexpected treat.

As we were leaving we asked if we might swim in the pool and were told it was completely safe. It was the clearest, most tempting water imaginable and we stood on the bank savouring it as we prepared to jump in. Then somebody pointed to the *Canje Queen* which was tied up by the bank. Clearly outlined in the water we could see, projecting from one end of the boat the head of an anaconda. Its tail was just visible at the other. The *Canje Queen* was 20 feet long. We decided not to swim.

That evening after supper as Teach sat with us drinking coffee, he told us that we need not have feared the water camoodi, as the Anaconda is known locally. It would not have done us much harm, he said, because it takes quite a long time to arrange itself to kill its prey. Having wrapped itself round one of us it would have had to find something suitable to fix its tail to, in order to be able to get sufficient leverage to tighten its hold and so crush its victim. Meanwhile, of course, the rest of us would have had time to chop it with a cutlass.

It seemed to make sense and it was quite a while before I bethought me that it would not have had to look far for something to tie its tail to—there would always have been the other eight of us to choose from.

Teach told us that he had seen a camoodi kill a chicken in the pool at Santa a few days before and had noticed that the prey died of submersion before it was crushed. When the camoodi has made its kill it swallows it whole and the outline of its meal can sometimes be seen quite clearly bulging out its otherwise svelte body. But, said Teach, drinking another cup of coffee which, being made of creek water, always looked rather stronger than it really was, it was very unlikely that the camoodi we had seen would have attacked us anyway. It would go for a child, perhaps, but hardly a group of adults. The children in the party did not seem to find this very reassuring and refused to go swimming in the creek for the rest of the holiday.

The next day was Easter Sunday and after a rather better night we got up in a leisurely way suitable to the sabbath and set about making ourselves unusually clean and tidy ready for church.

High up in its aeroplane fuselage, the bell of Santa church began to toll as we made our way down the sandy path from our house. The congregation, like most church congregations, was predominantly female. Looking around Santa church I recalled that I had as a child thought for a long time that a 'religious sect' meant women. The religious sex was certainly in the majority here, for only about half a dozen men sat on a bench together at the back. Apart from their conversation it was very still in the church, which Teach had risen early to decorate. It was made gay also by the women's colourful dresses and modish hats.

Teach came in now and moved us forward so that we were sitting just beyond the front two rows of children who, he told us, formed the choir. Suddenly a horrific bombardment began. Heavy objects seemed to be crashing down on the church. Nobody showed the slightest trace of astonishment or concern, but we must have looked alarmed, for Teach began the service by reassuring the visitors that they need not worry about the strange noises that beset us. 'It is but the fruits of the trees falling upon the roof of the House of God,' he explained. It had a Biblical ring and was also quite accurate, so long as one bore in mind that the fruits of the trees were coconuts and the roof of the House of God was made of corrugated iron.

Teach conducted the service with tremendous verve. His interest in every member of his little congregation was such that he made sure that each one in turn had found the right page of prayer or hymn book and if any appeared lost he called them to the front and found their place again for them. To do so he had temporarily to leave the organ, but he kept the refrain going with such use of his powerful voice that one could scarcely tell the difference.

He talked, in his sermon, of the year in the village, praising the women for their loyal support of the church, chastising the men for their neglect. There were all kinds of jobs they could do, he told them, such as mending the bench they were now sitting on. By an almost too perfect piece of timing, the bench immediately collapsed and we turned round to see a row of legs rising in the air as the men somersaulted backwards.

I would have suspected some kind of stage management had not Teach been so patently astonished and delighted. His usual volubility was silenced. Not normally a man at a loss for words, he stood now, his mouth hanging open and said nothing. Then at last his excitement broke loose, 'I told you, I told you,' he repeated several times. 'It is a judgement, a judgement.'

Sheepishly the menfolk of the village got up and dusted their knees and put the bench together again as best they could. Some of them sat down rather gingerly; others preferred to remain standing for the rest of the service.

After the sermon, the Captain took the collection while we sang a hymn. It was a long hymn and he had completed his task and presented himself at the top of the church before we were half way through. He waited a few seconds by Teach, looking at him hopefully. Teach continued to play the organ and sing lustily. The Captain fidgeted for a while and then put down the bag of money on the bench. Teach turned and glowered at him, shaking his head, but the Captain took no notice, and strolled away down the aisle. Teach got up from the organ and the hymn faltered a little. Then he caught the Captain's eye and with a sharp flick of his finger indicated the spot at the top of the aisle where the Captain must come and stand. For what seemed a long time they looked at each other, then Teach returned to his organ and the Captain came slowly back, looking, I thought, rather cowed. He picked up the bag and stood waiting obediently, his head down, until the end of the hymn.

I wondered what thoughts were going through that bowed head, what re-enactment of the ancient church versus state controversy we had just witnessed. My own sympathies were with the Captain, but then I have never been able to care much for Thomas à Becket.

The Preacher's zeal was not something which appeared only on Easter Sundays; he was always full of plans for his church and the village and his enthusiasm was the more remarkable for being so unaccompanied by any answering zeal in his congregation. After twenty years of their polite apathy, one might have imagined that he would have stopped caring very much about decorating his church, polishing its few treasures, composing sermons of such length and delivering them with such force. It was not as if there was even any exciting evil to be fought, to stimulate his enthusiasm.

In the afternoon we had further evidence of Teach's zeal and interest. If we had nothing planned, he told us, he would take us to The Field, a phenomenon which was well worth a visit and lay not far off, just across the creek. So after lunch we all crowded into a little canoe, with Teach and a guide and made our way a very short distance down stream and landed on the far bank. There was a little landing stage where we had previously seen people swimming and washing clothes as we passed on our way up to Santa. Teach explained that there was a very small village here, whose children came up by canoe to his school each day. The people used to come across to his church on Sundays too, but now they were building their own.

They were busy on it now, we saw, when we reached the village. They were laying its foundations: that is to say that the women were all pulling out the weeds from a patch of sand and the men were watching.

We had assumed that once this village had its own church, Teach would cross over to take its services, but he told us that this church was to be of a different denomination so that another clergyman would have to see to it. The proliferation of Christian sects is one of the absurdities which astounds the visitor to Guyana—we once counted twenty-six announcing themselves in the Sunday paper. Every branch and sect and denomination is represented, some supported, like the missions, by American finance, and each has its following, particularly among the Africans, though they often allowed themselves a certain amount of latitude in interpreting the rules of their chosen creed. Myra, who was a Seventh Day Adventist, once told me, 'I very strict Adventist, mistress, but I does likes to dance and eat meat.' Even in Europe or the United States, where their historical and liturgical differences have some significance and may be appreciated by their followers, the existence of so many sects, each claiming for itself a monopoly of the truth, may seem somewhat ridiculous, but to get the full savour of their absurdity one has to see them competing in a country where their differences are utterly incomprehensible to their congregations.

Teach explained to the villagers that he was taking us to The Field and they saw us off on our way through the bush, assuring us that it was well worth the journey. It was very hot in the early afternoon and none of us—except, of course, Teach and the guide—quite understood the purpose of the trek. The children particularly could not understand why it was being made instead of the lazy afternoon splashing in the creek which we had originally planned. We asked Teach to tell us more about the wonderful Field.

'Ah, it is a great expanse,' he explained, opening his arms wide, 'of—grass.'

We nodded, tried to look impressed, and pressed him for more information.

'There is no tree,' he went on. 'There is no bush, no water, no swamp—just grass. You have never seen anything like it.'

We had of course; we had seen fields of grass all over England, but in this part of Guyana what he described was indeed a rarity.

After walking for a very long time through uncomfortable terrain, stooping under low branches, catching ourselves on prickly bushes, always thirsty because we had not thought to bring anything to drink and constantly having to encourage the children who were getting steadily less restrained in their criticisms, at last we came upon it. It was just what Teach had promised; a field of grass which was about two feet high.

We stood and looked at it. The children straggled up and their parents glared at them, defying them to make derogatory and acid comments. They contented themselves by looking at it coldly and asking, 'Well, what do we do now?'

'We cross it,' Teach said, as if it was the greatest imaginable treat.

If we did have thoughts of rebelling against this proposal, his air of kindly enthusiasm, his zeal to show us all the sights of the district and have us enjoy them, overcame it. After all he was only making the mistake we all make when we show foreigners our own country; we take them to see what is unusual to our eyes. I once showed an Italian friend a beautiful avenue of cypress trees and was surprised when she scarcely looked at them, but could not take her eyes off a perfectly ordinary English oak.

So we set off dutifully across the hay field; there was absolutely no protection from the sun and the long grass was full of insects that attacked us ferociously. It was sharp too, for there was a great deal of razor grass among it which lacerated our legs. Even Teach was silent and exhausted as we made for the far side, which had a way of constantly receding, but he still looked around and said in wonder, 'All around us, see, nothing but grass, no trees, no swamp. . . .'

When at last we reached the other side we subsided on to the ground under the trees, taking great gulps of the cooler air. We soon realized why Teach and the guide had remained standing; the ground was swarming with giant ants.

When Teach pronounced that it was now time to start walking back, the children could no longer refrain from expressing their astonishment that the adults of the party should pander to such folly. Their silence had to be bought by carrying them back to the village, where we were welcomed like returning explorers and questioned about what we thought of The Field. When it was noticed that our throats were too dry to allow us to speak a little boy was sent up a tree to throw down coconuts. Their tops were slashed off with a cutlass and we were given them to drink.

It was dark when we climbed back into the canoe and crossed over to Santa. After supper that night I strolled down to the creek under a huge and brilliant moon. The sand gleamed white and unreal and the place was silent except for the gentle lapping of the water. The silk cotton tree shone like silver in the moonlight and its gaunt, ragged branches were pale and wraithlike. Seeing it in this ghostly setting, I understood at last its reputation for mystery and magic.

The next morning Granny came to meet me as I came down the steps of the house. I had never seen her so excited.

'We got baby,' she explained, taking my hand. 'We work all night and de baby she born dis morning early.'

The mother, it seemed, had been confined in Granny's house and would stay there with her baby. Granny must have delivered hundreds of babies in her long life, but she was as thrilled about this one as if it had been the first. Her tired, lined face was radiant and her eyes shone. She kept squeezing my hand in her excitement.

'Later—you shall see she,' she whispered and then walked quickly away with her characteristic long loping stride.

We spent the morning packing and carrying our belongings down to the creek where the more methodical stowed it all into the *Canje Queen*. The rest of us were employed as pack horses to carry the innumerable boxes, string bags and thermos flasks down the sandy path from the house.

I had lost my sandals somewhere in the course of the packing and was going bare-foot despite Teach's oft-repeated warnings against doing so for fear of jiggers. These are tiny sand fleas which, when the time comes to lay their eggs, love to do so in the human flesh. They penetrate the soft skin down the side of the toe nail, because, I suppose, that area is the most easily accessible to them. I regretted not heeding Teach's advice when some time later in Georgetown my foot began to swell and tickle. I had forgotten all about walking in the sand and went to our East Indian doctor who immediately diagnosed eggs. They had not hatched yet but were festering and digging them all out was a laborious business as it was important not to leave one egg behind. He told me that an Amerindian, without the advantage of such an array of sharp and sterile instruments as he himself had, would have made a much better job of it, lifting out the whole sac of eggs unbroken.

As I made my unshod way down to the creek I noticed that the children of our party were teaching the Amerindian children to play cricket, a game with which they were not as familiar as the children in Georgetown would have been. On the coast the game is almost an obsession; when the M.C.C. came for the test match an unofficial holiday was assumed. The stands were packed and there were even more people outside than in, for the road outside Bourda cricket ground is lined with tall trees from whose branches an excellent view of the game can be had. Hours before play was due to start the branches of these trees were black with spectators. They did not always ration the seating space up there as carefully as they should, for once, during an exciting over, a huge branch, laden with spectators, crashed into the road. By some miracle nobody was seriously hurt. I remember seeing, on my way to the ground, a very dapper African dressed like a city gentleman in dark suit, bowler hat and gloves, walk to a tree, take off his gloves, methodically hang his umbrella on a low branch and proceed to shin up the tree with the greatest agility to join his friends on the topmost branch.

The children of Santa were evidently not so keen, for none was watching the game. They were flying kites, a traditional Easter pastime in Guyana and the sky above the silk cotton tree was alive with their marvellous dragon shapes and long, beflowered tails.

I was not sorry to be interrupted on one of the long trails from the house to the creek, bearing all sorts and sizes of unmanageable parcels, by Granny, who suddenly appeared from apparently nowhere, took my arm and hurried me off to her house. I realized from her secretive manner it must not be customary to look at the baby so soon after its birth. She left me at the bottom of her steps and ran up into the house. She came out again carrying a big bundle of clothing, embedded in which, she carefully revealed, was a tiny little wistful face, as aged and wrinkled as her own. Puffy eyelids opened to reveal sad eyes and the baby gazed at us, looking as dejected and world-weary as only a new baby knows how. She seemed to be wondering why she had left the luxury of the womb, where all things were done for her, for this world where she had to breathe and feed for herself. Her long struggle had begun and we gazed at the baby, Granny and I, with wonder and compassion.

Granny wrapped up her charge again and carried her carefully into the house to the darkened room where the mother lay. Nobody would be allowed inside the house until the mother and baby came out together and returned to their home. Strangely moved and honoured by being allowed to see the youngest inhabitant of Santa, I rejoined the packers and found, to my relief, that they had finished carrying everything down to the creek. The house was quite empty and, feeling that I had perhaps got off rather lightly, I looked for a pointer broom to sweep the floor. A pointer broom is a Guyanese sweeping brush. Made of a bundle of springy twigs tied to a stick it raises a quite impressive amount of dust which hangs about in the air for a while before settling and so gives a temporary illusion of cleanliness.

Since a pointer broom was the one thing we had not thought of bringing with us from Georgetown I went across to our nearest neighbour's house to borrow one. The room had no sides and I could see that the mistress of the house was not there and remembered that the women of Santa often gathered at about this time for a chat in the centre of the village—at least they sat together in companionable silence which seemed to be their equivalent of a chat. A little girl of about three was in the room and I asked her if I might borrow the pointer broom which stood in one corner. She picked it up with some difficulty—it was taller than she was—and as I held out my hand to take it, she carefully and with considerable expenditure of energy turned it round in order to present me with the handle rather than the twigs.

It was the kind of little gesture one often noticed among the Amerindians, revealing their instinctive courtesy, for their children seemed to have natural good manners. There was nothing constrained or 'civilized' about their behaviour, which seemed to spring from an intuitive consideration for other people.

I thought, as I swept the little house, raising clouds of dust of which some found its way outside, of a story we had been told in Georgetown about an American missionary who had chosen to flex his spiritual muscles upon an unspecified Amerindian village in the Interior. He bullied its people into wearing clothes, tried to alter their eating habits because his sect was vegetarian and generally made a thorough nuisance of himself. When the Amerindians could bear it no longer, they did not argue or raise objections which might upset their self-appointed moral guide. They suffered him as long as they could and then one night they quietly melted away into the forest. When he awoke next morning the missionary found that the village had disappeared. The Amerindians had preferred to face such an upheaval themselves rather than upset a foreigner who had shown so little compunction about upsetting them. Sad to tell the evangelist went out and pursued them by helicopter and we never heard what happened when he found them.

This gentleness seems to be a characteristic of the Amerindians of whom there are about thirty thousand living in the Interior of Guyana. They belong to many different tribes, speaking different dialects and having different customs. They vary too in the extent to which they have been touched by civilization. The ones we knew at Santa were, of course, much affected by the modern world; they lived too near to Georgetown for it to be otherwise. We met others who were much less affected by it and there exist tribes in the far Interior, whom we were not able to visit, who retain their way of life unaffected by the outside world. At the far extreme from the villagers of Santa, with their Church of England services and Sunday hats, are the Wai-Wais who live in the Southernmost part of Guyana between the Rupununi and Brazilian frontier, who retain their customs unaltered, wearing bead aprons and feather head-dresses and painting their faces very colourfully. Between these two extremes there is a wide variety of tribes, affected to a varying extent by the influence of Government, traders and missionaries.

All these tribes present the administration with the same problem of how to integrate the Amerindians into the rest of the country without destroying their individuality. Although they are often regarded by travellers as being the most interesting feature of Guyana, they are still looked down upon by many of the Guyanese. The latter are still too much aware of the need to prove themselves the equal of the white man to be proud of these 'bucks' —who are not even civilized enough to wear proper European style clothes and sleep in beds. For so long have the white man's ways been accepted as the correct standard that any deviation from them tends to be regarded as a sign of inferiority.

The main difficulty for the central administration has always been that the Amerindians do not have an organization or representatives with whom the Government could work. The idea of making the Interior part of the administration of the whole country only began in 1946 when the Department of the Interior was set

Vatching cricket in
ieorgetown. The trees
utside Bourda cricket
round provide excellent
ee seats.

hildren playing
icket at Santa.

Gamblers in
a dark corner
of Georgetown.

Exploring the
Kamuni creek
in the
Canje Queen.

up to try to develop it and to protect the Amerindians. The Department began the system of appointing Captains, for the intensely individualistic Amerindians did not appoint leaders among themselves. One aim is to persuade them to live in larger villages, which has obvious advantages over the tiny scattered communities which have developed in the past. The work is not easy for though the Amerindian is gentle he is not malleable or easy to organize. As W. H. Segger wrote in *Timehri,* the journal of the Royal Agricultural and Commercial Society, in 1959, 'If he feels that there is the slightest intention to push him around he will quietly fade into the bush.' This instinct of the forest people to disappear into the bush when life becomes difficult contributes to the problem of trying to help them to found viable communities which in turn are part of the rest of the country. In 1965 a Department of Amerindian Affairs was set up under Mr. Stephen Campbell to try to help Amerindians participate in Guyanese society.*

One constantly heard the problem discussed and there are some who feel that the Amerindians are best left alone and that the Government should not try to interfere with them in any way. The trouble is that they cannot be left alone; civilization is for ever pushing and extending and it will reach them whether we like it or not, either in the shape of Government officials, traders or missionaries. It is simply a question of whether the process should be left to chance, in which case the interests of the Amerindians will probably not be the main consideration, or should follow a Government policy which has the Amerindians' welfare as its only object.

It so often happens, not only in South America, that when primitive people make contact with civilization they take only its worst and shoddiest features, losing their own time proven values and gaining nothing of worth in return. Commonly it is explorers, traders and prospectors who are held most reprehensible, for in pursuit of their own interests they have in many parts of the world debased the life of indigenous people. It has suited them to make these people dependent upon them for cheap foreign goods to the detriment of local crafts and they have deliberately introduced the horrors of drunkenness and prostitution into tribes in which such perversions of civilization were unknown.

*Mr. Campbell, who died in 1966, was himself an Amerindian. For years he worked for the cause of the Amerindians, particularly for their rights of land tenure. He was the only Amerindian member of the Legislative Council and represented them at the Independence conferences. At Independence, he became a Parliamentary Secretary.

Santa. Children playing with kites on the white sand.
Standing among the immense roots and buttresses of the silk cotton tree.
Sheltering in Granny's kitchen.
Sunrise over swamp land on the other side of Kamuni creek.

If civilization must come it might seem better that the contact should be made through missionaries, who come for the sake of the people, rather than through traders whose concern is profit in the pursuit of which local people may be exploited and corrupted. Yet corruption comes from unexpected sources. The missionary's motive may be entirely good, but he brings with him a concept of morality which is all-important to him and which he inevitably regards the natives as somehow not quite living up to. He does not, therefore, respect them or their ways and traditions, which he seeks to alter wherever they do not coincide with the message he is bringing.

It is perhaps as difficult to transplant a religious way of life as it is to transplant a constitution. A mystical belief may call down the ages and across the oceans but embodied into say, 'a Christian way of life' it is too closely involved with the ways of the civilization in which it has developed. Because they come from a prurient European or American society missionaries find the Amerindians' nakedness disgusting and teach the Amerindians to find it disgusting too. They have to create a sense of guilt about certain things where there was none before. Like latter day gods they have invented sins and then found the Amerindians guilty of committing them. Then, of course, they can offer the consolations of redemption and forgiveness.

It seems to require far greater knowledge and understanding than most of them have in the past possessed to distinguish between what truly belongs to the faith and what are simply standards which have suited their own society and to which therefore the generations of their fellow countrymen have wisely given the sanctions of religious backing. It takes a brave and unconventional man to jettison the latter when he goes to a society whose needs are different. Unfortunately rigidity in matters spiritual has often been the rule as in matters temporal. There is a certain false pride in demanding the same kind of behaviour from one's flock in the bush as in Basingstoke. It is the religious counterpart of the British colonial administrator who always dressed for dinner even in the heart of tropical Africa.

To take but one example: monogamy has best served the needs of Western Society, protecting the family which is the basic unit of the community and Christianity has lent to it the great strength of its support. A strong religious sanction has endorsed what was good for the well-being of society. But this situation is not necessarily universal. Some Amerindian tribes have been threatened with extinction by becoming less fertile. Malaria, which much reduced fertility, has in the past affected most of them. They knew instinctively what other societies have been slow to discover: that subfertility affects both sexes and that a couple who are childless may both have children if they change partners. The childless couple therefore sometimes parted and sought other partners. Sometimes, if it was more suitable, the woman stayed with her original partner and conceived by another man. In some tribes a couple did not marry until the woman had conceived.

To a missionary who comes bringing a different way of life and determined to impose it in toto, these habits seem shocking—and perhaps they would be in London and New York, whose inhabitants lack the Amerindians' gentle tolerance which enables these arrangements to take place without bitterness, jealously or violence. It makes sense to the missionary to insist upon monogamy and then regret the extinction of the tribe.

It seemed to me that one of the great differences between the communities the missionaries knew at home and those they came to convert was that the latter have no strong sense of possession. Our Western civilization has long held personal property to be a sacred right to the protection of which we have given religious sanctions. Nicholas Guppy in his book *The Wai-Wai* tells revealingly how the tendency of the Amerindian to steal from the Mission shocked the missionary, yet to the Amerindian it was shocking that anyone could keep a private store of food in excess of what he needed. To a primitive tribe the holding of things in common, the constant sharing of food and all basic requirements is fundamental to the life of the community. It is a basic unwritten law. Therefore stealing cannot exist. It is only when a Western conception of individual property is introduced that a crime called stealing can appear.

How ironic it is that this 'stealing' should shock a so-called Christian conscience. The early Christians who held all things in common were nearer in outlook to the Amerindians than to the missionary whose harking back to the Mosaic law really springs from his background of a capitalist society in which since the Middle Ages the all importance of property has been sanctified by the backing of religion.

It is sad to think that the piety, the self-sacrifice, the prayers and the work that goes into fund-raising by churches all over Europe and America can sometimes lead to such destructive activities among primitive tribes. It seems a pity that they cannot restrict their activities to those who have already lost their own heritage and urgently need help as they flounder in civilization. For here the work of the missions in providing medical care, education, training in crafts and agricultural skill is wholly good. Unfortunately there seems to be a strong feeling particularly among American evangelists who get tremendous support from big business that what really matters is to take the Gospel to people who have not yet had the opportunity of being baptized. This tendency to see things in grossly oversimplified terms vitiates the work of many good people. To count the heads of the converted is a simple and triumphant operation; to take a humble and disinterested view of what exactly these people have been converted from and to and to what purpose is a more exacting task.

It has been tempting in the past for those who were setting up missions to attract Amerindians to them by offering them foreign goods such as tinned milk and cheap cotton materials upon which they then became dependent and so have to come to the Mission to get them. In consequence many tribes have lost the skills which they once had. This has led to a loss of independence and self-sufficiency. One can imagine that it must have been tempting to use the resources of one's own advanced country in this way; besides the missionary would not see it as a temptation he should resist but as a weapon which God had put into his hand.

For these reasons restrictions on the activities of missions have been imposed by the Government and one gets the impression that the dangers are now fully realized. Indeed so loud were the criticisms of the harm that the missions had done to the Amerindians by people who had themselves never shown much inclination to do them any good that one began to wonder if the missions were not being made something of a scapegoat. It seemed to me that missionaries might still play a great part in helping the Government with its policy of maintaining the strength and numbers of the Amerindians without either making them curiosities in a reserve or letting their keenly individual way of life be lost in that of the rest of the country. They could do much to help the Amerindian adjust himself to civilization if they could dispense with the prejudices which belong to their own country and with the accretions of Christianity and take only that sense of love and service which is at its heart. Then their censoriousness might be replaced by respect for the Amerindian character and they would find themselves able to work within the framework of that way of life which already exists. They might do worse than read and ponder the words which Richard Schomburgk wrote in his *Travels in British Guiana* in 1884. 'Morality and virtue need not be brought from civilized Europe—Indians have far greater regard for them than we have.'

CHAPTER TEN

Orinduik – Kamarang – Kaieteur

We had been in Guyana for about a year when Eric and Susan Hiscock landed at Georgetown on their way around the world in *Wanderer III*. Guyanese hospitality being what it is, they found themselves welcomed and fêted everywhere. Indeed in order to get any writing done at all they had to beat a retreat nine miles up the Demerara and drop anchor in midstream to escape the invitations.

Before doing so they kindly asked anybody who was interested to inspect the boat. I was unwell at the time but Dick was delighted to have the opportunity to examine *Wanderer III* at close quarters and came home full of enthusiasm for the way in which the Hiscocks had organized their boat so that not only was she an efficient craft, but also a safe and comfortable home for them on their long voyages. He was very emphatic about the safety, knowing my landlubber's fear of small craft on high seas. Even the primus stove, he told me, was so cleverly designed that if the boat turned upside down the flame and pan would remain the right way up and cooking continue uninterrupted. I was more interested in which way up the cook would be.

I had expected the Hiscocks to be a frightening couple. It seemed likely that people who spent their lives battling with the elements and outwitting nature at her nastiest would become stern and forbidding in the process. I pictured them as stony-eyed and commanding, uncompromisingly stern in conversation, utterly humourless and inclined to shout orders every now and then. It was something of a shock, therefore, to find the skipper of *Wanderer III* light-hearted to the point of frivolity, and as unassuming about his exploits as about his writing. An even greater surprise was to find that his wife, whom I had pictured as being composed of muscles and bits of steel, was in fact gentle and feminine. It took me some time to superimpose the image of these real people on the one that I had created in my imagination.

The Georgetown Sailing Club, of which we were members, decided to celebrate the arrival of the Hiscocks by chartering a plane and taking them to Orinduik on the border of Brazil. The Hiscocks were delighted; usually, they told us, when they landed at a port the local sailing club welcomed them with, 'What shall we do to celebrate? Go for a sail?' And that, though they did not like to say so, was always just about the last thing they wanted to do.

The aeroplane that took us to Orinduik was a very old Dakota. We sat facing each other on benches which ran the length of each side. This and the fact that it was a very rattly vehicle, gave it the feel of one of the old trams of industrial cities in the north of England. The whole thing seemed somehow too loosely put together and once during the flight the door flew open. I wondered if we should all be sucked out one by one, but Dick said we should not be as the plane was not pressurized like the one I had read the story about. All the same I was glad when somebody shut it.

The plane had been standing grilling in the sun for several hours and by the time we got in had become a cylinder of hot metal in which we sat and panted for air. By the end of the journey, however, we were bitterly cold and realized that air a few hundred feet up is cool, even when it is over Guyana. I had hitherto believed that flying—or rather being flown—is the most boring of all forms of enforced inactivity. This was the first flight I ever actively enjoyed. In this plane we seemed as close to the countryside as if we were in a bus or train, only seeing it all from a fascinating angle as we flew very low over the tree tops. We seemed to be looking down upon boundless seas of foliage; mile after mile, as far as we could see in any direction, there stretched below us the infinite green. Its surface looked soft and rounded, cushioned like green cauliflowers. Sometimes we could see clearings where there was a village or timber reserve or follow the winding thread of a river, but they were only tiny scratches on an otherwise uninterrupted green canvas.

Suddenly we were among mountains, the Pakaraima mountain range, which we had heard of, but in whose existence we had somehow ceased to believe after months of living on the flat coastal strip with never so much as a rise in a road to remind us of what a hill looked like.

These mountains were extraordinary, sheer uprights, slices of rock, top hats of land, crazily cut in unnatural fret-saw shapes. Sometimes we would fly beside them, staring out into their straight-cut sides, sometimes we would be deep in a ravine, seeing them tower above us. Some were quite square, like mountain boxes, others like long turrets; whatever the shape they none of them had the look of mountains that have been worked upon slowly and gently by time and weather. They seemed to have been cut out in a great hurry by a giant with a penchant for geometry.

We bumped about wildly as we prepared to land and I noticed that most of our fellow passengers, though their normal complexions varied from white to glossy black with every intermediate shade of yellow and brown, now shared a fine greenish bloom on their cheeks. I usually feel sick in the ordinary kind of stuffy, padded aeroplane because I suppose there is nothing much else to feel, but this wonderful bouncing bean of a Dakota, which flew over tree tops and up ravines and along the sides of cubist mountains was altogether too exciting to inspire me with feelings other than those of wonder and delight.

Apparently our aeroplane was normally used for transporting beef from the savannah ranches to Georgetown. For to the south lies the great savannah area of the Rupununi, bordering on Brazil, which has its centre at Lethem. Cattle raising there is organized by private ranchers and the Rupununi Development Company. Since the pasture is poor and can only support about a dozen animals to the square mile, these ranches are of enormous size. The first real cattle rancher was a Scot called Melville who came prospecting to Guyana at the end of the last century. He was taken ill with malaria and left by his men near the Essequibo, where Amerindians found him and looked after him. Later he travelled with them to the savannahs and settled there, marrying two Amerindian wives from whom are descended today's great ranching families. These families, such as the Melvilles and Harts and others with whom they are connected by marriage, form a powerful oligarchy, employing Amerindians as stockmen to look after their herds. The ranchers have maintained a great deal of the independence of pioneers and we were told that they both resented interference from Georgetown and complained of lack of help from the central government. We hoped to be able to visit the Rupununi, whose savannahs contrast so magnificently with the dense forests and jagged mountain ranges which adjoin them, but we were not able to do so and Orinduik was the nearest we ever got to the savannahs of the Interior of Guyana.*

*On 2nd January, 1969, an attack was made on the Police Station at Lethem and on Government personnel by ranchers drawn mainly from the Melville

At Orinduik we came down on a little landing-strip like a red cricket pitch and found ourselves being greeted by African policemen. Apart from the policemen, there was a police house, the border and the great falls of the nearby Ireng river. Some of the party crossed over to the other side of the river and found that in Brazil also there were policemen, a police house, and the same falls of the same great river mocking the man-made frontier. The falls were wide and symmetrical and fell in three great tiers like an amphitheatre. The air was cool and light as we sat near the highest, up in the Gods, and breathed the intoxicating air.

The one disadvantage of Orinduik was the Kaboura fly, a black, vicious little creature whose blood-sucking activities leave sore patches on the skin for many days afterwards. But it was a small price to pay for a day in the peace of this remote river plain, the memory of whose falls and the cooling white spray that arose from them into the invigorating air remained with us long after our scars had healed.

The short day in Orinduik had so refreshed us that we determined to take any chance that arose to get into the far Interior again. The difficulty is that the only way is by aeroplane which is of course very expensive. We were fortunate, however, in hearing of an enterprising Guyanese who had decided to charter a plane if he could find about twenty people willing to fly up to Kamarang, North West of Orinduik, in the heart of the gold and diamond area of Guyana.

The flight was similar to that we had made to Orinduik, being

and Hart families. Security forces soon regained control but the incident was more sinister than one of pure terrorism. The ranchers, with the (probably unwilling) support of their Amerindian employees, had plotted with the Venezuelan authorities to establish a separate state which would secede from Guyana. They were given seven days' training in Venezuela and armed with automatic weapons and bazookas. Although the Amerindians were probably acting under duress, the Venezuelan press and radio reported the affair as an uprising of Amerindians who wanted to come under the sovereignty of Venezuela. The incident supports Guyana's previous accusations that Venezuela is trying to subvert her indigenous people and to claim the Essequibo region. Venezuela has also laid claim in 1968 to Guyanese territorial waters. Another disturbing feature of the incident was the part played by the United Force election candidate, Mrs. Valerie Hart, which lends force to the fear that politicians, as well as ranchers, were involved in the plot and that the Amerindians have been used as pawns in the political game by party leaders in Georgetown. It is perhaps significant that this attack, in which nine people were killed, was launched so soon after the results of the General Election (in which Mr. Burnham's government won by a large majority and the U.F. was defeated) became known.

over forests and mountain ranges. Kamarang is, however, a much bigger place than Orinduik. It is a Government station, which lies at the confluence of the Mazaruni and Kamarang rivers, near the Venezuelan border. From it can be seen Mount Roraima, the great mountain of the Interior which inspired Conan Doyle's *The Lost World,* crowning the border of Guyana, Brazil and Venezuela.

We were a typical Guyanese mixture in the party: there were English, Portuguese, Africans, East Indians and Chinese in roughly equal proportions with several mixtures of all five. As we touched down on the air strip most of the village seemed to have turned out to watch our arrival. We clustered under the wings, trying to find some shade while the plane was unloaded, for it was grillingly hot. We began to look for bottles and openers and fruit. Somebody killed a snake under the plane. At last the luggage was unloaded and we went and poked and probed among the huge mound of it until we found our own belongings, or at least some of them, and set off for the rest house which had been allotted to us.

The houses were new and lay back in a long line from the air strip. The village was very tidy and well-ordered. The air strip was newly laid and ours was one of the first planes to land on it. Until now everything that was needed for the Government station had to be brought by canoe taking days to reach Kamarang though occasionally supplies could be brought in the little Grumman amphibian aircraft. The achievement of the station was due to the enthusiasm and devotion of the only English District Commissioner, William Seggar, whose reputation is well known throughout the country. We were sorry that he was on leave when we went to Kamarang, but we talked to his local deputy who spoke of him with that respect and admiration which his work seemed everywhere to command.

The Government station at Kamarang had been established to carry on agricultural research in the area, for the soil here is known to be good and it is hoped that the Amerindians living nearby will be persuaded to grow more fruit and vegetables which could then be marketed for them in Georgetown. Many attempts have been made by private individuals to develop parts of the Interior as agricultural land for it is here, not on the coast, that both soil and climate favour plant growth. We constantly heard stories of enterprising men who had come from England and other parts of the world and started schemes to grow vegetables which would replace the imported ones, or fruit which could be tinned and exported or pineapples whose juice could be canned, but all had foundered in the face of the enormous natural difficulties and the isolation of the place. It seems that only large scale Government planning and long term policy can hope to overcome them.

We had been offered two buildings at the end of the village for our short stay: the larger, the rest house, had a kitchen in which we could prepare our meals and a big room where we could eat them and where the men could sleep. Not far away was the school house, where the women were to sleep. We slung our hammocks and went down to look at the nearby Mazaruni, black and narrow here, very different from the wide river set with islands that we had explored near Bartica, some hundreds of miles nearer the sea.

We ate our supper sitting on benches at long trestle tables, lit by what seemed a great luxury in the Interior—a single electric light bulb, for electricity was provided by the Government station. In this, the possession of electric light, we were better off than in Georgetown where recently the electricity supply had become inadequate to meet the demands upon it and constantly failed. Great debates were conducted about what should be done to improve the electricity supply in Georgetown and our hopes rose when the Government appointed a Controller of Electricity, whom we all welcomed with a round of parties in the belief that he was going to save the situation, but it turned out that his task was simply to organize the rationing of electricity. Thereafter we seemed to have even less electricity than before. For two days a week each area was without it. Lighting turned out to be the least of the inconveniences; lack of refrigeration was a far greater hardship. The failure of electricity was, however, easier to bear than the occasional failure of water supplies in a land where unwashed pots and pans are located in seconds by marauding ants and smells seem to multiply and abound and take on a life of their own.

In the Interior, however, we luxuriated in the knowledge that we had safe supplies of electricity and creek water. I pondered, as I had often done before, upon the sheer perversity of it. The population of Guyana is about three-quarters of a million and of these the great majority huddle together on the narrow coastal strip, which varies in width from ten to forty miles, is mainly below high tide level, necessitating the maintenance of an expensive system of sea defences, and has a humid and unhealthy climate. Yet the total area of the country is eighty-three thousand square miles. In this great expanse live a mere thirty thousand Amerindians.

It might make sense if the coastal strip was more agreeable or healthy or fertile than the Interior, but the reverse is true. It was always a wonderful release to us to get into the fresher air of the forests and mountains, though we could never convince the coast-bound that the Interior was more comfortable than the coast. Travellers and writers have so exaggerated the dangers and discomforts of the Interior that the advantages have been lost sight of. It is true that there is more chance of being attacked by a jaguar or of tripping over a deadly snake or standing on a scorpion, but they are after all only remote possibilities, and the advantages, the freshness of the air and absence of mosquitoes, these are real and assured. While we were in Guyana it was visited by a team of Cambridge scientists whose leader, when they emerged from a few months in the bush, gave a lecture on their findings and prefaced his talk by stressing how much pleasanter life had been there than in Georgetown. We agreed with him wholeheartedly, but most of the audience just thought that he was being agreeably and unusually modest about the hardships he and his party must have endured.

So we sat, on our first evening at Kamarang, under our electric light bulb, most of us leaning our elbows on the table, one or two already in their hammocks. An East Indian stood in the corner and played his violin. The conversation was as varied as the company. Easily the most loquacious was an African pork-knocker, the name given locally to gold and diamond prospectors, deriving possibly from their traditional diet of salted pork-tails. I had read about these men in the novels of Edgar Mittelholzer and Jan Carew, but apart from that had got no nearer to one than examining what I took to be a stuffed pork-knocker in the museum. They are adventurers possessed by the love of the uncertain life of hunting for gold. If they do strike rich they can dispossess themselves of their wealth with amazing rapidity, for it is not so much the gold they love as the excitements of seeking it.

The prospectors are essentially Africans from the coast who visit the Interior; they do not belong there. Indeed there are no African descendants of escaped slaves living in the bush, as happens elsewhere, for under both Dutch and English rule there was a highly organized system of recapturing runaway slaves. The Amerindians were employed as slave hunters and so expert were they in hunting and tracking that the slaves could not escape them however far they fled into the bush. For many years after the emancipation of slaves the memory of this was one of the factors making for ill-feeling between African and Amerindian.

The pork-knocker, who was called Mr. Caesar, was a tough, rough looking African who to judge by his greying hair and heavily lined face must have been well into middle age. He told me, in confidential undertones, that he had not come on this trip as a tourist like the rest of us, but for business, in order to make contacts with some of the divers in the diamond camp we could visit next day. He spoke very mysteriously and since he was always acting a part I took this just as a burlesque of the businessman's self-importance, but discovered later that the activities of these prospectors are in fact very closely controlled and they are not allowed to enter Amerindian reserves without permits which are hard to come by, so perhaps he was indeed smuggling himself in by joining our party. In which case by dressing up his business as a pleasure trip he was reversing the more usual process. We had observed that a great many English business executives seemed to find urgent business must be done in the Caribbean islands just when the weather in England turned really nasty. The swanning season, as it is locally known, lasts from January until March.

The pork-knocker told us a great deal about diamonds and casually took out a screw of paper from his pocket and tipped the contents into the palm of his hand. They were diamonds worth several hundreds of pounds, he told us, but we found that they were disappointing to look at in their raw state, at least to our inexperienced eyes. He told us innumerable stories of life in the bush in which fact and fiction were so inextricably interwoven that it was impossible to disentangle them. Just when a story seemed most likely to be a total fabrication some chance fact would come out to substantiate it. He was a born story teller and we might have stayed all night listening to him had not somebody suddenly pointed out that the light would be extinguished in a few minutes when the power was turned off at the Government station. It was a signal for the six women of the party to walk over to our sleeping place in the schoolroom, escorted by husbands who chastely left us at the doorstep in a way which carried me back to university days and nights.

We had only a minute before the light would be turned off but it was long enough to see that since we had left the room in the late afternoon it had been taken over by cockroaches. The floor was black with them and they scuttled up the walls as we came in. Our cases and rucksacks were alive with them and they inhabited the nightclothes we had left ready in our hammocks. The little wash room where we had put buckets of creek water ready for washing was even more infested. One had even arranged itself neatly along the length of the bristles of my toothbrush.

We viewed the cockroaches with varying degrees of horror, the Guyanese accepting them more stoically than the English. Only the wife of the Controller of Electricity and myself were badly afflicted and began shaking them out of our clothes, chasing them across the floor, throwing stones at them and stamping on them. When the light flashed three times, in warning that the electricity was about to be turned off, we found a torch and continued the search by its pale yellow beam and eventually got our clothes and hammocks clear, while the rest of the party grumbled at us from their hammocks. They grumbled even more in the morning when the floor was found to be liberally dotted with the crushed black and yellow corpses of cockroaches.

It was misty the next morning as we walked across the wet grass to the guest house and the air was cool. We looked hopefully in the direction of Mount Roraima, for we had not so far been able to catch a glimpse of the famous mountain. All the previous afternoon a mist had hung over it and although members of the Government station had twice come across to tell us it was visible, both times it had disappeared again by the time we reached the spot from which it can normally be seen.

We set off after breakfast in little boats with outboard engines to travel up the Mazaruni to the Peaima Falls where diamond divers and gold prospectors were busy working. The banks of the rivers were black with huge boulders which often came down very steeply to the water's edge. A look-out man squatted in the bows to give warning of tacoubas, which present a special hazard in these swift-flowing waters. The current was much stronger than we realized; when we trailed our cups in the water to rinse them after drinking, they were instantly snatched out of our hands and disappeared down stream.

We were in the territory of the Akawaio Amerindians and several of them passed us in woodskins, a distinctive kind of dug-out canoe. We could see sometimes on the bank a little path marked with sticks which showed that in a clearing beyond there would be an

Amerindian house. We stopped twice on the way to see them. Both houses were at the top of steep and muddy slopes; their inhabitants were shy but hospitable and showed us their houses, conical in shape with open sides, rather like a big coolie hat. Inside they pointed to their large gourds, the biggest we had seen, which make ideal containers for water, keeping their contents astonishingly cold. By contrast they had also acquired galvanized buckets. Both families had many children and in each there was a baby carried in a sling round the neck either of its mother or elder sister. They were very charming, these shy Akawaioan children and we asked if we might photograph them. The first family seemed pleased that we should, but the second hesitated, so we did not press the request. Some primitive people have strong feelings and superstitions about photography, believing that a picture taken of them takes away something of themselves and so weakens them. There are African tribes whose members will not write down their names for fear of losing strength by parting with something which is uniquely their own. We heard of one who would not even tell their names to the contractor for whom they were working for fear that its repetition might diminish them. Second names had to be invented for the purpose of their employment.

After travelling all morning we reached the falls, beyond which the river is impassable. The prospectors' camp lay on the right bank and two very battered-looking pork-knockers came down to the water's edge to help to pull us in. They presented a frightening spectacle, bits of them being wrapped in dirty bandages and their faces criss-crossed with sticking plaster. They had been celebrating bank holiday, they told us, and were still full of the party spirit.

The river here, just above the rapids, was shallow and the bottom was composed of fine sand. The prospectors 'panned' this sand for diamonds, sifting it gently through their pans as they sat in the water. We changed into swim suits and joined them, sitting in the cool water of the rapids and panning the sand through our fingers in the hope of spotting a diamond or two.

Suddenly there was a great bustle of activity on the bank and the preparations for diving began. The water was shallow but by wearing diving equipment the prospector can stay under long enough to examine the bed of the river carefully to see if it is worth bringing up sand for panning. Preparing the diver was complicated by the fact that all the pork-knockers were drunk. They encased the diver in all his equipment with the utmost deliberation and with many interruptions for hand shaking and speech making. A diver dressed for the water is a curious spectacle at the best of times, clumsy and dehumanized. A drunken diver is even more extraordinary. We watched, fascinated, as he lumbered about, leaden-footed and unsteady. His comrades began slapping him on the back and kept on doing so, even though the object of their attentions can scarcely have felt them. Finally they tired of this and tipped him unceremoniously over the side. They had told us that by wearing a diving suit he would be able to spend about half an hour working on the alluvial sand, but he did not make very good use of his time, for he kept bobbing up to the surface to wave to us and every now and then executed a dance in the water. It was a relief to all of us when he finally decided he had done enough diamond prospecting for one day and staggered out of the river. They all abandoned their equipment in the boat and went off to finish their celebrating.

Our own pork-knocker, Mr. Caesar, had left us immediately we landed. He did not return until we were about to leave in the late afternoon. He was evidently very pleased with the results of his afternoon's business, and was in high spirits. We gathered that he had spent his time more profitably than we had as we sat among the rapids panning sand through our fingers. I showed him two pieces of glassy-looking stone that I had picked out and he examined them carefully under his magnifying glass and pronounced them of some value. There were plenty of stones, he said, which were valuable but not enough to be worth while exploiting commercially. Excited by my find I pressed him to be more specific about the value of my stones. He pursed his lips judiciously, 'Well,' he said, with his usual air of dead-pan seriousness. 'I should not like to commit myself too precisely. The markets are constantly in such a state of flux that one does not like to feel inclined to say one can promise a certain price. But for these two together, roughly, I repeat roughly, I think it possible that you might get about one half of one farthing.' Suddenly his rubbery face crumpled up and with a roar of delight at his own fooling he threw the stones into the Mazaruni.

All the way back to Kamarang he kept us entertained with stories of his pork-knocking days, his finds and his failures. Now he had given it up, he said, for he was too old for the rough life and he screwed up his face so that he looked like a very old monkey. Then he straightened it out again and told us that he had become

Typical savannah country in the Rupununi
An Amerindian woman making a cassava grater
Baking cassava bread

instead a business man, a real business executive in the bush, and he looked very important and knowing. Even as he talked about his wealth and business connections he seemed to be laughing at himself for talking such nonsense. Yet his tales of his visits to New York to market his diamonds had the ring of truth.

He told us too about the Amerindians' way of life, relating with relish how the women made their cassiri drink by chewing cassava and spitting out the juice into a bowl. We knew this already, but he added all kinds of embellishments, assuring us that it was most hygienic because only the young women did the chewing as their teeth were still firm in their mouths and so not likely to be spat out into the drink by mistake.

As he talked the sky was darkening and the black water appeared to thicken. The steep sides of the bank closed in on us and the distant mountains seemed to grow nearer. It was night when we landed at Kamarang.

In the morning we set off for a trek along a forest trail. It was difficult going yet once or twice we saw evidence that others had been at work before us. For along the trail we would see a railed-off enclosure where a bore hole had been sunk to test the ground, for it was hoped that the Kamarang area might be rich in low grade bauxite. It hardly seemed possible that one day the dense forest might draw back and the place be noisy with machinery and full of the activity of a modern industry. Indeed there was a profound sense of remoteness from the world in the deep forests beyond Kamarang. More than any kind of terrain the bush gives this sense of isolation; in it one finds that international crises become completely unreal and impossible to believe in. I had recently reviewed a book on nuclear warfare, which explained with inescapable logic how atomic weapons would spread until their use in war was simply a matter of time. In Georgetown, as in Europe, it was not difficult to believe. But here, where as far as the eye could see in any direction nothing was visible but infinite forest. the place seemed too impenetrable for even destruction to penetrate, too distant from civilization for the events of the outside world to influence it in any way.

Yet in such remote places one gets a strong sense of the smallness of man, of the very short time he has spent on this earth. One really can believe that of its two thousand million years of existence, he has occupied the world for less than one million. In civilization, surrounded by human achievements, the world seems too man-

The waterfalls at Orinduik on the Brazilian border.
Kamarang by Dakota. Mr. Caesar third from right; author extreme right.
Nightfall over the Mazaruni at Kamarang.

dominated for this to be quite credible. Like the distance of the stars, one knows it as a fact but does not really believe it. It does not exert the kind of influence on one's outlook that a fully comprehended truth does.

In the bush, however, as in all places where man has made little impression, where rock and tree are dominant, it is quite easy to realize that man is no more than a short episode in the long history of the earth. The dinosaurs ruled the world for a hundred million years before their great size and strength proved insufficient compensation for their tiny brains. They gave way to mammals whose enlarged craniums enabled the development of far greater brains until man, the most intelligent of all the mammals, inherited the earth so successfully that we sometimes forget that it has not always been so. In the bush we remember it. I found myself wondering, as I walked under the giant trees, what kind of creature would evolve next, once man, his intelligence having proved of no avail without the capacity to live with his own kind, has destroyed himself. Presumably it would need to be a creature devoid of the instinct to destroy. Perhaps its reproductive functions would be more fairly divided between the sexes (assuming that there still were sexes) so that all the race had an inbred sense of how precious a thing is a life, instead of only half the race, as under the present arrangements. But now I was in the realm of fantasy and found myself a long way behind the rest of the party, so I left the contemplation of the next stage of evolution and concentrated instead on grappling with the thick undergrowth and long lianas which hung down from the trees and tripped us up like ropes strung across our path.

We had to be back at Kamarang by midday as the plane was due to come and pick us up at two o'clock in the afternoon. As we sat down to lunch a message came that the cloud had lifted from Roraima so we all dashed to the viewing place only to find that the cloud had come down again. After lunch we took down our hammocks, packed up our clothes and pots and pans and empty crates and boxes and walked back to the air strip. Here we waited and the plane failed to arrive. It was very hot and unshaded.

At five o'clock we we were told that since the plane was delayed we might have to stay the night, for planes cannot take off from these unlit strips after dark and it is anyway dangerous to fly through the mountains at night. There was no means, of course, of contacting families in Georgetown and those who had come without them became very concerned, knowing how anxious their relations would be when they failed to return. Moreover we had no more supplies. We had little energy either and the thought of unpacking and slinging hammocks again daunted us. We strained our eyes towards the west as the light began to fade, and then we saw it, the faintest dot above the horizon, our Dakota.

Even as he jumped out of the plane the pilot shouted to us that he could take off only if the plane was loaded and everyone on board within six minutes, otherwise we should have to stay the night. As it had taken us about three-quarters of an hour to unload when we arrived he seemed to be asking the impossible. However, with scarcely a word spoken the men made a chain and handed up the crates and boxes and cases for stowing and women organized themselves carrying the lighter baggage. Then the twenty of us filed into the plane with not an inch of space between us or a moment's delay. We were all in our seats and ready for take off five and a half minutes after the plane had landed. It was almost enough to make one believe that human beings have as much instinct for co-operation as they have for causing chaos. We left immediately and were safely out of the mountains before all light faded from the sky.

We did not expect to get to Kaieteur, the great waterfall of Guyana. We were of course familiar with its contours, the narrow straight sides and the tremendous perpendicular drop of more than seven hundred feet, which is five times as great as Niagara, for it is depicted on postage stamps and bedecks every piece of writing about Guyana. Yet this national symbol has never actually been seen by the great majority of the Guyanese people, for it is deep in the mountains of the Interior and the journey to it involves a week's strenuous travelling by boat, lorry and foot. We did not have the week. It can also now be reached by Grumman, an amphibian aircraft which holds six passengers, but that costs several hundred dollars.*

We had resigned ourselves to not seeing Kaieteur when it so happened, towards the end of our tour, that the work at the sugar terminal was inspected by visitors from London. In true Guyanese style the first thought of our clients was how the visitors should be entertained and we were asked what we thought they would most like to do. Whereupon we naturally gave it as our considered

*The Kaieteur air strip has now been repaired so that the Grumman is no longer the only aircraft that can land at the Falls.

opinion that they would more than anything like to fly by Grumman to Kaieteur—with us, of course. And so it was arranged.

I had often seen the Grumman taking off from the Demerara but the sight never failed to be exciting. The little craft ran down the runway, churned into the water and just when it seemed impossible for it to do anything but go on being a boat it rose gradually from the water and took to its wings. The more technically minded did not seem to feel this wonder at the dual character of the amphibian craft, but I always found something a little uncanny about a boat flying, or an aeroplane chugging through the water.

Our pilot, Harry Wendt, manipulated the Grumman as if it was a part of himself: one felt he could literally do anything with it. With Colonel Art Williams, an American like himself, he started in the early thirties the air company, consisting originally of one old Ireland Wasp and expanding until it included three Dakotas and one Grumman, to fly people to the Interior which had hitherto been inaccessible except by foot or boat. Their enterprise thus made possible the exploration of the Interior. They acted as pilots, mechanics and organizers, doing everything themselves. Their company was bought by the Government in 1955 and Art Williams returned to America but Harry Wendt remained as a pilot. We looked down at the uninterrupted forest below, in which there would be small hope of survival if one was forced to land and asked him if he had ever had an accident. Once, he said, he had found himself obliged to make a forced landing in the old Ireland Wasp. He had looked around for somewhere to land but the bush was impenetrable and he could not make out the smallest clearing, so he looked again and chose a nice comfortable looking tree and brought the craft down on the top of that. A perfect landing it was, he told us, and nobody any the worse. 'Well,' he added as an afterthought, 'one chap did break his leg, but that was when he was climbing down the tree.'

We flew over the forests and mountains, seeing even more clearly than we had in the Dakota. We flew up rivers and saw other great falls, for in this land of vast mountain ranges there are many great falls in level of water as one plateau of rock gives way to another. As we flew over we could see their spray rising white above them. At last we flew up the Potaro river and saw Kaieteur in the distance. We flew over it and then up the river above for about half a mile, dropping lower and lower until suddenly the water seemed to rise and hit us underneath. Foam flew up all round us and then as it settled we found ourselves sitting calmly in the Grumman, now turned boat, on the river.

There was a little clearing by the river with a house whose owner now came down to the water to help us out. There were some shy children outside the house and a few very confident parrots but we did not stop as we had only a short time to see the fall, so set off immediately down the path that led to it.

It was a wide, mossy path, green and cool and dark under the trees. It was hard to believe that we were in the same country as Georgetown; we only had to shut our eyes to feel we were back in an English wood, smelling of peat and damp vegetation. There were ferns growing under the trees at the side of the path and everything that grew was thick and lush and green. A tame trumpet bird followed at our heels like a dog, running alongside now and then to peck at my red canvas shoes, trumpeting cheerfully as if it had found something good to eat. It followed us for a while, pecking and trumpeting but then found the going too fast and stopped in the middle of the path and watched us disappear round the corner.

We walked about half a mile through woodland that smelled of peat and home and all the time we could hear the crashing of water in the distance and suddenly came upon Kaieteur. The effect was startling despite the fact that we had thought ourselves prepared for the phenomenal, which I suppose we should have realized is impossible. We stood on a little natural platform of rock on a level with the top of the fall. The river above us looked quite shallow and toffee-coloured with its tawny vegetation. It seemed to move steadily towards the fall and then hesitate, almost to stop flowing on the very brink—as if what it saw made it want to draw back—and then crash over the edge to drop straight down into the rocks seven hundred feet below, gathering momentum as it fell. The effect of the water was hypnotic. Our eyes caught up in its fall, we stood, mesmerized, lost in this giant cascade of water, which above the fall was just a calm river and below no more than a pile of rocks with foam and mist rising for a few hundred feet above them. But in between Kaieteur seemed to have a life of its own, wild and raging and awe-inspiring. One could not but feel its colossal power, which drew the spectator towards it. Alone on the rock platform, it would be hard to resist the impulse to let oneself be drawn over the edge to make the journey with the water down to the rocks. The effect is heightened by the complete isolation in which Kaieteur performs this ceaseless miracle, unbeholden and unexploited in the thick, unchanging forest. Orinduik, wide and serene, was certainly far more beautiful. Niagara, which we saw on our way home, more spectacular and showy. But Kaieteur was in a quite different category from either. They were as one imagines great waterfalls to be: Kaieteur was something mysterious and inexplicable.

There is always a rainbow over Kaieteur and when we were there we saw also a completely circular rainbow on the sheer side of the gorge below. It formed for a few minutes only and was gone. As we walked back down the path I knew that the chance of ever seeing again such a sight as Kaieteur was as remote as seeing again a circular rainbow. We walked back under the arched trees, silenced by what we had seen.

Back at the riverside we said goodbye to the shy children, were bitten by the confident parrots and saw no sign of the trumpet bird. We climbed into the Grumman and made our way down the river, moving steadily towards the fall. We approached so near that it seemed inevitable that we should crash over the edge, but just as we shut our eyes and waited to be dashed to pieces the Grumman slid off the surface of the water and we were in the air. Soon we were flying over mountains and forests and finally we found our way home to the muddy waters of the Demerara and were back in the world of everyday things.

CHAPTER ELEVEN

Sugar, Rice and Bauxite

These expeditions by aeroplane into the far Interior were necessarily few and far between. Usually we explored nearer home and went by boat. The going was slow and the distances relatively great so it was only worth while making all the arrangements that such outings involved if we could manage to go when a public holiday was tagged on to a weekend. Fortunately Guyana has more of such holidays than any other country. We once reckoned them up and found that there was only one month in the year that was not so relieved. On all of them—from Labour Day to Commonwealth Day—we would think pityingly of our friends and relations in England going unwittingly to work as we organized our stores and began to pack the *Canje Queen*.

It was on one of these holidays which fell on a Friday that we chugged our way across the Demerara and out to sea, following the coastline northwards, across the wide estuary of the Essequibo where we picnicked on an uninhabited island. By evening we had reached Adventure on the far coast. We stayed in the court house at the nearby village of Suddie, which was free of criminals and judges as the law was on vacation. We spent the next day exploring the waters of the Ituribisi which are notable for their hot and cold lakes. We followed the river until it opened out into what seemed to be a wide lake. It was shallow and we grounded on a sand bank well away from the shore. We got out of the boat and began to wade through the cool water to the land. Suddenly the water was warm and then uncomfortably hot. Various explanations have been put forward for this natural phenomenon, but none of them seems altogether convincing. The most likely, we thought, was that there were springs in the lake, but if so nobody has managed to locate them.

Two incidents only from this expedition remain fresh in my mind. The first was coming to a low bridge over the river as we made our way back to Suddie at the end of the day and finding that the *Canje Queen* was too tall to go under. We debated what we should do; if we went back and found another way we should not be back at the court house that night. We decided that without her sturdy wooden canopy the boat might just go under the bridge. We unpacked all her contents and carried them round to the far side of the bridge while the men got to work on the *Canje Queen,* unpicking her superstructure. This piece of carpentry took a good hour and they were very weary as they carried it to the other side of the bridge and dumped it down on the bank. Dick went back to bring the somewhat stunted-looking *Canje Queen* under the bridge. We were astonished to see that she slid under easily with several feet to spare. While we had been working on her, the tide had turned and the level of the water had been quietly dropping until, had we only noticed, the boat would have gone under easily top and all. Hot, oily, exasperated, the men got to work on restoring the boat and the rest of us decided that it was one of those occasions when it is more tactful not to laugh till breakfast time the next morning.

The other incident concerned our journey home, when everything went wrong. We began by striking a sand bank and sticking on it for two hours. By the time we had got going the tide was against us and the sea so choppy that the *Canje Queen*'s engine got clogged with sand and failed. In the sudden, frightening silence and with night approaching we began to drift out to sea. We held torches while the men probed and cajoled the engine back to life. This happened three times: the third time it was pitch dark and the engine took half an hour to repair. Just as the engine got going the last of the torches failed.

A more peaceful expedition was one up the Abary to try to observe the Canje Pheasant, a rare creature which is only to be found in this limited area. We went by car along the East Coast Road, with which we were now so familiar that it no longer shocked us. It still, however, made us uncomfortable with its mounds and pot holes which had to be avoided by adopting a wild, swerving course. The car was constantly on the bounce as we were tossed about on the uneven surface. There were periods of relief when we came to two parallel strips of concrete down the centre of the road, one made for each wheel. Suddenly the going became smooth and pleasant and dust no longer choked us. There was only one snag: sometimes we met a car coming in the opposite direction. The highway code lays down no rules about who has the right of way in such a head-on encounter and the system seemed to be that the smaller and weaker vessel gave way, the reverse of the more chivalrous law of the sea. The honour of both sides was only satisfied, however, by hanging on until the last available moment before skidding off the tramlines down into the dust.*

After about an hour the land became increasingly marshy; the draining of the coastlands was one of those problems about which much was spoken but little done. Village after village was surrounded with water, each house isolated on its stilts with a plank across to the privy. They seemed desolate and very unhealthy and the children most wretched as they stood wherever there was a pile of mud just out of the water to accommodate them.

This proved to be the wettest of all our outings. The savannahs up the Abary, where Bookers have a cattle ranch, is always a damp spot and as we made our way up the canal which leads to them we could see all around us the partly flooded fields. The cows stood knee deep in water, but appeared to take no harm. In the past many calves used to be lost as they were drowned immediately they were born. Now, however, embankments have been built and the cows climb to the top when they are about to give birth so that their calves are delivered on dry land. The cows were beautiful beasts compared with those we were accustomed to seeing in the rest of Guyana, but there was something strange and unreal about them as they stood in the water, staring at us as we passed. One could almost imagine that they were hiding webbed feet.

We kept a constant look out all the way for the Canje Pheasant which we had been warned is an elusive bird, easier to hear than to see as the trees make a perfect camouflage for its brown body. We were disappointed that we did not even manage to hear its call.

The little house where we stayed had the canal on one side and the river on the other. The other two sides were surrounded by flood water. We went as near as we could by boat and then the rest of the way over planks. One by one I noticed the party break into a dance as they walked the last plank to the house. They jumped about in an inebriated way and disappeared with a final leap up the front steps. As I reached the spot I suddenly felt red hot jabs in my feet and ankles. The attack was ferocious and soon I too was leaping and jumping as the rest had done along the narrow and uncertain piece of wood. The plank was covered with savage red ants which had been forced on to it by the rising water and were

*This road has now been hard-topped.

now doubly annoyed at being walked on by this succession of human feet. In the sanctuary of the house we slapped and brushed and killed until the last of the ants was slaughtered. We felt strangely marooned with water all round us and the one bridge to the outer world occupied by red ants. However, within half an hour they had disappeared without a trace and we were able to venture out.

It poured continuously for two days and nights, but having come so far we felt obliged to see what we could and, steaming under polythene capes and wrapped about with raincoats and plastic sheeting, and holding umbrellas over our heads, we set off by boat next day, with the superintendent of the ranch, downstream.

He took us, on the way, to see an old East Indian who had formerly worked on the ranch and now had been given a light job as night-watchman, for the river has to be closely watched for cattle thieves.

This stretch of the river was infested with pirai, as we had discovered when they persisted in biting through the steel hooks of the fishing lines we hopefully trailed behind the boat. We were, therefore, horrified, as we approached the East Indian's house to see the old man come down to the river and wade out to meet us. He stood in the water, among the rushes, talking to us, in a most animated and friendly way, quite disregarding all our entreaties that he should get out of the water. 'Pirai?' he said. 'Day don't touch me. Day don't never do me no harm. I tell you dis ting,' he went on confidentially, resting his chin on the edge of the boat, 'Maybe is de juju, maybe is dat me too little and tough, but pirai day don't touch me all dese years I been walking in de water.'

He was completely confident in his inviolability but we were less so and hurried on so that he had no cause to put it any longer to the test.

Further downstream we found an empty house which had once belonged to one of the ranchers. We decided to land there and so be able to eat our sodden lunch unencumbered by our waterproof trappings. It was a relief to get out of the noisy, teeming rain and we thought how pleasant this remote and peaceful house must be in drier seasons. As we sat on the verandah we noticed that several doors led off it and after lunch, it was discovered that behind one of them lay a proper working water closet. Knowing my horror of those awful little excursions into the bush which were a necessary part of all our outings, I was invited to be the first to enjoy this unexpected amenity.

It was a dark little place and I was well installed before my eyes, adjusting themselves to the blackness, began to make out certain shapes on the walls. I heard piping notes, gobbling noises, squeaks and grunts and suddenly realized that I was in some kind of frogs' home. There were little tree frogs on the ceiling, frogs all over the walls and huge toads in the pan. They must have come to regard the little room as their own dark and shady pool and been surprised at this invasion of their privacy. For me it was a moment of indescribable, immobilizing horror as I waited for them to fall on me from all sides. Then I rose into the air, powered by some electric current of fear, and, clothes still in immodest disarray, leapt into the midst of the astonished company outside. It was, I realize on reflection, a frog-like exit, a leap made still in the squatting position, with bulging eyes and only a long dry croak by way of explanation.

Having seen no sign of the Canje Pheasant on the way up to the Abary, we lost hope and did not even try to see or hear it on the way home. We were completely taken by surprise, therefore, when we suddenly heard its call. Although it seemed very near we could not see it among the foliage but soon heard and saw many others which obligingly flew about between the trees so that we could locate them despite the fact that their big brown bodies merge so perfectly into a background of branches. Fortunately the rain had stopped and we took yards of cine film showing the rare creatures among the trees and an extravagant number of coloured slides. Later, when the photographs returned from being developed in England, we found we had a fine record of trees and banks, close-ups of thick foliage and dense undergrowth, but not one sign of a bird. We looked at them from all angles, we twisted them around and turned them upside down, we showed the film so slowly that we practically set it alight, but still there was not a Canje Pheasant to be seen. We tried to discover a beak or a tail, we searched among the trees as if we were trying to solve one of those puzzle pictures for children where animals are drawn at unlikely angles in unlikely surroundings, but all in vain.

The boatman whose job it was to look after the *Canje Queen* was an East Indian called Krishnon. I remarked to him once that it was a pity that there were not more places one could get to from Georgetown in a day. We particularly wanted a gentle day's outing as we had an old lady staying with us and we wanted to show her something of the country without inflicting too much physical discomfort on her. Krishnon promptly assured me that there were such places. We might, for example, go up a sugar canal off the East Coast Road, not far from Georgetown. He warmed to his theme and with typical Guyanese optimism assured me that it would all be all too easy. His aunt, who lived on the canal he had in mind, would lend us her friend's horse, a very quiet one that she had borrowed before and which would walk very gently along the tow path by the canal pulling us in a canoe which his aunt would hire for us. We must make it a Sunday for that is the only day when the estates were not cutting cane, otherwise the canal would be blocked with the big punts which carry the sugar cane. All we had to do was drive up the East Coast Road and he, Krishnon, and his aunt would have everything ready.

On a prearranged Sunday, therefore, we bumped our way up the East Coast Road, the sea wall on our left, paddy fields on our right and dust all round us. In the flooded swampy land just off the road women were wading up to their waists in water, trailing nets to catch fish no bigger than minnows to add interest to their rice dinner. Now and then another red earth road joined us on the right and a canal with a few houses alongside.

Soon we turned up such a road and found, among the row of little wooden houses, the one that belonged to Krishnon's aunt. She turned out to be a highly excitable East Indian lady, much preoccupied with her new granddaughter whom we went inside to admire. She had several daughters in there too and they were all so equally proud of the baby that we never discovered which was the mother. They all talked a great deal and offered us refreshments and it was altogether rather difficult to get the conversation round to punts and horses. Krishnon, who had said he would travel up with us, had not appeared and we heard that he was indisposed, which we knew from experience meant that he had been celebrating with rum the night before. When we did finally broach the subject of our promised transport, his aunt rushed away saying she had everything ready and would be back just now, a common Guyanese expression which does not guarantee celerity of any kind. She returned about half an hour later leading a wild-eyed, rearing horse. She explained that the very gentle one that Krishnon had referred to was unfortunately not available, but this one was also an excellent animal. Of course, she admitted, clinging desperately to the end of an inadequate length of rope as the horse moved up into a perpendicular position, he was a little bit more lively than the other, but all the same he was a good horse, a very good horse indeed. Besides, she added optimistically, he would soon tire and calm down when he had been pulling us for a while. The horse reared up again, as if to deny it, and waved its front paws about and showed its long yellow teeth in a vicious grin.

Krishnon's aunt then told us that there was another little difficulty; the big punt she had hoped to hire for us was not available either, but never mind, she had hired two small ones instead and if we tied them together and the horse pulled the front one then of course we should all get along nicely. As for the horse, we need not worry, she had sent for another nephew to guide him on the tow path since Krishnon was indisposed.

We loaded up the second punt with all our crates and hampers and one member of the party while the rest of us got into the first one. Dick tied the two together with a length of rope and then tied our punt to the horse. Being tethered to such an animal gave me a strange sense of insecurity which was not dispelled by the sight of Krishnon's aunt's other nephew. We had imagined that he would be somebody of approximately Krishnon's vintage, forgetting the wide range of East Indian families. He turned out to be a tiny little boy who hardly reached to the horse's knees. But he looked very confident and brandished a stick in a manly fashion.

For the first hundred yards of our way the canal ran through the village and our progress was observed with some interest. This was not surprising, for no sooner had we jerked into motion than we realized that Krishnon's aunt's optimism about the smooth progress of two punts tied together was ill-founded. As the horse dashed forwards and our punt plunged ahead in the water it created such a wash that the second punt, attached unfortunately by a hook at the side, was hit so hard by the wash that it could only progress very jerkily sideways in a manner more befitting a crab than a punt. Not since my own abortive efforts on the Isis have I seen a punt behave in such an extraordinary way, twisting from side to side, gyrating at great speed, almost standing on its end. Its sole occupant tried valiantly to keep a straight course, dabbing at the water with his paddle.

Neither had we realized that when we left the village the tow path would become very narrow, overgrown and frequently blocked with trees. The horse invariably chose to go at full canter on the far side of any obstacles and the punt would crash up against the bank, while we all watched to see if the horse would take off into the bush, dragging the punts and all of us across the tow path after him. 'Cutlass' the boy would cry and Dick would stand with the cutlass poised ready to sever our connection with the horse if need be. He always postponed doing this until the last possible moment for he is fond of rope, and averse to cutting a good piece of it before he is quite convinced that the only alternative is certain death.

In fact the horse usually did repent at the last moment and, after subjecting us to a terrifying succession of bumps and crashes against the bank, would stand still stamping and snorting, and finally reverse back on to the tow path. Only once did it take off into the bush and that was when the little boy, tired of waiting when it was having one of its snorting sessions, decided to hit it with his stick. The horse can hardly have felt the infantile blow, but possibly understood the intention and, rearing up, plunged off among the trees. The punt rose on its end and was almost perpendicular with its passengers hanging on to its sides, before Dick could bring himself to do irrevocable damage to his rope. He regretted it instantly for the horse, evidently deciding that the sortie into the bush was no fun without the punts, quietened and returned obediently to the side of the canal.

After this we made our way peacefully for a while observed only by an occasional child fishing with a huge net on a hoop, who would stare at us with solemn brown eyes. It was then that we encountered the last—and insoluble—problem. When Krishnon told us that on Sunday the canal would be free of sugar punts because the estates would not be working, he had forgotten that on that day the village people are allowed to cut their own cane and take it in the punts to the factories where it is bought from them by Bookers. We rounded a corner to find the canal completely blocked by massive steel punts being loaded with sugar cane.

We disembarked so that we could go over to the field and watch the cutting operation. We had to push our way through a stretch of undergrowth that bordered the canal, wobble over a bridge that was no more than a thickish pole laid over a river and cross a field of stubble which remained after the cane had been cut.

Since it was the season of cane cutting we had for days previously seen the fields on fire. Before the cane is cut the fields are set alight in order to get rid of the leaves and 'trash 'as well as to clear away rats and snakes. Not all sugar growers do this; the practice is, I believe, frowned on in the West Indian Islands, but in Guyana it is universal; the traveller can only be grateful, for to see these great fields burning with a marvellous orange glow is an unusual and beautiful sight.

The cane cutters then hack down the smoke-darkened cane with their cutlasses and carry it in great bundles on their shoulders to the punt. In this case, that involved, as I have said, walking a distance across a field of stubble, swaying over a pole bridge and finally stooping through the undergrowth to reach the canal. We who walked unburdened found it hot and tiring and we watched the cane cutters with respect as they made their way under their great unwieldly loads doggedly and without pausing for rest. It is desperately exhausting work and we realized now why one of the problems into which medical research is being done is how to avoid collapse from exhaustion by the men who do this work, the heaviest of the sugar industry.

The barges into which the sugar cane was thrown are pulled by mules which plod with massive strength along the tow path pulling a chain of perhaps ten barges, each one of which may weigh ten tons when laden. The greatest effort is to get the punts moving; once they are under way the mules seem to pull without over-exerting themselves.

Later we saw what happened when the barges reached the factory. Across the bottom and sides of the barge are chains on top of which the cane has been thrown, so that when the chains are raised they lift up the whole barge-load of cane in one huge bundle. A crane places it on a weighing machine and then drops it on to a conveyor belt which carries it into the factory building. Here the cane is crushed by a succession of huge rollers so that more and more juice is extracted. The fibrous stuff that remains—the 'bagasse'—is then used for burning as fuel in the factory, thus providing energy to work the boilers.

The sugar is now in the form of dirty juice which must be purified by boiling. Further boiling converts the juice into brown crystals. A by-product of this process is molasses which is fermented to make rum, Guyana's national drink. Each sugar factory therefore originally had a distillery attached to it, though Bookers have now centralized their distilling at Uitvlugt and Rose Hall.

After further processing, conveyor belts carry the sugar to the far end of the factory where it is put into sacks, tied up, weighed and loaded into punts or, in some cases, lorries if the rest of the journey is to be made by road. When the sugar terminal was finished the sugar was no longer put into sacks but sent in bulk for storage at the terminal before being loaded automatically into bulk sugar boats.

The sugar at this stage is a dirty grey colour. One of the things that surprised us when we got back to England was the startling whiteness of the sugar for we had so completely forgotten what refined sugar looks like. Since no sugar is refined in Guyana, we used to get it clean before making it into drinks, or anything else where the foreign bodies would show, by melting it in water and straining it. Otherwise the lime juice would be afloat with debris. I realized one of the reasons why it was so dirty when I went round a sugar factory and noticed the scant respect with which the sugar is treated. As we climbed up steps made of metal bars or walked along high metal gangways, I noticed the scrapings from the shoes in front falling down on to the conveyor belts of sugar below.

Canals are all important in Guyana's sugar industry, both for transport and irrigation; on each estate there are hundreds of miles of canal which have to be constantly maintained for they very quickly become overgrown. Apart from the main canals, such as the one we travelled on, which take the sugar barges from the fields to the factory, there are others, fed by ditches which run across the sugar fields, which are designed entirely for drainage and carry waste water out to sea.

We made our way back in the evening rather more sedately than we had travelled in the morning, for the horse was feeling less frisky and the little boy had abandoned his stick and was now riding on the horse's back. Krishnon's aunt was looking out anxiously for us and seemed surprised at our safe return. Beside her stood Krishnon himself, now quite recovered from his little indisposition.

When Krishnon told us that he had an uncle who lived up the Mahaicony river and whom we might visit if we would like an interesting and pleasant day's outing, we were naturally not very enthusiastic. However, it turned out that we should not this time be dependent on transport provided by any of Krishnon's relations; in fact it was simply a matter of going to see him and his rice farm.

Rice was introduced into Guyana by the East Indians who came to provide indentured labour on the sugar estates after the abolition

Sugar. East Indian workers cutting the cane with cutlasses.
Loading cane into punts.
Cane being unloaded and weighed at the factory.

Cellular rafts being sunk as foundations for the sugar store in Georgetown.

Inside a modern sugar store: the sugar has been dropped from a conveyor belt and awaits export by bulk carriers.

of slavery. It had been their staple diet at home and they naturally grew it in the land of their adoption. In Guyana, of course, they were only allowed to grow it on the poorest land which was not wanted for sugar. It was usually the worst drained. The fact that rice land lacked good drainage made its production a very chancy business, very much dependent on the weather. The output varied from year to year far more than one might reasonably expect. This uncertainty very much delayed the use of modern methods and machinery in the industry; farmers were naturally unwilling to take too many risks.

For the great difference between the production of sugar and rice is that whereas sugar is grown on great estates, owned by Bookers and the much smaller Demerara Company, rice is for the most part cultivated by small farmers of East Indian descent holding about seven acres of land.

There are, however, some few who hold hundreds of acres cultivated by modern mechanical methods. These men are among the richest in the country. One owned a house on the East Coast Road where we had noticed that the burnt earth surface of the road, elsewhere dry and dusty, was always kept damp. Jubraj told us that the farmer was so rich that he could employ men to water the road in front of his house all day to prevent dust from being raised in the vicinity of his house and garden.

We travelled along this road again to get to Krishnon's uncle, for he lived on a large farm up the Mahaicony river. This is the main rice growing area of Guyana and the centre of the Rice Development Company which was established in 1953 to pioneer the large-scale production of rice by mechanical means. The company runs two rice mills which process not only its own paddy but also that of individual farmers. The company also lends machinery to farmers. All the rice, except that retained by the farmers for their own use, is sold to the Rice Marketing Board, which markets it. It used to be sold almost entirely to the West Indies, but since 1961 a great deal has been sold to Cuba and other markets. An American firm has recently offered to sell any surplus rice and has found purchasers in West Africa.

As a result of drainage schemes, increased mechanization and guaranteed markets, there has been a phenomenal rise in the production of rice. It has doubled in the last decade and since so much is exported this has been of great importance to Guyana's economy. Although sugar is, of course, still the most important crop, the value of whose exports was sixty-two million dollars in 1967, rice is now a second crop which, with exports worth twenty-five million dollars in 1967, accounts for fifteen per cent of Guyana's exports. This is a most encouraging development and helps to reduce the country's former dependence on sugar, for at one time it was virtually a one-product colony. Now, although sugar production is increasing steadily, sugar, which once accounted for about seventy per cent of Guyana's exports, now accounts for only thirty-three per cent. This is a far healthier position for the economy to be in.

We had noticed as we drove through the East Indian villages of the coastlands that most of the people we saw were daubed with pink patches. It was the feast of Phagwar, a Hindu celebration. Originally Hindus sprayed each other with red water to symbolize the shedding of Homolcar's blood, but now it has, among the majority, become simply an excuse to chase anyone they can and throw pink liquid at them. It is a holiday time of much drinking and jollification and giving of presents, reminiscent, both in the manner in which it is celebrated and in the way its original meaning has become somewhat remote to the majority of people, of Christmas.

When Krishnon had arranged our outing he had forgotten about Phagwar. No work was going on at his uncle's farm: everyone was either celebrating Phagwar or recovering from the previous day's celebrations. We were taken to see a great machine, however, a combine harvester which Krishnon's uncle had recently bought for thousands of dollars and met also his grandfather who was in charge of it. We found him perched up high on the machine and the family told us that he spent practically all his time up there. He spoke very little English and could not read or write. He showed us the impressive tome of instructions that had come with the harvester and smiled as he remarked that he could not read them. Yet his son, who could do so, left the care of the machine entirely to the old man who seemed to have some kind of instinctive understanding of mechanical things.

Krishnon's uncle had also recently bought a motor boat and insisted upon taking the men up the river in it while the rest of us prepared a picnic lunch. They were away for two hours and, what was worse, had taken the tin opener and the bottle opener with them. We paced up and down on the bank wondering what accident had happened to them, and getting hungrier and hungrier until we remembered that we had sausage rolls. Thereafter we gazed up the river and ate sausage rolls. One of the children of the household approached and we offered him one which he took with interest, but before he could eat it one of his elders appeared and took it from him. He did not query its removal and guiltily I remembered that Hindus are forbidden to eat beef.

At last the rest of our party returned, in high spirits; indeed so high that when the boat stopped rather suddenly they all fell overboard. They told us that they had not gone far up river when they had been hailed by one of Krishnon's uncle's neighbours who was having a Phagwar party on the bank. They had had to drink an immense amount of rum; apparently it is bad manners to drink less than a pint at Phagwar.

The ownership of motor boats seemed to be the latest status symbol up the Mahaicony river. In the afternoon we were taken to visit a neighbour who had just bought a speed boat in which he took us in turns for a spin on the river. He was a very solemn and dignified East Indian and his boat was called *Elvis*. It seemed an incongruously modern way of celebrating Phagwar even though good old-fashioned rum was also much in evidence. Afterwards we made our way back to Krishnon's uncle's house for refreshment which turned out to be more rum.

I noticed that the children of the household were extremely well disciplined. In the afternoon when we all sat in the big living room of the farm, they brought out their new toys, presents for Phagwar, to show the children in our party. When the latter began to treat them rather roughly one of the little East Indian boys quietly collected them up and took them away, returning with older toys for the guests to play with. He did it so unobtrusively, with such adult tact, that I do not think anybody else noticed. The children responded at once to the slightest word from their elders and there was no evidence of the casual equality of English families.

This strong family sense and the patriarchal status of the father was something we had often remarked upon in Hindu families. Singh stood in awe even of his rapscallion father and any instructions that his mother gave him about our garden were carried out much more promptly than my own. I was aware of it again at the wedding we were invited to in Basdeo's family. His elder brother was to marry a girl from the other side of the Demerara and we were invited to the wedding.

We had no idea what kind of ceremony or occasion it would be and no way of finding out since direct questions are somehow very hard to ask of an East Indian peasant and would not, anyway, get a direct answer. It was unfortunate that the ferry we were to cross by was so crowded that we had to wait for the next one and so arrived, as we thought, a few minutes late. We need not have been anxious for as we drove along the road at the other side we were hailed by a crowd of men who were also on their way to the wedding and to whom we gave lifts both inside the car and on the roof and bonnet. They showed us the way to the girl's home, but there was no sign yet of any particular gathering. Basdeo met us, however, and put us in charge of his cousin who, he said, would look after us.

The cousin was a curious youth with the knowing smile of a Leonardo satyr. He led us up the steps to the house and presented us to a large, elaborately dressed lady who stood at the top.

'She is supposed to be the bride's mother,' he pronounced enigmatically, leaving us in some doubt as to whether she really was the bride's mother or if we were seeing some kind of pageant in which she was playing the part. In turn we took hold of her limp and unresponsive hand and moved it up and down slightly, before letting it fall again to her side.

The cousin then led us to a man at the other side of the verandah. 'He is supposed to be the bride's father,' he said. This time we did not try to shake hands but murmured something about its being nice to be there.

The cousin then opened a door off the verandah and pushed us into a tiny room which was full of women and clothes. One of them was in a frightful state of disarray, her clothes and hair looking as if they had recently been subjected to a force eight gale. Her eyes were wild and she seemed to be undergoing some kind of unpleasant treatment from her room mates.

Basdeo's cousin singled her out for introduction. 'She is supposed to be the bride,' he intoned with his ambiguous smile.

The atmosphere was strained to breaking point; indeed the whole house felt so curious that we still did not know if we were among the real wedding party or play actors. The three of us now walked back across the verandah. Looking over the edge we saw that many more people had arrived and were walking about under the house, around the yard and over the few flowers and vegetables that were struggling to maintain some kind of life in it. 'And those,' Basdeo's cousin observed sadly, 'are supposed to be our friends.'

Still bemused and wondering what kind of elaborate charade

we were involved in, we were greatly relieved to see Basdeo's familiar face. He was real enough anyway. He said he had come to take us to another house and we followed him, wondering if the wedding which was due to have begun an hour ago had already taken place. He led us to a house where we were given a big leaf like a rhubarb leaf and taken to sit on a verandah. Basdeo's father now appeared and we all sat down round a little table holding our rhubarb leaves on our knees. Soon various delicacies of curry were brought in and put on to the leaves for us to eat. We were given spoons, although East Indian peasants usually eat with their fingers, a habit which our African staff used to deplore, but which, it struck me, must seem to those who are accustomed to doing so much more hygienic than using a fork or spoon which a great many other people have previously had in their mouths. Basdeo, excited by having his employer to entertain, kept pressing us to eat more and more even when we refused. His father rebuked him quietly, 'It is not good to ask visitors again and again. You must accept when they say no.'

He was a big gentle man, whom we knew quite well for he lived near to us in Campbellville and in the evenings would bring his cows to crop along the roadside. He had a slow, charming smile and an air of quiet authority. He looked after us with the greatest courtesy, and we soon relaxed and stopped worrying about whether we had missed the ceremony we had come so far to attend.

When we did finally ask him if he thought it was time for the wedding, for it was now over two hours since the time we had been told it would begin, he rose slowly and said we might perhaps go to see. He took us back to the bride's house and there handed us over once again to Basdeo's cousin. A circle in front of the house had been marked out with poles and cloth hung over them to make a kind of tent. Inside this circle, we gathered from Basdeo's cousin, the ceremony would take place and outside it the supposed guests would sit or stand.

We had hoped to be able to find somewhere inconspicuous to put ourselves for the service and the sight of two wooden chairs of the kind one sits on at school in the centre of the circle rather worried us. We were afraid that this guest of honour treatment was intended for us and it turned out to be the case. We consulted urgently with Basdeo's father who had the two chairs lifted outside where we were allowed to sit with the other guests. We need not have worried, however, in case we should be conspicuously unable to follow an unfamiliar service for there is no sense of being part of a congregation at a Hindu wedding. Indeed we were not quite sure when it began or ended.

In the circle there squatted Basdeo's brother, the bridegroom. He was dressed in a pink robe which reached to the ground and on his head he wore a most elaborate crown of tinsel and shiny materials, with many dangling pieces, rather like an elaborate bird cage. These crowns are made specially for the occasion, worn only once and later buried near water.

Next to the bridegroom sat his page, also wearing a pink gown. Basdeo and his father also sat in the ring and two priests moved about, talking softly, so that we began to wonder if the service had already started, when it at last dawned on us that it would not be heralded by the arrival of the bride. The key role played by the bride in England was here taken by the groom, who was also the recipient of all the presents.

We noticed now that people were beginning to go into the ring with their gifts. They took off their shoes before doing so, because, we imagined, the ground was sanctified by the religious ceremony that was taking place on it and must therefore be given the same treatment as a temple. The presents were laid down at the feet of the groom who ignored them and their donors. I took our parcel, kicked off my shoes and entered the circle. It seemed unnatural just to dump it down in front of Basdeo's brother, so I said I hoped he would be very happy and he allowed a faint flicker of recognition to pass over his face.

We saw that many of the people gave money and soon there was a pile of it at the bridegroom's feet. There was absolute silence throughout the present giving transactions and this part of the ceremony seemed very business-like. One old lady gave a large note and asked for—and received—change.

By the little entrance to the ring sat a clerk noting down what everyone had given and its value, if it was not money. This, we were told, was in order that when the donor was married, today's groom could give a present of the same value plus ten cents. It seemed a sensible if somewhat inflationary arrangement.

We noticed that everyone gave money to the little page also and soon he too had a pile in front of him. I paid a second visit to the ring and added a belated contribution to his pile of notes.

There was now a commotion near the house as a huge white bundle appeared at the top of the steps. It was the bride wrapped in a sheet. Her mother held her firmly round the waist and steered her down the steps and into the circle where she was put to sit on a little stool next to her future husband.

It seemed that they had a priest each, like a solicitor representing each party. Seven vows were taken, the priest saying them first in Hindi and then in English for our benefit. When a vow such as the wife's promising to keep a clean house and to cook was made, the groom's priest repeated it to the girl and made sure she understood what she was promising, as if pressing his client's interests. Her priest did the same when the groom vowed to work to keep his wife and her children. One felt that the vows were clear and practical and that the marriage was meant to be as lasting and as strong as human beings could make it.

The bride and groom were then both covered with a cloth and nothing was said. After a while they were brought out and, the bride still shrouded, were tied together, the hem of the groom's robe being knotted to the corner of the girl's sheet. Thus knotted together, with the bride holding on to her husband's hips for guidance, they walked around the fire that burned in the centre of the circle, stopping at the end of each round to perform such a symbolic rite as throwing rice on the fire, to represent the food of their household. Various offerings of this kind were made and vows taken; for each one the couple walked slowly and solemnly round the fire. Nothing was hurried and there was a great deal of talk and consultation throughout the proceedings.

The assembled friends and relations did not follow what was going on very closely: they chatted among themselves, greeted friends, walked about. The chief distraction was provided by the arrival of the entertainers who kept the guests amused while the long rites were being carried out in the circle. The entertainers were two men who danced, or rather wriggled very energetically to the sound of their drum. They kept it up for several hours but the onlookers seemed not to tire of the rather unvaried diet. Afterwards the priests sauntered out of the circle and watched them too with quiet, benign smiles. Soon we concluded that the wedding must be over.

We were wrong; only the first stage was over. Hindu weddings last about a week. The bride spends a testing time with her mother-in-law to make sure that she is suitable and if not she can be returned. If she stays, however, there are more parties at the groom's house.

The following Sunday, therefore, we were asked to Basdeo's home, near to us in Campbellville. We were given a meal and introduced to a great many relations. The atmosphere was much more relaxed and normal than it had been the previous Sunday. A young, smiling East Indian girl was presented to us as the bride. We could not recognize in her the poor harassed creature we had found in that crowded little room last Sunday. Evidently she did not recognize us either for she was surprised to hear that we had been at her wedding. It seemed strange that she should have been unaware of the only two Europeans who had been introduced to her that day and I should have liked to have been told more about the prenuptial treatment of the leading lady but was afraid to ask.

The little page appeared and told us that he had bought a new suit of clothes with his wedding money and still had some left over. He had evidently found the wedding an exciting and profitable experience. He was looking forward to the next brother's betrothal.

We had asked if we might take photos during the wedding and the idea had been greeted with delight. When the cine film was returned from being developed in England, a few weeks later, we asked Basdeo's father and his family if they would like to come to see it, bringing with them the bride's family and any of their friends who might be interested. We arranged an evening and set up the projector and chairs under the house. A great many people arrived and we came down to find that they had turned all the chairs round and were sitting facing the projector.

We persuaded them to turn their backs to the machine and face the improvized screen on the wall. They watched the opening shots very quietly, but immediately anybody they knew appeared on the screen they began to laugh. All the events which they had observed without any trace of mirth when they actually happened were now greeted with hilarity; the bride and groom walking round the fire, myself taking off my shoes, the clerk valuing the presents, all were greeted with appreciative guffaws when shown on celluloid. I was interested to note that they laughed most uproariously at the antics of the entertainers whose wrigglings had amused us at the time but had been watched by the other guests with solemn absorption. As they watched the entertainers now they rocked like an audience at a Chaplin film.

Even the priests permitted themselves a laugh; they were both very impressive, handsome men who seemed to enjoy seeing their flock enjoying themselves. They really came into their own when the supper was brought on, for all our guests consulted them about what they could eat and what they could not. I had in fact been careful to see that I served only permitted foods, but one very persistent old lady refused to believe that there was not beef in her curried shrimps and was not at all happy about eating them until the priest confirmed what I had told her. Towards the end of supper one of the priests remarked that what he would really like was more film which provoked some laughter and agreement so we put it through again and this time there was even more hilarity.

It was not the first film show we had had. One evening in our very early days in Guyana we had looked at a few slides of the house and countryside that we had had developed and suddenly realized that Myra, who had been washing up, was now standing behind us in the kitchen doorway, watching entranced. The slides showed the interior of the house and she could not get over the fact that they were so exactly the same as the real thing. 'Is marvellous,' she kept saying. 'Mistress, if even day was nearly de same it would be good, but day is exact, even de pattern on de drapes is just like we have in dis room.' We thought that it would have been rather more remarkable if the pattern had come out different, but it was no good trying to explain anything like that to Myra. Instead we asked her if she would like to come with Lucille and their children to watch properly the next evening. The next day at about seven in the evening I went downstairs to find a long queue which stretched from the front door, right round the house. There were nephews and nieces and friends' sons and daughters and only three adults between them.

Many of the children were far too young to understand at all, but they enjoyed watching the projector. The youngest was called Winston, a chubby little boy of about six months. He lay happily on the floor and emptied his bladder at frequent intervals. The first time this happened, Myra, whose nephew he was, rushed out and had mopped up the pool with the dish-cloth before I had realized what she was doing. The next time Lucille, who always had a keener sense of hygiene than Myra, administered with the floor-cloth. She was particular about the floor, a lovely greenheart one which she kept highly polished. At about the sixth expedition into the kitchen for the floor-cloth she looked at Winston and exclaimed with justifiable amazement, 'Lord, madam, how dat chile do wee-wee.'

We were invited to spend our first Whitsuntide in Guyana with some English friends, a doctor and his wife, at Mackenzie, the second largest town in Guyana. It lies some sixty miles up the Demerara river and the journey there by the steamer *R. H. Carr* takes the best part of a day. It is a hot and tedious way of travelling and as we went we wondered how long it would be before the projected road from Atkinson to Mackenzie would be completed.*

There was not much to see travelling up the wide river. The first diversion was at Atkinson field, where we stopped to take on passengers and goods and to buy from the fruit vendors who crowded the stelling. Since the *R. H. Carr* stood high in the water we were well above the vendors' heads and the passengers had to lower baskets for the fruit and throw down the money. Some managed to leave their purchases until the last possible moment, so that as the boat moved away, they drew up their baskets of fruit and shouted apologies for not being able to pay.

This was the only long delay of the journey. Usually we would stop just for a few minutes in the middle of the river while a little boat or canoe joined us to take off a parcel or letters. Sometimes passengers would leave us; it was strange to see them, part of the steamer in their Georgetown suits, but suddenly incongruous in a dug-out canoe disappearing up one of the creeks into the densely wooded banks.

I was hanging over the rails idly watching two or three Africans and their luggage being helped off the *R. H. Carr* and into a canoe. One of the cases interested me; it was an unusual, silver grey coloured one.

'Look,' I remarked to Dick who was lying with his eyes closed in a deck chair. 'There's a case just like yours.'

'Yes,' he replied absently, not looking.

'It's the same queer shape—and it's got the same kind of yellow tag thing.'

'Has it?' he murmured, not moving in the deck chair.

'And do you know it's even got the same kind of square red label stuck on one side and I can see—'

Suddenly I realized he was not there any more. Something seemed to have upset him for he rose into the air, vaulted over the little rail and jumped down a flight of steps and began shouting

*It was in fact finished in 1968. The U.S. Government provided more than nine million dollars to build a bituminous surfaced road from Georgetown to Mackenzie. Plans for its continuation to the Rupununi are well advanced and will do much to open up the Interior. Mackenzie has been renamed Linden.

at the Captain. Soon the Captain was shouting too and the *R. H. Carr* was hooting and the little canoe with the familiar-looking case on board was pulling steadily away towards the bank.

The hullabaloo was suddenly hugely magnified by an amplifier. It roared and spluttered and made loud subhuman noises which the canoe was apparently able to interpret for it turned back obediently to the steamer. There was much laughter and excitement and exchange of compliments and Dick reappeared up the steps carrying his case. He put it carefully down in front of his deck chair so that he could use it as a foot rest.

'Did they tell you why they'd taken it?'

'No, you never get reasons in Guyana. Lucky I spotted it, wasn't it?' he said, settling down into his deck chair with immense satisfaction.

Not only human beings and their baggage disembarked from the *R. H. Carr*. Once a canoe drew alongside and after a passenger had climbed into it, a cow was pushed overboard. This involved falling several feet and a cow is not designed for graceful diving. With a fearful splash the poor thing disappeared and the brown waters of the Demerara closed over her head. She emerged after what seemed enough time to drown a herd of cows and began swimming frantically after the canoe. Only then did we see that she had a calf attached to her by a piece of rope. Together the two paddled desperately after their owner towards the bank. It was a pathetic sight; I was glad that Singh was not there to witness it.

Apart from such occasional excitements the river was quiet. We were passed now and then by a charcoal barge or a raft with timber and saw several little thatched houseboats. They are owned by families who earn their living by buying fruit from people who grow it in small clearings just back from the river bank and then selling it at other villages. They spend their whole life moving up and down the river and live entirely on their little fruit boats.

It took us nearly eight hours to reach Mackenzie. It was mid-afternoon when we saw on the left bank the town stelling, the row of houses behind and, in the background, the tall chimneys of the bauxite company. It was strange after hours on the river, moving between what seemed uninhabited country to round a bend in the river and find ourselves looking at a modern, orderly town.

It is an artificial town whose *raison d'être* is bauxite, even its name deriving from that of the American prospector G. B. Mackenzie who first realized the potential wealth of the area in 1914.

Bauxite had been known to exist there in the nineteenth century, but it was only after methods of turning it into aluminium were discovered that prospectors became interested. Now Guyana provides one tenth of the world's bauxite and although it is among the most expensive in the world to produce it is also of uniquely fine quality and so holds its own in the international market.

The Demerara Bauxite Company—or Demba, as it is always known—is a subsidiary of the Aluminum Company of Canada and the majority of the non-Guyanese population of Mackenzie is Canadian. The labour force is mainly African. Demba, which owns seventy-seven per cent of Guyana's bauxite, has mines on both sides of the river south of Mackenzie and at Ituni, thirty-five miles to the south-east and at Karakara. The rest of the bauxite is mined by an American company, Reynolds Metals Company, which gets its bauxite from Kwakwani, one hundred miles up the Berbice river. The difficulty there is that the Berbice river is not dredged for ocean going ships so that the ore has to go by barge to Everton, near New Amsterdam, and then be trans-shipped for export. The company, which employs about one thousand people and has installed a calcining plant, exports about half a million tons of bauxite a year, mainly to the United States. Demba, however, which supports at Mackenzie a population of about twenty thousand people, is the Bookers of the bauxite industry.

The doctor met us at the stelling and took us to the Guest House, where we were to sleep, to drop our luggage. It was the coolest and most spacious building we had seen in Guyana. From there we went on a tour of the hospital. The standard of living and the welfare services at Mackenzie are far better than the average in the rest of the country and the wages are higher. There are excellent primary and secondary schools, a well-equipped hospital, a library, recreation hall, churches and a cinema.

The doctor's house overlooked the river and differed from Georgetown houses by being quite open all the way round so that we seemed to be on a verandah. After months of steaming evenings in Georgetown, it was wonderfully refreshing to be able to sit after dinner and feel positively cool and enjoy hot coffee. The great difference between the climate here and on the coast is that although the temperature climbs higher during the day it drops sharply at night.

Looking at the open sides of the house (rain shutters can be drawn in storms, but are normally left open) we asked about 'teef-men'. In Georgetown we knew nobody would have dared lay themselves so invitingly open to burglars. The doctor said they had been visited only once. It happened that he was away up country and his wife was alone with their three little girls, in the house at night. She awoke to hear somebody creeping into her room. She is at normal times no mean figure of a woman, but it happened that she was then eight months' pregnant. Feeling nothing but rage that anybody should dare thus to invade her privacy, she jumped out of bed, turned on the light and must, she admitted, have presented a pretty terrifying spectacle to the African who had just climbed in. As he stood horror-stricken she looked about for the handiest thing to throw and her eye fell upon a double-edged axe which the chief of some head-hunting tribe had given her husband as a present in gratitude for the removal of a grumbling appendix. It stood, as an ornament, on a table by the bed, so naturally she picked it up now and hurled it at the intruder. Fortunately she missed and the axe buried itself three inches in the door frame. Had she been a better shot, her husband assured us, he would have returned from the Interior to find her on a charge of manslaughter. It took a long time to extract the axe from the door frame; the 'teefman' did not return.

As we were talking a message was brought for the doctor that an African woman had been brought into the hospital. She was unconscious, appeared to have nothing wrong with her but could not be brought round. While he was out his wife told us that such cases were not uncommon, all normally accepted methods of restoring consciousness proving ineffective, but her husband found that the assertion that he was going to give a strong injection (although in fact he only gave a hefty injection of water) was usually successful. Subsequent talks with the patient usually revealed some insuperable domestic difficulty; she was perhaps a woman deserted by her husband with no means of feeding her children. He felt it was the equivalent of the more sophisticated person's nervous breakdown. Faced with a situation that the personality could not cope with, nature simply opted out. The long term treatment was to try to help the sufferer deal with the problem; the short term one was an injection with a blunt needle.

The next day we were to be taken to see round the bauxite works, but first, at the doctor's children's request we went to 'speed on the air strip'. This involved driving along a sandy road through trees until we reached a tarmacadam run built during the war set high above the Demerara river, surrounded by white sand. We tore up and down the air strip, the children shrieking with joy at the unaccustomed speed.

To get to the mining area we had to travel by jeep, for the way through the forest was rough. It was startling suddenly to come out of the quiet forest into a great cleared area and find it a centre of activity. Mountains of white sand, which had been removed from the surface of the ground, lay to the left. Then there was red and grey clay which had been removed from beneath the sand and finally the bauxite itself had been revealed. The scene reminded us of the slag heaps of northern England, alleviated by the variety of the colours and with a touch of the skiing holiday provided by the slopes of snow-white sand.

Dick was much taken by a mechanical excavator worth over a million dollars, which was busy removing the land above the bauxite. When the top sand, which is loose, has been washed away by powerful water jets, this excavator, known as the Lord Dragline, moves in to deal with what lies beneath. It does not stay still like most excavators but walks about on two skids which lift themselves up like feet. The ore, now revealed on the floor of the quarry, is blasted out and mechanically loaded on to the trucks which take it by rail to the Mackenzie plant. We were not able to see what happened there as the plant was closed for the holiday. The mines, we were told, work all the year round.

We gathered that at the Mackenzie plant the ore is crushed and then either dried for export as bauxite or else heated to the point of incandescence and then exported as calcined ore which is used in the abrasive and refractory industries. By far the greater part, however, is exported as dried bauxite to the Aluminium Company of Canada's smelting plants in Quebec where it is made into aluminium. In the past bauxite, like sugar, has not been refined in Guyana, but in 1961 a vast and very successful alumina plant was opened so that part of the ore can be processed into alumina which is a half-way stage between the ore and aluminium. It is hoped one day to produce aluminium itself in Guyana and this, it seems to me, would be a great advance both economically and psychologically, showing how very far Guyana has travelled from the days of the old colonial system when the colonies were regarded as a cheap source of supply of primary materials for the manufacturing industries of the more advanced nations.

Even apart from this, the bauxite industry makes a tremendous contribution to the economy of the country, providing about twenty per cent of the value of Guyana's exports. The only other mineral which can be described as commercially exploitable is manganese, a rare metal used in steel making, which is mined in the north west of Guyana, again by a Canadian company. It produces about two hundred thousand tons a year and exports the ore to the United States and Norway.

In the evening we sat on the verandah again and watched the Demerara and wondered why we had to go back to Georgetown the next morning. On our way back to the Guest House we walked under a full moon to the accompaniment of a frogs' chorus even louder than that we were used to at home. We found our room had been further cooled by the addition of a large electric fan which had been installed while we were out during the day. We were rather wary of fans; a few Georgetown houses have them suspended from their ceilings. They are huge things, about five foot in diameter with whirling arms. Unfortunately the first one we encountered was fixed about six foot four inches from the ground and Dick being just a little bit taller than that, walking absent-mindedly across the room, was almost scalped.

It was now my turn to do battle with a fan. I had on a long white negligée, relic of my trousseau, which floated out behind me as I walked across the bedroom. Suddenly I felt myself seized from behind and jerked backwards. The fan had caught a corner of the garment in its jaws and was tearing at the rest of it with fearful flapping sounds. Fortunately it had bitten off more than it could chew and now slowly growled to a standstill, its works clogged with yards of white negligée. Gingerly we disentangled the torn and oily material and then I spent our last night at Mackenzie sitting nursing my bruises while Dick mended the fan.

The next morning we went early to say goodbye to our friends before catching the *R. H. Carr* back to Georgetown. It seemed so strange to be cold, but we were so, for at Mackenzie the mornings are cool and often misty until about ten o'clock. As we stood in their garden they suddenly suggested that we might like to take a few things back with us for planting in the one we were still busy making in Campbellville. Thereupon there broke out a great deal of activity, with everyone hunting for spades and scissors, digging up cuttings and rooting about for seedlings, heaving plants into old buckets and tying earthy bundles up in brown paper with yards of hairy string. Some orchids were wrapped in tree bark and bound up with an old torn up skirt. We took three hydrangeas too, for they do startlingly well at Mackenzie, loving the bauxite. They do not grow in Georgetown so we took a large supply of Mackenzie soil in the hope that the hydrangeas would not notice that they had been moved. The ploy was successful; the hydrangeas flourished in oil drums in our Campbellville garden to the amazement of our neighbours.

We only just caught the steamer and our friends were still holding an assortment of garden implements as they waved us off. We sat on the deck of the *R. H. Carr* surrounded by our plants and bags of Mackenzie soil and drifted down the river. An old African came and sat with us. He came from Wismar, a village opposite Mackenzie on the far bank of the Demerara, as sprawling and natural a place as Mackenzie is tidy and artificial. He was very knowledgeable about flowers and told us what treatment to give to our assorted hydrangeas and orchids. He himself had a fine collection of the latter he told us, especially of the midnight orchid which flowers only in the dark. Most people find it hard to grow and anyway are not able to enjoy its nocturnal beauty to the full. He was one of the few people who could do so, he told us with a smile, for he was a night watchman.

Journey to Mackenzie. Thatched houseboats of a family of fruit vendors on th[e] Demerara rive[r]

Fruit sellers at the stelling at Atkinson Field offering their wares to the passenge[rs] in the boat above the[m]

Bauxite mining. The ore is loaded on to rail trucks to be taken to the pla[nt]

CHAPTER TWELVE

Departure

Soon after we arrived in Guyana, I was told, by the wife of a member of Booker's staff, that she had the previous morning attended the trial of a man accused of murder, talked to him in prison in the afternoon, when she took books to him as part of her work for the prison library, and in the evening sat next to his judge at dinner. It struck me at the time as an extraordinary coincidence but later I realized that it was not so strange in Guyana, where everything was on a much smaller scale and people in power more easily accessible.

There is a curious, toytown feeling about the administration of Guyana: it is all there, the Government of Britain in miniature, the same legal system, the same civil service and the same political pattern. It is fascinating to observe, for one can see the workings of a modern democratic state at much closer quarters than in England and since it is on a smaller scale get a much better all round view.

Interesting as it may be to observe, one cannot but wonder if the arrangement is altogether sensible. Guyana may be the size of Great Britain but its total population is only that of a large English town; it seems doubtful if it requires, even if it could afford, the kind of administration suitable to a modern European state.

One resultant disadvantage is that changes come about slowly as they have to work their way through a bureaucratic system which rightly belongs to a more complex industrial society.

Guyana is a land much visited by experts. Projects are discussed ad nauseam while the achievement remains discouragingly small; it is a very difficult place to get things done. Sometimes one had the feeling that the Guyanese actually preferred to talk about things rather than to do them. The climate of course is not one which encourages vigorous or sustained activity. Moreover government by expatriates had perhaps fostered a curious contradiction which we noticed in the national character; a meticulous attention to the manner in which things were done sometimes prevented their

Planting rice on the west coast of Demerara.
Working in the rice fields.
A village in the flooded coastlands of the Courentyne.
N

being done at all. Everything was sacrificed to form. Possibly a colonial people, as they begin to manage their own affairs, have a deeply felt need not to lose face by doing something incorrectly. Even being punctual seems to be regarded as a face-loser.

Not long before we left we received a notice of a meeting inviting us to a nearby house to discuss the setting up of a Residents' Association. It struck us as being a good idea and worth supporting for the little time we had left. Many new houses were being built where we lived, but the roads were bumpy, unlit and unnamed, there were many rough spaces of waste land, the whole area was flooded in the rainy season and nobody did anything about getting rid of the wild dogs. There was much that a group of people might achieve, either by organizing improvements themselves or working together to persuade the Georgetown authorities to do so.

Dick was late home the night of the meeting, and unshaved and unfed he accompanied me to the house, apologizing for being five minutes late. The lady of the house seemed surprised to see us and said her husband had gone out for a drive but would no doubt be back soon. After about half an hour one or two other people arrived and the business actually began an hour after that. The company was a cross-section of middle class Guyanese. The man whose house we were in, a Portuguese, acted as Chairman and explained that other associations had been set up which had achieved a great deal and so he and a group of his friends had thought that something similar might be done here. We all agreed, and it was decided that a Committee should be chosen to decide what kind of things might be attempted.

We were about to vote when an African schoolmaster, well-versed in Committee procedure, said in rather pained tones that he presumed we should have a secret ballot. The Chairman hastily said that of course that was exactly what he had intended and a great hunt began for pencils and paper. When they had been located and distributed we proceeded to vote for a long list of officials, each one being nominated and seconded and then voted for by secret ballot. It took a long time, but the African waited until we had worked our way through the list of officers and members of the Committee before raising another difficulty.

He pointed out that we had not yet voted to set up an Association; how, therefore, could we have a Committee for an Association that did not, strictly speaking, exist? It was, he said, a real point, for the association could not act if it did not legally exist. It could not sue or be sued.

The election of the Committee was therefore declared invalid by the Chairman and we started again. More paper was found and we took a vote on whether we should form an Association or not. The Chairman made a short speech supporting the motion, the African seconded it; we were about to vote when somebody asked how we could say if we wanted to form an Association when we did not know what it was for. It might do things we did not approve of. Surely we should not vote in the dark, as it were? We put our pencils down and waited.

The African pronounced this to be a very real problem. After much discussion it was agreed that the only correct procedure would be to draw up a list of the aims of the Association that everybody could study and agree upon and then vote whether or not they wanted to set up a Society with such aims. Then and only then —could a committee be elected. The African rubbed his hands and declared himself satisfied that it was the right procedure.

Thus shown the way, the Chairman now invited suggestions for the aims of the Association. Somebody proposed, amid murmurs of approval, that street lighting should be installed. One by one everyone bore witness to the difficulties of getting about at night with the roads unlit and then all the holes and the danger of lurking thieves. It was not safe for women either. After everybody had contributed something to the general discussion of the hazards of the unlit roads, it was agreed by show of hands that installing street lights might be one of the aims of the Association.

The African now made the point that had been fairly obvious from the start—but I suppose if it had been made then it would have prevented all the enjoyable talk—that street lighting was not the kind of thing that the Association would find easy to see to. It would need Government engineers and a great deal of money and then it would need electricity and there was not enough of that already. And it would need to be joined up with other lighting and so should really be handled by Georgetown.

A Portuguese girl then asked, in a high-pitched voice which was almost smothered by giggles of embarrassment, what about all those coils and posts down by the canal—perhaps they were going to be used for street lighting? A pale little Civil Servant then agreed that something was afoot about lighting for this area, but he had not liked to mention it before because he only knew of it through his position of trust in the Civil Service and of course all people in such positions of trust in the Government of the country must swear to be secret about what plans they knew of, but of course since the matter had now been raised by somebody else, he was not afraid to say. . . .

The installation of street lighting, therefore, did not stand as a possible aim of the Association. Others were invited and the clearing of ditches was suggested. They were smelly, everyone agreed, and did not take away the water, so that in the rainy season all the yards were flooded and all the plants ruined. There were in the room, at the most, three of us who had made any attempt to create a garden, but a stranger might have been forgiven for thinking himself in a room full of horticultural enthusiasts. Suddenly everyone seemed to be suffering terrible losses of flowers, vegetables and lawns. I wondered if we were all to go out and dig the drains but somehow, although it was easy to imagine the assembled company discussing until doomsday the fascinating topic of the clearing of the ditches, one could not imagine any of them actually doing anything about it with a spade. A sad-eyed Chinaman now pointed out that we had already paid in the rates for the ditches to be dug; surely we did not want to pay for it twice? This met with unanimous and immediate agreement. The Civil Servant said knowledgeably that it was a matter for the Ministry of Health. Discouraged, everyone agreed that in that case it was not a matter for the Residents' Association.

Another aim was now put forward: the destruction of the wild dogs. In Georgetown a van went round picking up strays and taking them to be put to sleep. In Campbellville people left puppies in the road, 'for de cars to mash up.' We had twice rescued these pathetic little objects and taken them to be destroyed in Georgetown. Word gets around quickly in Guyana and thereafter we frequently found puppies tied to the gate in the hope that we would oblige. We did; at a dollar a time it became quite an expensive operation.

A verbal onslaught was now launched against the wild dogs: it was impossible to get a wink of sleep at night and they were always in the dustbins; it was not nice the way they went round copulating all over the place. In fact it was very disgusting, especially for children. They should be destroyed so that there would be no more puppies. The oldest inhabitant said that when she first came there was only one wild dog, but she could not catch it even though it was pregnant. And now there were hundreds.

At least, the sad-eyed Chinaman, pointed out, it would not cost anything, for the R.S.P.C.A. destroyed the dogs free. But, somebody else said, if you paid a dollar they were put to sleep painlessly with chloroform. If you did not pay a dollar the dog did not get chloroform. This extraordinary statement was accepted quite seriously with slow nods of agreement. If necessary, it was decided, the dollars must be found, but then it needed an expert to catch the dogs in the first place, they were so quick and crafty. Reluctantly it was agreed that it was really a task for the R.S.P.C.A. and not for the Residents' Association after all.

Somebody remarked that it was midnight, which was received with much astonishment. The Civil Servant said that we could call for candles, ha-ha-ha. This statement caused instant panic since everyone took it to mean that the lights were about to go out through a power cut, and rushed to go home before it happened. He had to explain his joke at some length before they sat down calmly again. They listened to the Chairman proposing that another meeting should be held at which the aims of the Association could be drawn up and somebody offered to have the meeting at his house next time and it was about to be agreed when the African said, 'It is correct and customary for the Secretary to send out notices. I propose that that is what we should do.'

There followed a long discussion about who should act as Secretary and it was finally agreed that it would be constitutional to allow the one who had formerly been elected to act on this occasion and for the expenses to come out of subscriptions to be voted and paid next time. It was a typical Guyanese ending to a typically Guyanese meeting. Because notices were sent out about meetings, it was forgotten that they were only sent to convey information which if it could be conveyed without them by settling the time and place of the meeting immediately, so much the better. The correct form must be followed, even if it caused delays. As far as I know there never was another meeting. Again and again we found in public as in private life that practical courses were lost in a welter of abstractions and legal niceties. People seemed so easily side-tracked. Debating points were scored and facts established which were often true but always irrelevant. The tendency may have been fostered by an over-large bureaucracy and by the fact that colonial people have to accustom themselves to the idea that they may have the right to debate issues but not to decide them, but it owes something to the Guyanese love of philosophizing and theorizing.

This respect for the outward forms rather than the inner meaning was at the root of much of the veneration for education. As in most developing societies there was among the mass of the people a desire for education often stronger than their understanding of what exactly it was for and about. We had an African neighbour whose son was for ever consulting us about his career. He and his friends were addicted to sending away for correspondence courses which promised to make learning very easy and very quick. One day he would be excited at the prospect of getting A level physics in a year. The next he would tell us he was going to do O level Latin in three months by an American method which made it quite painless. To be educated was marvellous and if you could be it without too much work or even thought that was even more marvellous.

At one point he thought he might take a correspondence degree course in Engineering. He came to ask us what he would earn when he obtained his degree. When Dick told him that after he himself had qualified he got £5 a week as a very junior Engineer on a site, he was frankly incredulous. It was no good explaining that a graduate straight from college has a lot to learn before he was of much practical value on a site. As far as he was concerned there was no point in slaving away for a degree if its possession did not bestow the immediate right to give orders and be well paid. Education mattered more than anything else as a status symbol.

Such people fall easy prey to the propaganda of those who make money out of running such correspondence courses, especially if they had some academic ability but were not among the privileged few who gained a place in a grammar school. Those who did, received an education comparable to those at similar schools at home. Indeed it was a curiously English education altogether. Even seeing the children in the streets we were struck by this from the very first; in their familiar navy tunics with box pleats worn over short sleeved blouses, the girls were replicas of English schoolgirls, if not perhaps the most modern ones.

Later, I was asked to help out with some teaching while one of the English staff was away on Long Leave and I found that in the school the syllabus was predominantly imported; *Silas Marner, David Copperfield, Vanity Fair* were, I remember, among the set texts in English. I took over in the midst of exams and one of my first tasks was to mark a set of Comprehension papers on a passage which described a cosmopolitan railway station in central Europe. Some of the children did not even know what was being described. It was not an easy piece of writing, but a European child would probably have caught most of the references. To a Guyanese it was almost incomprehensible. These were VIth formers, but the problem existed throughout all age groups; I remember the youngest children being puzzled by a story about going out to tea with Granny. Accustomed to a three or four generation family living together they never thought of Grannies as people to visit; they lived with you at home. They made about as much sense of it as an English child would of a story about a visit to Mummy's house.

Of course, it is good for children to read about other lands and of things they have not actually experienced. English children read stories of jungles and deserts which can only take shape in their imagination. But the difference here was that these strange places and things were not presented as foreign, but as their normal fare, and later as part of their G.C.E. syllabus. It is not easy to suggest alternatives. As inhabitants of an English-speaking ex-colony they must clearly be led to read the best that the language can offer. Fortunately now many of the writers from the Caribbean area are among the best and one hopes that children will be encouraged to study them. In fact Guyanese children should be well placed to receive the best of English and American literature as well as modern West Indian writers, for the country is influenced by all three cultures.

In history too the syllabus was a predominantly European one. The teaching of West Indian history in its own right has been made more difficult by the lack of suitable text books, but the real problem is that it is in fact a by-product of European history. Its course has been shaped by European wars, by European expansion, by European treaties. It is hard to see, if history is to be true to the past, how it can be presented as anything other than a European dominated subject.

For better or for worse the pattern of life has been laid down by Europeans and the end of colonial rule cannot radically alter that pattern. Europeans brought in the African slaves, they indentured labour from India and Madeira. They shaped the economy to suit their own needs and the social structure to counterfeit home. One should not therefore be surprised at finding these children of the tropics being taught exactly as if they had been brought up with an English suburban background, but it did none the less sometimes seem startlingly inappropriate. In the next few years considerable changes are likely to be made and the aim here, as in other fields, should be to adapt what is best, to keep what is most suitable and jettison the rest.

The great majority of children, however, do not go to grammar schools. The burden placed on the education system by the rapid increase in population has fallen on the primary schools; it was hard to believe that the one near us could possibly contain the number of children who crowded through its doors in the morning. They were all taught in one room, the classes being separated by putting the children back to back. In the past the education that they received there was a narrowly academic one, utterly unsuited to their needs and by training them for the kind of work they would never find, brought them bitterness and unemployment. A sensible move is now being made to give a more practical bias to education in primary schools, with emphasis on wood work and domestic science and all the crafts which Guyana lacks. There are no indigenous crafts such as exist in other underdeveloped countries. Africans in their own continent produce fine carving in many materials, basket work and many other works of art, but torn away from their homeland the slaves lost all heart for such pursuits and any skills that were brought over with them have long since been forgotten.

Possibly one of the reasons why life in Georgetown has a hollow ring is that one senses the lack of local crafts and skills and traditions, of that solid background which should give life in any country a sense of permanence and reality and its people self-respect. 'It's the best—it's imported,' the shop girls would say of anything from meat to furniture. It struck me as being terribly sad, the casual way in which they said it, as if it was self-evident that any product of their own land must by definition be inferior.

We had remarked upon the low standard of craftsmanship when we moved into our newly built house and found throughout our stay that little care or skill was put into any practical job. This was in part the result of a low standard of life. Things are shoddy and there is a feeling that anything will do. The local papers were a mass of misprints, of pictures printed upside-down and wrongly captioned. As readers we found it greatly added to their interest. The very first paper we opened in the country, I remember, carried a rather pompous article by a bishop, which concluded, 'Life, my friends, is not all beer and shittles.'

Later, when I wrote weekly book reviews, I found it rather less amusing and fought long and frustrating battles to have them correctly printed. At first I thought it would be enough to correct my own proofs, but having pointed out twenty errors and left them to be altered, I was horrified next day to open the paper and find that they were all there plus several new ones. After that I used to spend hours with the type-setter in the printing house explaining alterations, shouting above the roar of the machines, dripping with sweat, for it was rather like working in a factory inside a very overheated greenhouse. I was aware that I was regarded as eccentric; so long as the printing was near enough to correct for readers to get the gist of the thing, nobody else seemed to think a few mistakes mattered. Moreover, with the rest of the paper full of mistakes it seemed a bit pointless to bother so much about one article. The idea that it must be done right for no other reason than that was the only satisfying way of doing it was quite alien to them. Here, as elsewhere, there were no standards with which to compare, nothing against which to measure one's work.

Yet, as sometimes happens, there was an exception to prove the rule: in this case an East Indian, who was fanatically careful. He had never been out of Guyana, so the argument that the Guyanese must travel abroad to acquire standards certainly did not apply to him. He was simply intensely interested in his work. He loved words and respected them enough to make sure they were printed correctly. He was on duty about one week in four and I always knew that it was enough in that week to mark the mistakes in the proof and leave it with him. I still spent as long in the printing house, for he loved to talk and wanted to know about the books and how they were published. All this had to be discussed above the roar and clatter of machinery with men working all round, shouting to each other and bumping into us as they carried great trays of type about the place. He loved to increase his vocabulary and any unfamiliar word had always to be explained in great detail and its etymology speculated upon. He was on duty when I took in my last article and as we were about to say our farewells he suddenly remembered there was a word he had to ask about. 'Dis word,' he shouted through the racket of machinery in full pelt, stabbing at the proof with an oily finger, 'dis word, "Phallic." Please for de meaning, application and derivation.' I still cherish a picture of him, leaning forward, his bright brown eyes eager for knowledge, his ear cupped towards me as, above the noise of the machines and the rush of human beings, I shouted across to him as succinctly and as modestly as I could, the required information.

It joined a host of other memories of the last few weeks, when ordinary things were suddenly sad because we were doing them for the last time. We spent our last Sunday at Santa. Thinking we might not be able to get there again, Granny had sent us a present of a fan with Teach who had gone to Georgetown the previous weekend. Such arrangements have a way of going awry. A kind friend of ours took Teach to the cinema and when they came out the contents of the car had been stolen, including Granny's fan. Despite this calamity, we spent a pleasant day at Santa making a leisurely round of farewells, chatting under the silk cotton tree, swimming in the creek. We drank creek water and ate labba, a kind of large rabbit, which had been prepared for us, for the consumption of these two things guarantees that the traveller will return.

It was the saddest farewell of all to say goodbye to Granny, whom we knew we should not see again. European friends we knew we could see again in England and there was a good chance of meeting many Guyanese ones in the same way. Besides it was always possible that we might one day return. But with Granny it was final and it struck me that one so rarely says adieu that one does not know how to say it. I was silent as Granny took my hand. She said simply, 'We meet on the other side.' It was not said as a pious hope, but as a simple statement of fact.

She stood waving on the top of the hill as we set off down stream in the *Canje Queen*. Then she went to her house for something and ran down the slope with it. She handed it to a little boy who put it in his mouth and swam after us. As he came alongside we saw it was a fan which we took carefully out of his mouth and waved to the little group of people by the side of the creek, until we turned the first bend.

Our house in Campbellville was not a very cheerful place to return to; stripped of our personal belongings, of books and pictures, it had an abandoned look. As we walked about our footsteps echoed hollowly. Our trunks were packed and crated under the house and we avoided going there as one might avoid in a house of mourning going into the room where the body lies. Mable and Lucille added to this impression by going about with funereal faces and speaking only when they had to and then in whispers. They treated us with gentle solicitude as if we were invalids.

Basdeo and Singh made more effort to be cheerful and were kept busy as it had for some reason or other become a point of honour to leave the garden looking its best. The house was in great confusion with packing, so the garden had to make up for it by being especially tidy. In the evenings we would sit in the bare room or on the verandah listening to the orchestration of frogs and crickets and try to realize that we should soon be in England sitting over winter fires, shut in from the outside world.

We spent our last night at a hotel, but I returned unexpectedly to our house the following morning and found Lucille sitting dejectedly under the house. It was all locked up but she had found an old plank in the garden and was squatting on that. I felt helpless and guilty at deserting her in this way, for the life of somebody in her position depends utterly on her employer. For Mable it was different; she had a husband with a good job. Although she was saddened by the parting, as we were, after nearly two years working together, it would not change her life very much. But for Lucille it was little short of catastrophe. Widowed with five children in a land which provides no help for the widowed or unemployed, without friends or relations in any position to help, her only hope was good employment. Her sense of security was now lost. True I had found her another job, knowing that difficult though it was for me to do so it would be much harder for her after we had gone, but she knew as well as I did how easily maids are dismissed. I had written testimonials for them both which they carried round like a talisman, but I had less confidence in those than they had for I had heard too many remarks of the 'Testimonials! They all write their own, of course,' variety to feel that they would carry much weight if ever Mable and Lucille had to go knocking for jobs on European back doors. We persuaded her to leave the house and took her home. Jubraj drove us back to Georgetown, passing Bourda market with its rows of vendors squatting behind their piles of fruit and vegetables on the pavement. As we drove I thought how we now took for granted the behaviour of Guyanese traffic which had once horrified us: bicycles swerved across the highway, cars ignored the rules of the road, donkeys did unpredictable things with an air of stolid determination. Near the centre of the city, traffic lights had recently been installed. Since their like had never been seen in Georgetown before, pretence ones had been put up for several months beforehand so that the populace could get used to the sight of them. It was a psychological mistake, the only result of which was to get people so used to driving through them that they continued to do so even when the real lights were put up. This greatly increased the chances of an accident and Jubraj now always went a long way round to avoid the danger zone around the traffic lights.

Safely through Georgetown, we drove through La Penitence and past the sugar terminal. Work on the superstructure was now under way and the site was still stiff with the angular forms of derricks and cranes. A few goats found something to eat between the concrete and the buildings and machinery. We slowed down as we passed. 'Somethin' puzzlin' me, boss,' Jubraj remarked. 'You sad to be leavin'?'

'Yes, very sad.'

'Den why,' Jubraj asked, with true Guyanese logic, 'why den did you work so hard to get it finish so quick?'

We pondered this problem as we gazed out of the car windows and watched the sugar fields flip by. We knew this road well now; we knew where we should bump over the wooden bridges that spanned the canals, where we should encounter the sweet smell of molasses from the sugar factory near the road. We knew the names of the villages and recognized the mosques. Soon the vegetation began to thicken and then the trees began, just past the house where the man lived who sold stuffed alligators. Then we were slowing down to pass through the gates of Atkinson Field.

'In de war I was station here up at de base,' Jubraj told us for the first time. We were surprised; it was not easy to imagine Jubraj in the army, despite his habitual khaki shirt. 'I work on de lorries for de Americans,' he amplified. 'Once, day try to send me abroad to fight so I eats soap.'

'You ate SOAP?'

'Yes, mistress. Den day say, "Dis man too ill" and day leaves me here wid de lorries.'

'You didn't like the army?'

'No mistress. Is nasty. Very nasty. In de army all is orders. Well, I doan' mind doin' tings for people, mistress, but doan' want to *has to,* mistress. In de army all is *has to.*'

I was sorry he had left it so late to tell us about the army; I should have liked to have heard much more, especially about the soap, but now we were too engrossed in getting the luggage out of the car.

We had rather a lot of luggage. We were not flying straight back to England but going first to the West Indian Islands, then Canada and the United States and since it was November, we had to take with us everything we should need both in extreme heat and in extreme cold. We knew we were already very much over the weight allowed by the air line and the situation was made considerably worse by the arrival of kind friends to see us off, bringing with them presents which, though unexpected and exciting, turned out to be also bulky and very heavy. With great ingenuity we contrived to disguise as much as possible as hand luggage to be carried on to the plane with us. Dick unpacked a case and took out a raincoat and filled its capacious inner pockets with heavy objects until the coat weighed more than the case. We interpreted the permitted hand luggage in the widest possible way; reading matter for the journey, I remember, consisted of fifteen books hanging over Dick's arm on a strap. Finally, 'Just carry that nonchalantly as if it held your toothbrush and flannel,' he told me, dropping on to my shoulder a blue travel bag containing his oil painting equipment, including what seemed to be half a ton of lead paints.

Having left our official luggage to be dealt with by the staff and said goodbye to our friends, we staggered across the tarmacadam to the waiting plane, myself dreadfully deformed by apparently having one shoulder six inches lower than the other and trying hard to look nonchalant. As we toiled to the top of the gangplank, the air hostess met us with an international smile, tried—and failed—to relieve me of my little blue bag, seized Dick's coat to hang up and then sank almost to her knees beneath its weight.

We were not, as we quite expected we might be, put off the plane. Fortunately there were very few other passengers and we told ourselves that their absence compensated for our extra luggage. As we taxied down the runway we could just make out the little group of friends waving goodbye to us and, some way apart, the lone figure of Jubraj in his khaki shirt, one arm raised in salute. Then they grew smaller and were lost, with the air strip, among the trees.

INDEX